Nevada Guide to Genealogical Records

Diane E. Greene, AG
Accredited Genealogist
(Eastern States)

CLEARFIELD

Printed for
Clearfield Company, Inc. by
Genealogical Publishing Co., Inc.
Baltimore, Maryland
1998

Reprinted for
Clearfield Company, Inc. by
Genealogical Publishing Co., Inc.
Baltimore, Maryland
2000

International Standard Book Number: 0-8063-4816-X
Made in the United States of America

Contents

Preface

This book pulls together records from a variety of sources, including information from county court houses, Nevada internet sites, and various lists, which are in the first chapter on general information.

Each county chapter includes information (arranged alphabetically) on the cemeteries, churches, courthouses, funeral homes, libraries, newspapers, societies, and the holdings of the Family History Library for that county. When available, the phone, fax, and e-mail numbers are provided, along with addresses and hours of operation.

The listings for newspapers are from the Dickerson Library at the University of Nevada, Las Vegas, but the University of Nevada, Reno, should also have the same newspapers.

You will notice the lack of cemetery information as most of Nevada's older cemeteries are now abandoned. I would suggest that when you are seeking specific cemetery information you should first check to see if the Family History Library in Salt Lake City, Utah, has microfilmed the records. Always check the city and county listings as sometimes cemeteries from different locales are grouped together on one microfilm. This is especially true of cemetery records from the National Society, Daughters of the American Revolution, whose holdings were microfilmed by the Family History Department in the 1970s. Unfortunately, most of the early DAR records for Nevada are not indexed. I am currently indexing Nevada's DAR records, with copies going to the Family History Library in Salt Lake City, Utah, and the DAR Library in Washington, D.C.

In February of 1998 it was announced that Northern Nevada's new area code will be 775. Previously the entire state had the 702 area code. I have listed the new area codes, but use 702 until December 18, 1998, when the new area code becomes operational. It will affect only a sliver of southwestern Clark County, and the rest of Clark County will retain the 702 area code.

I visited many of the major libraries and archives, which is why they are covered in greater detail. I would like to thank all the librarians and archivists who patiently showed me their Nevada holdings.

Thank you to my friends and colleagues who took the time to review and critique this book.

CHAPTER ONE

Nevada
General Information

Nevada is one of the largest states, rated thirty-ninth in population, but seventh in size. Nevada takes its name from a Spanish word meaning "snow covered," which refers to the high mountain ranges.

It lies in the Great Basin and Plateau section of the United States, bordered on the north by Oregon and Idaho on the west and southwest by California, and on the east by Utah.

In 1857 Nevada was denied territorial status by the United States Congress. In 1861 it was finally organized as a territory. With the outbreak of the Civil War the Republican administration was eager to add Nevada's strength in Congress. In 1863 an act was passed to make Nevada a state, but a proposed state constitution was rejected by the voters of the territory. In 1864 Congress passed a second act and another constitution was accepted by Nevada voters. The entire constitution was telegraphed to Washington, D.C., at a cost of $3,416.77. Nevada was admitted to the Union on 31 October 1864, in time to ratify the Thirteenth Amendment. The state flag bears a scroll that reads "Battle Born," to commemorate Nevada's admission during the Civil War.

Historical Background

1775   Spanish Missionary Francisco Garces becomes the first European to enter Nevada, en route to California.

1801   Esmeralda County established with Goldfield as its county seat.

1825   The Humboldt River discovered by fur trapper Peter Skeen Odgen, of Hudson's Bay Company.

1830   The old Spanish Trail across Nevada is pioneered by William Wolfskill.

1833   Joseph R. Walker pioneered the California Trail from Utah, crossing the Sierra Nevada mountains.

1843-45 John C. Fremont explored Nevada.

1848   Nevada was acquired through the Treaty of Guadelupe Hildalgo which ended the war with Mexico. Nevada was then a part of California, known as Washoe County.

1849	Mormon Station, now Genoa, Nevada's first permanent settlement was established by H. S. Beatie.
1850	Most of Nevada included in the newly organized Utah Territory.
1851	Carson County created by Utah legislature, including all settlements in the western area. The inhabitants petition Congress to annex them to California.
1859	The Comstock Lode, a rich silver deposit, is discovered near Virginia City, generating a rush.
1861	Utah Territory is divided and the western part is designated Nevada Territory.
1864	Nevada is admitted to the Union as the thirty-sixth state.

Bibliographies

Lee, Joyce C. *Genealogical Prospecting in Nevada: A Guide to Nevada Directories.* Nevada Library Association, 1984.

Lingenfelter, Richard E. *Newspapers of Nevada, 1858-1958: A History and Bibliography.* San Francisco: John Howell Books, 1964.

Cemeteries

Burek, Deborah M. *Cemeteries of the U. S.* Gale Research, Inc., 1994.

Census records

Federal census records for 1850 and 1860 are with the Utah Territory Census.
Federal census taken in 1860 (with Utah), 1870, 1880, 1900, 1910, 1920.
   Territorial census 1862 (located at Nevada State Archives) for Douglas, Storey, Washoe, Lyon, Humboldt and Ormsby counties, and 1863 for Lander County.
Union Veterans and Widows 1890.
State Census 1872 and 1875, with index.

Church records

Church of Jesus Christ of Latter-day Saints, 50 East North Temple, Salt Lake City, UT 84150
Nevada Diocese of Roman Catholic Church, Catholic Chancery Office, 515 Court St., P.O. Box 1211, Reno, NV 89504
Protestant Episcopal Church, Nevada Dioceses 1862-1969, Nevada Historical Society, 1650 N. Virginia Street, Reno, NV 89503
United Methodist Church, Commission on Archives & History, 36 Madison Avenue, P.O. Box 127, Madison, NJ 07940

Court System

Nevada has several Municipal Courts of limited jurisdiction in the incorporated cities and towns. The state's Judicial Courts have limited jurisdiction over misdemeanors, small claims and civil cases. Each county seat has the District Courts which have general jurisdiction over major civil cases, felonies, equity, probate and guardianship, misdemeanors and juvenile matters. First Judicial District: Carson City (independent city) and Storey County; Second Judicial District- Washoe County; Third Judicial District- Churchill and Lyon counties; Fourth Judicial District- Elko County; Fifth Judicial District- Esmeralda, Mineral and Nye counties; Sixth Judicial District- Humboldt, Lander and Pershing counties; Seventh Judicial District- Eureka, Lincoln and White Pine counties; Eighth Judicial District- Clark County; Ninth Judicial District- Douglas County. The Supreme Court is the court of last resort.

Funeral Homes

1995 The National Yellow Book of Funeral Directors. Nomis Publications, Inc.

Gazetteers

Carlson, Helen S. *Nevada Place Names: A Geographical Dictionary*. Reno: University of Nevada Press, 1974.

Genealogical Research Guides

Spiros, Joyce V. Hawley. *Genealogical Guide to Arizona and Nevada*. New Mexico Verlene Publishing, 1983.

General

The Handybook For Genealogists. 8th Edition, Everton Publishers, Inc., 1991.

Histories

Nevada, The Silver State. Carson City: Western States Historical Publishers, 1970.

Davis, Sam P. *History of Nevada*. Las Vegas, NV, Nevada Publications, nd.

Compton's Living Encyclopedia.

Reproduction of Thompson and West's History of Nevada. Berkeley, CA, Howell-North, 1958.

Land Records

Nevada is a public-domain state with one principal meridian (established 1851 in California). The General Land Office (GLO) was set up within the Department of the Treasury in 1812 to administer all public land transactions except surveying and map work. In 1849 the GLO was transferred to the Department of the Interior, then in 1946 it was merged with the Grazing Service to form the Bureau of Land Management. This Bureau manages, classifies, and disposes of public lands and their resources. Nevada had four GLO land districts; the first opened in 1864 at Carson City.

Patents can be obtained from the BLM Nevada State Office, 300 Booth Street, Box 12000, Reno, NV 89520. This office has copies of the tract books. The National Archives in Washington has the land-entry case files (described in Inventory No.22) and the GLO headquarters original tract books and township plats. It also has a card index to Nevada patentees from 30 Jun 1908. The San Bruno branch of the National Archives has the records of the Nevada GLO district offices, including the originals of the local office township plats and tract books.

Libraries and Society Holdings

American Library Directory 1996-1997. New Providence, N.J.: RR Bowker, 1996.

Nevada State Archives & Records (2nd Floor of Nevada State Library)
Phone: 775 687-5210
Reference-Archive Phone: 775 687-5160 Fax: 775 687-8311
Created 1965 to administer programs for the creation, maintenance, preservation of records of the executive branch of state government. Records Management inventories the records of executive branch agencies. It preserves the records that document history, organization and function of Nevada state government. There are currently 8,650 cubic feet of territorial and state government records dating from 1851 to the present.
Special collections:
Department of Education, Retired teacher records: contain the names and schools of Nevada's teachers that retired from 1927 to 1949.
Military Records: Adjutant General, Civil War Muster Rolls and Descriptive Lists 1863-1866, indexed.
U. S. Selective Service Records: Service cards (Form DD 53) for persons registered or serving in World Wars I and II, Korean War and Viet Nam Conflict until 1972. DD 214 discharge papers for Nevada veterans, transferred for historical and informational purposes. Access restricted by Privacy Act to person of record or immediate family.
Name Index to Correspondence of Governor James Nye, 1861-1864

Nevada State Children's (Orphans) Home, 1870-1968
Newspapers: Indexes
Carson Daily Appeal, 1865-66, 1869-70, 1881, 1885, 1886
http://www.clan.lib.nv.us/docs/newsind.htm
Nevada Appeal, 1980-currently being updated (at Nevada State Library,
Carson City, NV)
Prisoner Name Index to Nevada State Prison Case Files 1863- 1950
Secretary of State, License Plate Registration 1913-1946.
Tax Assessment rolls- Ormsby County
Territorial Papers:
An Inventory and Index to the Records of Carson County, Utah and Nevada
Territories, 1855-1861 (Grace Dangberg Foundation, 1984) These records
include individual court documents regarding divorces, estate settlements
and child custody, bonds and oaths of office of elected or appointed
territorial officials.
Name Index to Territorial records, Carson City, Utah and Nevada
Territories, 1855-1864, compiled by Charles A. Maze, 1993
Transcripts of Storey County and Carson City Coroner's burial permits

Nevada State Library
100 Stewart St., Carson City, NV 89710
Phone: 775 687-8313   Fax: 775 687-8330 (ILL, Reference) Internet:
http://www.clan.lib.nv.us
Hours: 8 a.m. to 5 p.m. Monday through Friday, except holidays
Founded 1859
Research fees: $15.00 per hour for Nevada residents, $20 per hour for non-
residents
Copying fee: copies by staff .30 each, microfilm copies made by researchers are
.15 per copy
Special Collections: Nevada Collection, Nevada Newspaper Collection
Census Records: 1862-1875 Territorial & State Censuses
    Indian Census Rolls (National Archives microfilm)
        Walker River (Paiute) 1897-1912 & 1914-1924
        Fort Lewis (Ute) 1904-1908
        Fort McDermitt (Pauite) 1910-1923
        Fallon (Pauite) 1909-1924
        Bay Mills School
        Birch Cooley Agency
        Bishop Agency
        Western Shoshone (Shoshoni & Pauite) 1885, 1887-1890; 1892-1909;
        1910-1929
        Carson 1909; 1925-1930

County Records:
  Duplicate assessment rolls for all counties 1891-1892
  Lander County, Preliminary listing of Births and Deaths 1887-1910
  Lyon County marriages 1862-1887
  Ormsby County- Civil court records 1862-1926
  Assessment rolls 1862-1950
  Partial list of births in Washoe County, 1887-1911
  Marriage licenses 1862-1872
Military Records:
  Nevada Territory & State Adjutant General Civil War Muster Rolls
  Nevada volunteers 1863-1866
  Reports of Office of Indian Affairs
  Returns from US Military Posts- Nevada
  Territorial papers, Utah 1853-1873
Newspaper Indexes, Nevada
  Carson Daily Appeal, 1865-66, 1869-70, 1881, 1885, 1886
    http://www.clan.lib.nv.us/docs/newsind.htm
  Douglas County Banner, Oct-Dec 1865
  Nevada Appeal, 1980-currently being updated

Nevada State Museum and Historical Society- Cahlan Library
700 Twin Lakes, Lorenzi Park, State Mail Complex, Las Vegas, NV 89107
Phone: 702 486-5205 Fax: 702 486-5172
  Society Background- Related to the Nevada Historical Society in Reno,
founded 1904
Nevada Holdings:
Books: Non lending- covering Nevada and the Southwest
Census Records
  1870 U.S. Census NV (2 rolls microfilm)
  1880 U.S. Census NV (2 rolls microfilm)
  1900 U.S. Census NV (1 roll microfilm) Esmeralda, Eureka, Humboldt, and
    Lander counties
  1910 U.S. Census NV (2 rolls microfilm) Clark County
  1920 U.S. Census NV- (11 rolls microfilm)
Indexes
  1880 Soundex NV (3 rolls microfilm)
  1900 Soundex NV (7 rolls microfilm)
Directories
  McKenney's Pacific Coast Directory, 1886-1887
  Reno, Sparks Directory, 1904, 1906, 1911-1912
  Polk's Reno, Sparks & Washoe County Directory
    1913-1914, 1917, 1920-1921, 1923, 1925-1926, 1927-1928, 1929-1930

Polk's Reno City Directory
  1933, 1935, 1937-1942, 1944, 1946, 1948, 1950
State of Nevada Telephone Directory
  Jan 1943, Oct 1946-Oct 1951, Aug 1952-Aug 1956
  Misc: Las Vegas telephone directories (scattered 1931-1970)
  Manuscript Collection: Index to Nevada Historical Manuscript Collection in
  Reno and index to Cahlan Collection
Maps:
Sanborne Fire Insurance Maps 1918-1953 (microfilm)
  Aurora   1890, with undated corrections
  Caliente   1928, with corrections to 1940
  Carlin   1927, with corrections to 1952
  Carson City   1907, with corrections to 1923
  Carson City   1907, with corrections to 1952
  Dayton   1895, with corrections to 1902
  Gold Hill   1877
  Las Vegas   1928, with corrections to 1961
  Lovelock   1923, with corrections to 1952
  Mina   1917
  Pioche   1924
  Reno   1879
  Reno   1918, with corrections to 1933
  Reno   1918, with corrections to 1953
  Reno   1918/1955, republication, corrected to 1972
  Sparks   1925, with corrections to 1930
  Virginia City/ Gold Hill 1890, with corrections to 1904)
  Winnemucca   1912, with corrections to 1952
U.S. Geological Survey Topographic Maps of Nevada
  Amargosa Region   (NV-CA)   1906
  Ballarat Quadrangle (CA-NV   1913
  Ballarat Quadrangle (CA-NV   1913 (1933 reprint)
  Bullfrog Special Map   1906
  Bullfrog Quadrangle   1906 (1932 reprint)
  Camp Mojave Sheet (AZ-NV-CA)   1892 (1911 rept)
  Carson City Quadrangle   1893 (1949 reprint)
  Carson Sheet   1893 (1909 reprint)
  Carson Sink Quadrangle   1908 (reprint)
  Carson Sink Quadrangle   1910 (1934 reprint)
  Disaster Sheet   1886
  Disaster Sheet   1893 (1922 reprint)
  Ely Special Map   1907
  Ely Quadrangle   1910 (reprint)
  Furnance Creek Quadrangle (CA-NV) 1910

Goldfield Special Map	1906, 1909
Granite Range Sheet	1894 (1914 reprint)
Hawthorne Quadrangle	(NV-CA) 1901, 1911 (1921 rept)
Honey Lake Sheet	1894 (1899 rept.)
Ivanpah Quadrangle	(CA-NV) 1912
Kawich Quadrangle	1908
Las Vegas Quadrangle	(NV-CA) 1908 (1920 rept.)
Lida Quadrangle	(NV-CA) 1908, 1913 (1927)
Long Valley Sheet	1894 (1920 rept)
Manhattan & Vicinity	1916 (reprint)
Markleeville Sheet	(CA-NV) 1889 reprint; 1893 (1916 reprint)
Paradise Sheet	1893 (1920 reprint)
Pioche Sheet	1893 (1920 reprint)
Reno Sheet	1893 (1900 reprint)
Rochester Mining District	1916
St. Thomas Sheet (NV-AZ)	1886 (1908 & 1929)
Silver Peak Quadrangle	(NV-CA) 1900 (1906 & 1916)
Tonopah Mining Map	1904
Tonopah Quadrangle	1908 (1922 reprint)
Truckee Sheet (CA)	1895 (1914 reprint)
Wabuska Sheet	1891, 1894 (1906)
Wadsworth Sheet	1890 (reprint); 1894 (1906)
Wellington Sheet	1891 & 1893 (1911)
Yerington District	1915

Newspapers & Magazines

Basic Bombardier	7 May 1943-17 Nov 1944 (microfilm)
Basic Magnesium Newsletter	26 Jun 1942-22 Apr 1943 (microfilm)
County Review	1909-1926 (microfilm)
Las Vegas Age	1905-1940 (microfilm)
Las Vegas Morning Tribune	1 Dec 1944-31 Mar 1945 (microfilm)
Las Vegas Review	3 Mar 1922-31 Dec 1926 (microfilm)
Las Vegas Review-Journal	1930-1970 (microfilm)
Nevada Snookum Times	23 May 1908 (microfilm)
Pah-Ranagat Silver Mining Co.	(microfilm)
Pioche Record, misc.dates	1872-1885 (microfilm)
Searchlight Bulletin	6 Aug 1909-13 Jan 1913 (microfilm)
Nevada Newspaper Index	Jan 1991-Sep 1994 (microfiche)
Las Vegas Sun	Jan 1991-Nov 1993 (microfiche)
Las Vegas Review Journal	Jan 1983-1990 (microfiche)
The Las Vegas Age	1905-1940
Las Vegas Review Journal	1930-1962 (3 X 5 card)
Las Vegas Review Journal	Sep 1962-1970 (ongoing project)
Nevada Magazine	1936-present

Nevadan   1964-present
Pioche Weekly Record   1872-1904 (microfilm & card file)
Nevada Historical Society Quarterly- complete run + index through 1973

Oral Histories: Not indexed. Have most of University of Reno's oral histories
    that relate to Southern Nevada and have most of Nye County's Oral History
    Project.
Photographs: Not open for general public, but photo requests can be discussed
    by appointment.
Research Services: Mail requests, if small. Photocopy costs: $.10 per page

Military Records
The 1st Battalion of Nevada Cavalry and the 1st Battalion of Nevada Infantry are
the only organization of Union Troops from Nevada. The National Archives in
San Bruno, California has separate compiled service records for these troops.

Mining Claims
Nevada State Library and Archives: http://www.clan.lib.nv.us/docs/mining.htm

All mining claims are recorded with the county recorder. Taxes are assessed by
the county assessor and paid to the county treasurer. All disputes over mining
claims were decided in district court, whose records are filed with the county
clerk. The county assessor may have a claim description in the tax assessment
records.

Mining companies incorporated in the state filed their articles of incorporation
with the Secretary of the Territory from 1861 to 1864, and with the secretary of
state from 1865. The State Archives has some of these records from 1861 to
1926. Mining companies that incorporated in another state were not required to
file papers with the state until 1891. They did have to file information with the
county clerk in the county in which the corporation did business. The secretary
of state has records of all active corporations or those that disincorporated after
1926.

The state mine inspector kept card files which listed mines in operation from
1909 to 1974. The records for these years 1909-1974 are in the State Archives
with an alphabetical file of all company names for all years. This record series
includes some description of the mine operation, addresses of managers,
licenses of hoist operators (1922-1971) and mining accidents (1909-1971),
both fatal and non-fatal. The accident reports are now maintained by the
Nevada State Industrial Insurance System. (Las Vegas branch: 1700 W.
Charleston, Las Vegas, NV 89102, phone: 702 388-3100.)

National Archives
Pacific Sierra Region, 1000 Commodore Drive, San Bruno, CA 94066
Phone: 415 876-9009
Hours: Monday - Friday 7:45 - 4:15
Serves Nevada (except Clark County), California (except Southern), Hawaii, and the Pacific Ocean area
Nevada Holdings:
Ninth Circuit Court, District Of Nevada, Carson City & Reno, 1865-1911. RG21
Common law and equity cases-mining, railroad industries, and land claims.
"Registers, Dockets & Naturalizations, 1865-1952," microfilm 130.
"Minutes, Journals, and Orders 1865-1956," microfilm 133.
District Court (Reno Division) 1865-1963. RG21
Bankruptcy, common law, criminal, and equity cases, including mining company bankruptcy.
State District Court, First Judicial District, Fallon (Churchill County), 1877-1956.
Declarations of Intention and Petitions for Naturalization.
State District Court, Second Judicial District, Reno (Washoe County), 1864-1949.
Declarations of Intention and Petitions for Naturalization, and final naturalizations.
Indexes (Soundex) 1880 & 1900 Nevada federal census
Records Geological Exploration of Fortieth Parallel ("King Survey"), 1867-1881. RG57-M622
Records of the Bureau of Land Management. RG49
Records of the Nevada land and survey office, 1912-1954. Land entry serial numbers and patents.
Index to Compiled Service Records of Volunteer Union Soldiers Who Served in Organizations From the State of Nevada. RG94-M548
Records of the Selective Service System (World War I). RG163
State Department Territorial Papers, Nevada 1861-1867. RG59-M13
Records Geological Exploration of Fortieth Parallel ("King Survey"), 1867-1881. RG57-M622

Pacific Southwest Region, 24000 Avila Road, P.O. Box 6719, Laguna Niguel, CA 92677
Phone: 714 831-4220
Hours: Monday - Friday 8:00 - 4:30
Serves Clark County, Nevada, Arizona, and Southern California
Nevada Holding:
District Court, Las Vegas, 1954-1968, RG21
Naturalization, bankruptcy, civil and criminal cases.

Bureau of Land Management, Las Vegas District Office, 1936-1971, RG49
State Department Territorial Papers, Nevada 1861-1864, RG59-M13
Indexes (Soundex) 1880 & 1900 Nevada federal census

Naturalization Records
Nevada State Library and Archives: http://www.clan.lib.nv.us/docs/natural.htm

Naturalization records may be found in the state district courts, and in U. S.
District Court records at the National Archives, Pacific Sierra Branch in San
Bruno, CA.

Naturalization records have not been filmed for any Nevada counties, except
for Washoe County District Court Naturalization records, 1861-1908 (film
0977771 ff.) at the National Archives Regional Branch in San Bruno,
California. These records are also available through the Family History
Centers.

Contact the county courthouses for copies of the original records for all
counties, including the Washoe County Courthouse in Reno.

Newpapers
Nevada State Library and Archives:
http://www.clan.lib.nv.us/docs/newsind.htm - Nevada Newspaper Indexes
Newspapers in Microform. Washington, Library of Congress, 1984.
1994 Yellow Book Daily Newspapers & Hospital Supplement Guide. Nomis
  Publications, Inc.

The largest collections of Nevada newspapers are at the University of Nevada,
Las Vegas and at the Nevada State Library in Carson City.

Probate Records
Probate actions before 1861 were recorded in the Utah territorial courts.
Records located the Nevada State Library and Archives. Probate records after
1864 are in the district courts.

Tribal Organizations
"Indian Territory" *The Discover Nevada Bonus Book 1997*

Battle Mountain Band Council
  35 Mountainview Drive, Battle Mountain, NV 89820
  Phone: 775 635-2004 Fax: 775 635-8016

Duck Valley Shoshone-Paiute Tribes
  P.O. Box 219, Owyhee, NV 89832
  Phone: 775 757-3211 Fax: 775 757-2219

Duckwater Shoshone Tribe
  P.O. Box 140068
  511 Duckwater Falls, Duckwater, NV 89314

Elko Band Council
  P.O. Box 748, 511 Sunset, Elko, NV 89803
  Phone: 775 738-8889 Fax: 775 753-5439

Ely Shoshone Tribe
  16 Shoshone Circle, Ely, NV 89301
  Phone: 775 289-3013 Fax: 775 289-3156

Fallon Paiute Shoshone Tribe
  8955 Misson Road, Fallon, NV 89406
  Phone: 775 423-6075 Fax: 775 423-5412

Fort McDermitt Indian Reservation
  P.O. Box 457, 111 North Reservation Road
  McDermitt, NV 89421

Las Vegas Indian Center
  2300 West Bonanza Road, Las Vegas, NV 89106
  Phone: 702 647-5842

Las Vegas Paiute Tribe
  1 Paiute Drive, Las Vegas, NV 89106
  Phone: 702 386-3926 Fax: 702 383-4019

Moapa Tribal Store
  P.O. Box 340
  #1 Lincoln Street, Moapa, NV 89025
  Phone: 775 865-2787

Pyramid Lake Paiute Tribe
P.O. Box 256
208 Capital Hill, Nixon, NV 89424
Phone: 775 574-1000 Fax: 775 574-1008

Reno-Sparks Indian Colony
98 Colony Road, Reno, NV 89502
Phone: 775 329-2936 Fax: 775 329-8710

Stewart Indian Cultural Center
5366 Snyder Avenue, Carson City, NV 89701
Phone: 775 882-1808

Walker River Paiute Tribe
P.O. Box 220
#1 Hospital Road, Schurz, NV 89427
Phone: 775 773-2306 Fax: 775 773-2585

Washoe Tribe of Nevada and California
919 Highway 395 S., Gardnerville, NV 89410
Phone: 775 265-4191, 775 883-1446
Fax: 775 265-6240 E-mail: bwallace@itcn.org

Yerington Paiute Tribe
171 Campbell Lane, Yerington, NV 89447
Phone: 775 463-3301 Fax: 775 463-2416

Vital records

Nevada State Library and Archives: http://www.clan.lib.nv.us/docs.birth.htm

Nevada State Department of Health
Division of Archives and Records, 101 South Fall Street, Carson City, NV
  89710

Birth and death records: There were no birth or death records kept in Nevada until 1887, when the first vital statistics law was passed by the Nevada State Legislature. Birth and death records from 1887 to the present are recorded in each county, either in the county recorder office or the county health officer. The State Department of Health has birth and death records from July 1911.

Burial permits: From 1879 to 1911, incorporated cities required undertakers to obtain burial permits from the county coroner's office. Permits were issued when the death certificates were filed. These certificates exist for Virginia City and Gold Hill for 1879-1887, and Carson City 1893-1896.

Marriage and divorce records: The Nevada State Office of Vital Statistics has marriage and divorce records from 1968 to the present. Divorces are civil court actions and from 1862 to the present are kept at the county clerk office for each county. Civil court cases are filed by case number and indexed by plaintiff and defendant. Marriage certificates are filed with the county recorder in the county where the marriage license was issued, not where the marriage took place.

Nevada State Archives has some marriage and divorce records for Carson County, Utah and Nevada territories, 1856-1862, and marriage records for Douglas, Lyon Ormsby, Storey and Washoe counties for 1862-1900. The latter are available on microfilm, for research only.

FAMILY HISTORY LIBRARY (Salt Lake City, Utah) HOLDINGS

All microfilmed and microfiched records (unless restricted) are available to rent worldwide at branch Family History Centers and selected larger public and private libraries and societies.

Credit Line: Reprinted by permission. Copyright ©1987 by The Church of Jesus Christ of Latter-day Saints.

Nevada - Archives and libraries - Inventories, registers, catalogs

Nevada. Secretary of State. *Inventory of Territorial Documents, 1860-1863.* Q AREA 979.3 A1 no. 1, also on microfilm- 0824279 item 4

Nevada - Biography - Indexes

Parker, J. Carlyle, *Nevada Biographical and Genealogical Sketch Index.* Turlock, Calif. : Marietta Publishing, c1986. 979.3 D32p

Nevada - Cemeteries

Bible and Cemetery Records of Nevada.
Microfilm of original records in the D.A.R. Library in Washington, D.C., filmed 1971.
Microfilm- 0869278 item 2
Contains bible records of: Hillman, Daniel and Grace Haines; Menardi, Andrew E. and Mary Lemira; Norris, Moses L. and Annie L. Joy; Samuels, William L. and Annie Bell Conway; Sawin, Ethan A. and Lucina Remington; Stier, Eleanor; Walters, Reis and Margaret; and Andrews, William H. and Sarah J. Deveors. Also contains cemetery records of: Elko County, Nevada; old mining towns of Nevada; and Sierra County, California.

Card Index of Persons Buried in Nevada Cemeteries. Filmed 1990.
Microfilm- 1307667
Includes name of deceased, cemetery of burial, location of records, date of death and sometimes birth or age and other incidentals.

Taylor, Richard B. *The Nevada Tombstone Record Book.* Las Vegas, Nevada : Nevada Families Project, 1986.
979.3 V3n, also on microfilm- 1421848 item 5
Includes inscriptions from community cemeteries, newspaper obituaries, and selected family records.

Nevada - Cemeteries - History

Crabtree, Kathryn Rae. *Cemeteries in California and Nevada : A Western Thanatopsis*

979.4 V3c, also on microfilm- 1697406 item 9

The author's dual purpose is to indicate how to study cemeteries and why to bother with them, by recommending a procedure for recording western cemeteries, and gives examples of using above-ground cemetery data to understand past lifeways.

Nevada - Census - 1861-1862

Nevada Territory Manuscript Census, 1861-1864 and Nevada State Manuscript Census for Washoe County, 1875. Carson City, Nevada, 1991.

Microfilm- 1689341

Records located at Nevada State Library and Archives, Division of Archives and Records, Capitol Complex, Carson City, Nevada. Includes partial index to 1862 census for Storey and Ormsby counties, Nevada Territory; census report of Henry DeGroot, 1861 (summaries only); Churchill County census report, 1862 (summaries only); Douglas County, 1862; Humboldt County, Buena Vista, 1862; Humboldt County, Echo township, 1862; Humboldt County, Humboldt township, 1862; Humboldt County, Prince Royal township, 1862; Humboldt county, Santa Clara township, 1862; Humboldt County, Star township, 1862; Leander County, 1963; Lyon County, Dayton, El Dorado Canyon, Palmyra, 1862; Lyon County, Silver City, 1862; Lyon and Churchill counties, census report, 1863 (summaries only); Ormsby County, 1862; Storey County, Flowery District, 1862; Storey County, Gold Hill, 1862; Storey County, Virginia City, 1862; Washoe County, 1862; Wahoe County, 1875. Nevada Territory 1861-1864, Census 1875.

Nevada - Census - 1870

United States. Census Office. 9th census, 1870. *Nevada, 1870 Federal Census: Population Schedules.*

The 1870 census was filmed twice. The second filming (2nd) is listed first and is usually easier to read.

Microfilm- 0552333 (2nd filming) Churchill, Douglas, Elko, Esmeralda, Humboldt, Lander, Lincoln, Lyon, Nye, Ormsby, Pahute (Subdivision of Lincoln County), Roop (Subdivision of Ormsby County).

Microfilm- 0552334 (2nd filming) Story, Washoe, and White Pine counties.

Microfilm- 0014892 Nevada: (1st filming) Churchill, Douglas, Elko, Esmeralda, Humboldt, Lander, Lincoln, Lyon, Nye, Ormsby, Pahute

(Subdivision of Lincoln County), Roop (Subdivision of Ormsby County), Storey, Washoe, and White Pine counties.

Nevada - Census - 1870 - Indexes

Jackson, Ronald Vern. *Mortality Schedule Nevada 1870.* Bountiful, Utah: Accelerated Indexing Systems, 1980.
979.3 X2jm 1870

Jackson, Ronald Vern. *Nevada 1870 Territorial Census Index.* Salt Lake City : Accelerated Indexing Systems, c1979.
979.3 X2j 1870

Nevada 1870 Federal Census Index. Salt Lake City : Filmed by the Genealogical Society of Utah, 1979.
Includes transcription of all information found in the 1870 census arranged alphabetically by surname except for cards that were missed in filming and all Chinese entries are at the end of the last film.
Microfilm- 1206333 A - Dl
Microfilm- 1206334 Do - J
Microfilm- 1206335 K - Pf
Microfilm- 1206336 Ph - Wi
Microfilm- 1206337 Wo - Z; Chinese; Missed cards

Nevada - Census - 1875

Jensen, Genevieve S. *Persons Living in Nevada Who Were Born in New Jersey, Extracted From Nevada State   Census, 1875.* Salt Lake City : Filmed by the Genealogical Society of Utah, 1994.
Microfilm- 1598226 item 8
Surnames are in alphabetical order. Includes name, age, sex, color, occupation, value of real estate, value of personal estate, place of birth, father of foreign birth, mother of foreign birth, county, volume and page.

Census of the Inhabitants of the State of Nevada, 1875. Millwood, N.Y. : Kraus-Thomson, [198-?].
Fiche- 6016536 Counties: Churchill, Douglas & Esmeralda. No circulation to Family History Centers.
Fiche- 6016537 Elko
Fiche- 6016538 Elko (part) & Eureka (part)
Fiche- 6016539 Eureka (part)
Fiche- 6016540 Eureka (part), Humboldt & Lander (part)
Fiche- 6016541 Lander (part) & Lincoln (part)
Fiche- 6016542 Lincoln (part) & Lyon (part)
Fiche- 6016543 Lyon (part), Nye & Ormsby (part)

Fiche- 6016544 Ormsby (part) & Storey (part)
Fiche- 6016545-6016550 Storey (part)
Fiche- 6016551 Washoe (part)
Fiche- 6016552 Washoe (part) & White Pine (part)
Fiche- 6016553 White Pine (part)

Nevada State 1875 Census - Name Index. Carson City, Nev. : Nevada State Library, [1900?].
Each county is separately indexed. White County (fiche 6332701) is mislabeled as Hite County. Provides year, sex, race, occupation, vol. and page number.

Microfilm- 6332696 Churchill County
Microfilm- 6332697 Douglas County
Microfilm- 6332698 Elko County
Microfilm- 6332699 Esmeralda County
Microfilm- 6332700 Eureka County
Microfilm- 6332702 Humboldt County
Microfilm- 6332703 Lander County
Microfilm- 6332704 Lincoln County
Microfilm- 6332705 Lyon County
Microfilm- 6332706 Nye County
Microfilm- 6332707 Ormsby County
Microfilm- 6332708 Storey County
Microfilm- 6332709 Washoe County
Microfilm- 6332701 White County

Nevada - Census - 1875 - Indexes

Jensen, Genevieve S. *Index to Nevada State Census 1875 Appendix to Journals of Senate and Assembly, 8th Session, v. 2-3, Head of Family and Other Name.* Salt Lake City : Filmed by the Genealogical Society of Utah, 1994.
Microfilm- 1598226 item 11

Nevada - Census - 1880

Jackson, Ronald Vern. *Nevada 1880 Mortality Schedule.* Bountiful, Utah : Accelerated Indexing Systems, c1984.
979.3 X2n 1880

United States. Bureau of the Census. 10th census, 1880. *Nevada, 1880 Federal Census : Soundex and Population Schedules.*
Microfilm- 0378008 Soundex: A000 thru L261
Microfilm- 0378009 Soundex: L300 thru W666
Microfilm- 0378010 Soundex: Y000 thru Institutions
Microfilm- 1254758 Population schedules: Churchill, Douglas, Elko,

Esmeralda, Eureka, Humboldt, Lander, Lincoln, and Lyon counties.
Microfilm- 1254759 Population schedules: Nye, Ormsby, Roop, Storey,
Washoe, and White Pine counties.

Nevada - Census - 1880 - Indexes

Jackson, Ronald Vern. *Nevada 1880 Territorial Census Index.* Salt Lake City :
Accelerated Indexing Systems, c1979.
979.3 X2j 1880

Nevada - Census - 1900 - Indexes

Jackson, Ronald Vern. *1890 Nevada Census Index : Special Schedule of The
Eleventh Census (1890) Enumerating Union Veterans and of Union
Veterans of the Civil War.* Salt Lake City : Accelerated Indexing Systems,
c1983.
979.3 X22jv 1890

Jackson, Ronald Vern. *Nevada 1900.* North Salt Lake, Utah : Accelerated
Indexing Systems International, Inc., c1986.
Contains census index.
979.3 X22j 1900

United States. Census Office. 12th census, 1900. *Nevada, 1900 Federal
Census : Soundex And Population Schedules.*
Microfilm- 1245959 Soundex: A000 - thru C455
Microfilm- 1245960 Soundex: C460 - thru F525
Microfilm- 1245961 Soundex: F530 - thru J200/216 Frank
Microfilm- 1245962 Soundex: J200/216 Gee - thru M250 John
Microfilm- 1245963 Soundex: M250 John - thru P500/562
Microfilm- 1245964 Soundex: P600 - thru S553
Microfilm- 1245965 Soundex: S560 - thru Z635
Microfilm- 1240943 Population schedules: Churchill, Douglas, Elko,
Esmeralda, Eureka, Humboldt, Lander, Lincoln, Lyon, Nye, Ormsby,
Storey, Washoe, and White Pine counties.

20 Nevada Guide to Genealogical Records

Nevada - Census - 1910
United States. Bureau of the Census. 13th census, 1910. .*Nevada, 1910 Federal Census : Population Schedules.*
No Soundex was created for this date.
Microfilm- 1374871 Population schedules: Churchill, Clark, Douglas, Elko, Lincoln, Esmeralda, Eureka, Humboldt, and Lander counties.
Microfilm- 1374872 Population schedules: Lyon, Nye, Ormsby, White Pine, Storey, and Washoe counties.

Nevada - Census - 1920
United States. Bureau of the Census. 14th census, 1920. *Nevada, 1920 Federal Census : Soundex and Population Schedules.*
Microfilm- 1827174   Soundex: A000 - thru B650
Microfilm- 1827175   Soundex: (B651-B652) -thru (D452-D466)
Microfilm- 1827176   Soundex: D500 - thru (G631-G634)
Microfilm- 1827177   Soundex: (G635-G636) - thru (K130-K166)
Microfilm- 1827178   Soundex: (K200-K216) - thru M263
Microfilm- 1827179   Soundex: (M264-M266) - thru P362
Microfilm- 1827180   Soundex: (P363-P366) - thru (S341-S346)
Microfilm- 1827181   Soundex: S350 - thru T651
Microfilm- 1827182   Soundex: T653 - thru Institutions
Microfilm- 1821004   Population schedules: Churchill Co. (ED's 1-4), Douglas Co. (ED's 5-6), Elko Co. (ED's 7, 10, 8-9, 11-14, 16-17, and 15), Eureka Co. (ED's 18-20), Lander Co. (ED's 27-28), Clark Co. (ED's 1-5)-28), Esmerald Co. (ED's 19, 11, 7-10, and 6), Humboldt Co. (ED's 21-26), 7-10, and 6) Lincoln Co. (ED's 12-17 and 32), Lyon Co. (ED's 29-31) 7 and 32), Ormsby Co. (ED's 32, 68, and 33-34)
Microfilm- 1821005   Population schedules: Mineral Co. (ED's 18, and 20-23), Washoe Co. (ED's 42-43, 45-54, 58, 44, 57, and 55-56), Nye Co. (ED's 24-31), Pershing Co. (ED's 35-38), Storey Co. (ED's 41, 39, and 40), White Pine Co. (ED's 64-65, 59-60, 63, 62, 66, 61, and 67)

Nevada - Census - 1910 - Indexes
Dilts, Bryan Lee. *1910 Nevada Census Index : Heads Of Households And Other Surnames In Households Index.* Salt Lake City : Index Publishing, 1984.
979.3 X22n, also on microfiche- 6331388
No circulation to family history centers.

Jackson, Ronald Vern. *Nevada 1910 Census Index.* Bountiful, Utah : Accelerated Indexing Systems, c1984.
979.3 X22j 1910

Nevada - Church history
Loofbourow, Leonidas Latimer. *Steeples Among the Sage, a Centennial Story of Nevada's Churches.* Oakland, Calif. : Lake Park Press, c1964.
979.3 K2
Includes histories of Baptists, Catholics, Jews, Methodists, Mormons, Presbyterians and Episcopalians in NV.

Arrington, Leonard James. *The Mormons in Nevada.* Las Vegas, Nev. : Las Vegas Sun, 1979.
979.3 H2a, also on microfilm- 1059488 item 7
Index- Microfilm- 1421708 item 7

Loofbourow, Leonidas Latimer. *Cross in the Sunset : The Development of Methodism in the California-Nevada Annual Conference of the Methodist Church, and of its Predecessors with Roster of All Members of the Conference.* San Francisco, Calif. : Historical Society of the California-Nevada Annual Conference of the Methodist Church, c1966.
979.4K2

Tanner, Bette. *Latter-Day Saints In Southern Nevada.* Salt Lake City : Filmed by the Genealogical Society of Utah, 1986.
Microfilm- 1421590 item 2
Includes a brief history of the following stakes in southern Nevada: Moapa (Logandale), Las Vegas, Henderson (formerly Lake Mead), North Las Vegas Nevada, East, Las Vegas Nevada Central, Las Vegas Nevada South, Las Vegas Nevada Henderson West, Redrock, Paradise and Las Vegas Nevada West.

Nevada - Church records
Episcopal Register of The Bishop of Utah (Bishop's Personal Register) 1899-1946, 1951-1967. Salt Lake City : Filmed by the Genealogical Society of Utah, 1975.
Microfilm- 0908728
Contains confirmations, baptisms, marriages, burials.

Inventory of the Church Archives of Nevada, Protestant Episcopal Church. Reno, Nev. : Historical Records Survey, 1941.
979.3 K2he, also on microfilm- 1036524 item 2, also on microfiche- 6051184

Church of Jesus Christ of Latter-day Saints. Nevada Conference. *Annual Genealogical Report, Form E, 1908-1940.* Salt Lake City : Filmed by the Genealogical Society of Utah, 1953.
Microfilm of original records in the LDS Church Archives, Salt Lake City. The Nevada Conference of the California Mission included some local units in the state of California.
Microfilm- 0001787　Form E　1908-1941
Photocopies not permitted except for direct line descendants. Remove all other data from photocopy.
Reorganized Church of Jesus Christ of Latter-day Saints. Pacific Slopes Mission (California & Nevada).
Church Records, 1863-1878. Salt Lake City : Filmed by the Genealogical Society of Utah, 1994.
Microfilm- 1927791 item 6　Membership records 1864-1878, History 1863-1866

Nevada - Church records - Inventories, registers, catalogs
Historical Records Survey, Division of Professional and Service Projects, Work Projects Administration. *Inventory of the Church Archives of Nevada, Roman Catholic Church.* Reno, Nev. : Historical Records Survey, 1939.
979.3 K2hc, also on microfilm-1036527 item 7, another filming, 0982096 item 5, microfiche- 6051185

Nevada - Court records
Greathouse, Bill. *Nevada Local Court Records Project Records Inventory Sheet at Carson City, Nevada, March - September, 1987.* Carson City, Nev. : Greathouse, 1987?.
979.3 P23n
Includes state of Nevada minimum records retention schedule for district courts. Includes index.

Nevada - Description and travel - Guide-books
Hart, Herbert M. *Tour Guide to Old Forts of New Mexico, Arizona, Nevada, Utah & Colorado.* Boulder, Colo. : Pruett Publishing, c1981 (Fort Collins, Colo. : The Old Army Press).
978 E6h v. 2

Nevada - Directories

Kelly, J. Wells. *First Directory of Nevada Territory : Containing the Names of Residents in the Principal Towns*. San Francisco : Valentine, 1862.
979.3 E4v
Indexed in: An alphabetical listing of the first directory of Nevada territory- 1598348 item 16

Nevada State Gazetteer and Business Directory, 1907-08, 1914-15. Salt Lake City : R. L. Polk, 1907.
979.3 E5n, also on microfilm- 1000195 item 1

Knight, William H. *Handbook Almanac for the Pacific States : An Official Register and Business Directory, 1863*. Tucson, Ariz. : W. C. Cox Co., 1974.
Microfilm- 1000121 item 3
The register and business directory covers the state of California and Oregon; the territories of Washington, Nevada, and Utah; and the colonies of British Columbia and Vancouver.

Langley, Henry G. *The Pacific Coast Business Directory for 1871-73 : Containing the Name and Post Office Address of Each Merchant, Manufacturer and Professional Residing in the States of California, Oregon, and Nevada; the Territories of Washington, Idaho, Montana, Utah, Arizona and Alaska; and the Colony of British Columbia. Also a Gazetteer of the Counties, Cities and Towns With the Federal, State and Municipal Officers Attached Thereto, and an Exhibit of the Resources of the Pacific Coast.*
Microfilm- 1697369 item 11

The Pacific Coast Directory : Giving Name, Business, and Address of Business and Professional Men of California, Oregon, Washington, British Columbia, Alaska, Nevada, Utah, Idaho, Montana, Arizona, and New Mexico Together With Sketches of the Different Towns, Giving Location, Population, etc.. -- 1871-1884. Salt Lake City : Utah State Archives and Records Service : Microfilmed by the Genealogical Society of Utah, 1975, 1994.
Microfilm- 1004513 item 3   1871-1873
Microfilm- 1004515 item 2   1878
Microfilm- 1004517   1880/1881
Microfilm- 1697991 item 4   1883/1884 (pagination in order)
Microfilm- 1004519   1883/1884 (pagination out of order)

Business Directory of San Francisco, and Principal Towns of California and Nevada, 1877 : Containing Names, Business and Address of Merchants, Manufacturers and Professional Men. Salt Lake City : Filmed by the Genealogical Society of Utah, 1989.
Microfilm- 1597554 item 4

State of Nevada directory. -- 1871-72. Reno, Nev. : State of Nevada, 1871-72
979.3 E4pn, also on microfilm- 1425608 item 4

Nevada - Directories - Bibliography
Quebedeaux, Richard. *Prime Sources of California and Nevada Local History: 151 Rare and Important City, County and State Directories, 1850-1909.* Spokane, WA : Arthur H. Clark, c1992.
979.4 E43q
    Contains an annotated bibliography of the most important directories of California counties and state of Nevada. Includes brief historical sketches of each county and gives directory names, publishers and descriptions.

Nevada - Directories - Indexes
Thompson, J. S. *An Alphabetical Listing of the First Directory of Nevada Territory : Directory Compiled by J. Wells Kelly, Circa 1861-1862, for the Towns of Aurora, Carson City, Dayton, Empire, Genoa, Gold Hill, Jack's Valley, Silver City, Virginia City, Washoe.*
Microfilm- 1598348 item 16

Nevada - Directories - Inventories, registers, catalogs
Lee, Joyce C. *Genealogical Prospecting In Nevada : A Guide to Nevada Directories.* Nevada Library Association, 1984.
979.3 A1no.29
    Contains a list of the directories with holdings of Nevada archives and libraries.

Nevada - Encyclopedias and Dictionaries
Davis, Ellis Arthur. *Davis' Commercial Encyclopedia of the Pacific Southwest. California, Nevada, Utah, Arizona.* Berkeley, Calif. : E. A. Davis, c1914.
Q AREA 979 D3d, also on microfilm- 1000134 item 7

Nevada - Gazetteers
Fox, Theron. *Nevada Treasure Hunters Ghost Town Guide : Includes 1881 Fold-in Map of Nevada With Glossary of 800 Place Names, 1867 Map of Nevada.* San Jose, Calif. : Fox, 1961.
979.3 A1 no.23

Averett, Walter R. *Directory of Southern Nevada Place Names.*
979.3 E5a

United States. Office of Geographic Research. Branch of Geographic Names.
Nevada Geographic Names Information System Alphabetical List.
979.3 E2u, also on microfilm- 1320966 item 2

Nevada - Genealogy
Nevada D.A.R. chapters, 1953-1954. *Genealogical Records 1953-1958.*
979.3 D2d, also on microfilm- 1425613 item 6-8

Dawson, Alson W. *Greener Grass, a True Story of a Pioneer Family: A
Bittersweet Struggle for a Better Life on the Western Frontier.* Boise, Ida. :
Dawson Publishing House, 1984.
929.273 D323da, also on microfiche- 6089063
   Alexander Dawson (1796-1871) married Elizabeth Lunney about 1821,
   and moved to Dickinson Center, New York during or before 1828.
   Descendants and relatives lived in New York, Nevada, Idaho and
   elsewhere.

Daughters of the American Colonists (Nevada). *Bible and Family Records.*
Microfilm- 0176645

Nevada - Genealogy - Handbooks, manuals, etc.
Nevada : Research Outline / Family History Library. Salt Lake City : Corp. of
the President of the Church of Jesus Christ of L.D.S., c1988.
929.1 F21ro US-STATES no. 29, also on microfiche- 6105268

Nevada - Genealogy - Indexes
Bell, Connie R. *Index to Maude Sawin Taylor's From My Nevada Notebook.*
Salt Lake City : Filmed by the Genealogical Society of Utah, 1987.
Microfilm- 1421750 item 5

Nevada - Genealogy - Inventories, registers, catalogs
Spiros, Joyce V. Hawley. *Genealogical Guide to Arizona and Nevada.* Gallup,
N.M. : Verlene Publishing, c1983.
979 D23s, also on microfiche- 6049613

Nevada - Genealogy - Periodicals
Northeastern Nevada Genealogical Society. *Chart and Quill*. Vol. 1, book 1 (May 1979).
979.3 D25c
    Quarterly. Includes genealogical gleanings from the northeastern counties of Elko, Eureka, Humboldt, Lander, Pershing and White Pine. Library's holdings begin with v. 1, book 1 (May 1979).

Nevada - History
Averett, Walter R. *Through the Rainbow Canyon*. Grand Junction, Colo. : W.R. Averett, c1995.
979.3 H2a

Bancroft, Hubert Howe. *History of Nevada, Colorado and Wyoming, 1540-1888*.
979 B4b v.25, also on microfilm- 0982474 item 1

Dangberg, Grace. *Carson Valley : Historical Sketches of Nevada's First Settlement*. Reno, Nev. : Carson Valley Historical Society, 1979, c1972.
979.3 H2c

Edwards, Elbert B. *200 Years in Nevada : A Story of People Who Opened, Explored and Developed the Land; a Bicentennial History*. Salt Lake City, Utah : Publishers Press, c1978.
979.3 H2ed

Elliott, Russell R. ; line drawings by Jack Brodie. *History of Nevada*. [Lincoln, Neb.] : University of Nevada
Press, 1984, c1973.
979.3 H2e

Ellison, Marion. *An Inventory & Index to the Records of Carson County, Utah & Nevada Territories, 1855-1861*. Reno, Nev. : Grace Dangberg Foundation, 1984.
979.3 R2e
    Includes index. Includes history of early Utah and Nevada Territories. Consists chiefly of land records.
    Contains probate records.

Florin, Lambert. *Nevada Ghost Towns*. Seattle : Superior Publishing, c1971.
979.3 R2f
Includes cities of Aurora, Austin, Belmont, Berlin-Union, Broken Hills,
Candelaria, Dayton, Eureka, Fairview, Galena, Genoa, Gold Hill,
Goldfield, Gold Point, Goodsprings, Grantsville, Hamilton, Ione, Johnnie,
Manhattan, Midas, National, Nelson, Paradise Valley, Pine Grove, Pioche,
Rawhide, Rhyolite, Rochester, Rockland, Sutro, Tonopah, Tuscarora,
Unionville, Virginia City, Wadsworth, and Washoe City. Includes short
biographies of some early settlers.

Hulse, James W. *The Nevada Adventure : a History*. Reno, Nev. : University of
Nevada Press, c1981.
979.3 H2h

Johnson, David Alan. *Founding the Far West; California, Oregon, and
Nevada, 1840-1890*. Berkeley, Calif. : University of California Press, c1992.
979 H2a

Johnson, Robert Neil. *California-Nevada Ghost Town Atlas*. Susanville, Calif.
Cy Johnson, 1970, c1967.
979 A1 no.1

Koenig, George. *Beyond This Place There be Dragons : The Routes of the
Tragic Trek of the Death Valley 1849ers through Nevada, Death Valley, and
on to Southern California*. Glendale, Calif. : Arthur Clark, 1984.
979.4 H2k

Mack, Effie Mona. *Nevada : a History of the State From the Earliest Times
Through the Civil War*. Glendale, Calif. : Arthur H. Clark Co., 1936.
979.3 H2m

Mathews, Mary McNair. *Ten Years in Nevada : or, Life on the Pacific coast*.
Tucson, Ariz. : W.C. Cox Co., 1974.
Microfilm- 1000194 item 1

Murbarger, Nell. *Ghosts of the Glory Trail : Intimate Glimpses into the Past
and Present of Western Ghost Towns*. Palm Desert, Calif. : Desert Printers,
1971, c1956.
979 H2mg
Great Basin lies between the Wasatch Mountains of Utah and California's
Sierra Nevada. Includes stories of the people who settled cities which
grew up from the sage and directories locating and describing briefly 275
former boom camps.

Myron Angel, ed. *History of Nevada : with Illustrations and Biographical Sketches of its Prominent Men and Pioneers.* Tucson, Ariz. : W.C. Cox, 1974.
Microfilm 1000194 item 2, another filming 1841572

Paher, Stanley W. *Colorado River Ghost Towns.* Las Vegas, Nev. : Nevada Publications, c1976.
979.13 H2p

Paher, Stanley W. *Nevada Ghost Towns & Mining Camps.* Las Vegas, Nev. : Nevada Publications, c1970.
979.3 H2p, also microfilm- 1598077 item 2

Patterson, Edna B. *Nevada's Northeast Frontier.* Reno, Nev. : University of Nevada Press, c1991.
979.3 H2pat

Pompey, Sherman Lee. *1863 Census of Some Prominent Residents of the Nevada Territory.* Salt Lake City : Filmed by the Genealogical Society of Utah, 1970.
Microfilm 0823650- item 2.
List of names of individuals, including all County officers, members of the Legislative Council, Legislative Assembly representatives, Constitutional Convention delegates, "...as well as...doctors, attorneys, notary publics, dentists...and other business and professional persons..."

Pompey, Sherman Lee. *Nevada Territory Pioneers Who Stayed.* Salt Lake City. Filmed by the Genealogical Society of Utah, 1970.
Microfilm- 0823650 item 2.
Contains names of individuals, state or nation of birth, and position in Nevada county.

Roske, Ralph J. *Las Vegas : a Desert Paradise.* Tulsa, Okla. : Continental Heritage Press, c1986.
Q AREA 979.3135 H2r

Scrugham, James Graves. *Nevada : a Narrative of the Conquest of a Frontier Land Comprising the Story of Her People From the Dawn of History to the Present Time.* Chicago : American Historical Society, 1935.
979.3 H2s, also on microfilm- 1000194 item 3-5

Silverberg, Robert. *Ghost towns of the American West.*
978 H2sg

Smith, Grant Horace. *The History of the Comstock Lode, 1850-1920*. New York : Thomas Y. Crowell, c1968.
979.3 H25s

Tolman, Sybil. *Index to Leonard J. Arrington's The Mormons in Nevada*. Salt Lake City : Filmed by the Genealogical Society of Utah, 1987.
Microfilm- 1421708 item 7

Nevada, a Guide to the Silver State. Compiled by workers of the Writer's program of the Work Projects Administration in the state of Nevada. Tucson, Ariz. : W. C. Cox Co., 1974.
Microfilm- 1000196 item 1

Nevada, Official Bicentennial Book. Thomas C. Elgas, coordinator; edited and designed by Stanley W. Paher.Las Vegas, Nev. : Nevada Publications, c1976.
979.3 H2pa

Nevada : the Silver State. Carson City, Nev. : Western States Historical Pub., Inc., 1970.
979.3 H2n

Political History of Nevada 1990. Issued by Frankie Sue Del Papa, Secretary of State of Nevada. Carson City, Nev. : [s.n.], 1990.
979.3 N2p

Nevada - History - Indexes
Poulton, Helen J. *Index to History of Nevada*. Reno : University of Nevada Press, c1966.
979.3 B4u v. 6
This index can be used with the original 1881 ed. published by Thompson and West, and the 1958 reprint.

Nevada - History - Maps
Carter, Richard. *Mormon Colonies, 1847-1900*.
map case 978 E7caw

Nevada - History - Periodicals
Nevada Historical Society (Reno, Nevada). Nevada Historical Society Quarterly. -- Vol. 1, no. 1 (1957). Reno, Nev. : The Society, 1957.
979.3 H25n
Library has: Vol. 9, no. 1 (Spring 1966), v. 15, no. 1 (Spring 1972).

Nevada Historical Society Papers, 1913-1920. -- Vol. 1 (1913-1916)-v. 5
(1925-1926). Carson City, Nev. : The Society, 1917-1926.
979.3 H25p
Library has v. 1 (1913-1916) - v. 2 (1917-1920).

Nevada - Land and property

*In the District Court of the United States in and for the District of Nevada : in
Equity Docket no. A3, The United States of America, Plaintiff, vs. Orr Water
Ditch Company, et al. Defendants.*
Q AREA 979.3 R21u

Ellison, Marion. *An Inventory & Index to the Records of Carson County, Utah
& Nevada Territories, 1855-1861.* Reno, Nev. : Grace Dangberg Foundation,
1984.
979.3 R2e
Includes history of early Utah and Nevada Territories. Consists chiefly of
land records. Contains probate records.

Thompson, J. S. *Early Nevada Records : Certificates of survey, Carson Valley,
1856; 1862 Census of Churchill County; 1864 Census of Nye County.* Salt
Lake City : Filmed by the Genealogical Society Utah, 1995.
Microfilm- 1598348 item 1
Contents: List of names found on certificates in Carson Valley 1856
--Alphabetical listing of 1862 census of Churchill County with name, age,
gender, state of birth, occupation and residence -- Alphabetical list of
names and age of those in Nye County census, 1864 -- List of names
subscribed on 14 Feb 1863 at a meeting in Virginia City to organize the
Democratic party in Nevada.

Nevada - Law and legislation

Nevada. Governor (1861-1864 : Nye). *State Department Territorial Papers,
Nevada, 1861-1864.* Washington, D.C. : National Archives and Records
Service, [19--].
Microfilm- 1491200
Includes index. Includes rough draft of bylaws of territory, constitution of
state of Nevada, civil   appointments, numeral census report and 1864
Governor's message. (National Archives microfilm publications ; no. 13-1)

Nevada - Maps

Gray's Atlas, California and Nevada.
  map case 979 E7g
    Scale 1:2,280,000. [1874]. 1 map : col. ; 64 X 40 cm. Insets: The vicinity
    of San Francisco. Scale 1:633,600 -- Map of the Yosemite Valley,
    Mariposa Co., Cal. Scale 1:95,040.

Nevada. Chicago : Rand McNally, 1893. Scale ca. 1:[1,013,760]. 1 map ; 88 X
  57 cm.
  map case 979.3 E7rm

New Railroad and County Map of Northern California and Nevada. [S.l. : s.n.,
  1881?]. Scale ca. 1:[2,080,960].
  map case 979 E7n

Rand McNally & Co.'s New Family Atlas Map of Nevada and Arizona. [S.l.] :
  Rand McNally & Co., 1888.
  map case 979 E7na
    2 maps on 1 sheet ; 23 x 31 cm.

Nevada. [S.l.] : Rand McNally, 1881. Scale ca. 1:[1,393,920]. 1 map ; 65 X 42
  cm.
  map case 979.3 E7rm 1881

Carter, Richard. *Mormon Colonies, 1847-1900.* 1 map ; 34 x 52 cm.
  map case 978 E7caw

Mallery, J. C. *New Map of the Territory of Arizona, Southern California and
  Parts of Nevada, Utah and Sonora.* San Francisco : Britton, Rey, 1877.
  Scale ca. 1:[1,520,640].
  979 E7mj

Map of Public Surveys in Nevada Territory. San Francisco : Surveyor General's
  Office, 1862. 1 map ; 63 X 42 cm.
  map case 979.3 E7ns

Map of the Silver Mines of Nevada. New York : G.W. & C.B. Colton, 1865.
  Scale ca. 1:[887,040].
  map case 979.3 E7c
    1 map ; 41 X 44 cm.

Nevada and Eastern California Mining Towns and Railroads. [S.l.] : D. F.
Myrick, c1965.
map case 979.3 E7n
Scale 1:3,168,000. 1 inch to 50 miles. 1 map ; 29 x 21 cm.

Map of Utah Territory : showing the routes connecting it with California and
the east compiled in the Bureau of Topog. Eng. of the War Depart. from the
latest and most reliable data. Richmond : Ritchie & Dunnavant, 1858.
Scale ca. 1:[2,027,520]. 1 map ; 58 X 80 cm.
map case 979 E7us

Tackitt, Jim W. *1866 County Map of Utah and Nevada.* Concord, Calif. :
Tackitt Photographic, [1990?].
map case 979 E7u
Scale [ca. 1:3,168,000]. 1 map : 25 x 31 cm.

State of Nevada. Washington : U.S. Geological Survey, 1920-1922. Scale
1:500,000.1 map ; 157 X 106 cm.
map case 979.3 E7u

State of Nevada. New York : U.S. General Land Office, 1876. Scale
1:1,013,760.
map case 979.3 E7ug

Nevada - Maps - Inventories, registers, catalogs
Ansari, Mary B. *Nevada Directory of Maps and Aerial Photo Resources.* Santa
Cruz, Calif. : Western Association of Map Libraries, 1983, c1984.
979.3 E73a

Nevada - Military records
Pompey, Sherman Lee. *Civil War Veteran Burials From California, Nevada,
Oregon and Washington Regiments Buried in Colorado.* Independence,
Calif. : Historical and Genealogical Pub. Co., c1965.
978.8 M2ps

Thompson, J. S. *Records of Early Nevada Military Units and Personnel.* Salt
Lake City : Filmed by the Genealogical Society of Utah, 1995.
Microfilm- 1598348 item 12

Pompey, Sherman Lee. *Burial List of the Members of the 1st Nevada Cavalry.*
Kingsburg, Calif. : Pacific Specialities, 1972.
979.3 A1 no.14, also on microfilm- 0908752 item 7
Lists cemetery where soldier is buried, dates not given.

Nevada Historical Society (Reno, Nevada). *Revised and Complete Roster of Nevada Veterans, Civil War, Spanish American War, Nevada National Guards to 1914, State Militia, Home Guards.* Salt Lake City : Filmed by the Genealogical Society of Utah, 1994.
Microfilm- 1307686 item 3
   Original records at Nevada State Library & Archives, Carson City, Nevada. Alphabetical list of veterans by surname for years 1860's to 1914. Includes enlistment date and place, military rank, military unit (company), and mustered out information and date.

Nevada. Adjutant General. *Annual Reports, 1865-1930.* Compiled by the Nevada State Library and Archives Jeffrey M. Kintop, editor. [S.l.] : Filmed by Nevada Printing and Micrographics Division, 1991.
Microfilm- 1876595
   Microfilm of original: Carson City, Nevada : Nevada State Library and Archives, 1991.

Nevada - Military records - Civil War, 1861-1865
Pompey, Sherman Lee. *Civil War Veteran Burials from the Arizona Territory, Nebraska, Nevada, New Mexico, Oregon, Utah and the Washington Territory.* Salt Lake City : Filmed by the Genealogical Society of   Utah, 1975.
Microfilm- 0908986 item 2

Slagle, Eleanor. *Nevada Veterans, Civil War.* Salt Lake City : Filmed by the Genealogical Society of Utah, 1994.
   Microfilm- 1307686 item 2
      Microfilm of cards, arranged in alphabetical order by surname of Nevada veterans of the Civil War, companies A-F, at Reno Family History Center, Reno, Nevada. Companion information in Revised and complete roster of Nevada veterans.

Nevada - Military records - Civil War, 1861-1865 - Indexes
United States. Adjutant General's Office. *Index to Compiled Service Records of Volunteer Union Soldiers Who Served in Organizations From the State of Nevada.* Washington, D.C. : The National Archives, 1964.
Microfilm- 0821939
   National Archives microfilm publications ; Microcopy 548.

Nevada - Military records - World War, 1914-1918
Parkin, Nona. *Biographical Sketches from Nevada's Golden Stars : a Memorial Volume Designed as a Gift From the State of Nevada to the Relatives of Those Nevada Heroes Who Died in the World War Prepared Under the Direction of Maurice J. Sullivan, the Adjt. General of Nevada.* 1964.
979.3 A1 no.36

Nevada - Military records - World War, 1914-1918 - Registers
United States. Selective Service System. *Nevada, World War I Selective Service System Draft Registration Cards, 1917-1918.* Washington, D.C. : The National Archives, 1987-1988.
National Archives microfilm publications ; M1509. Original records in the National Archives in East Point, Georgia. Cards are in rough alphabetical order. Occasionally while filming, lost cards would be found. If these cards were found, they would be filmed after the Z's of the locality they belonged to. The draft cards are arranged alphabetically by state, then alphabetically by county or city, and then alphabetically by surname of registrants.
Microfilm- 1711534   Churchill County, A - Z; Clark County, A - Z; Douglas County, A - Z; Elko County, A - N
Microfilm- 1711535   Elko County, O - Z; Esmeraldo County, A - Z; Eureka County, A - Z, Humnoldt County, A - Z
Microfilm- 1711536   Lander County, A - Z; Lincoln County, A - Z; Lyon County, A - Z; Mineral County, A - Z   Nye County, A - O
Microfilm- 1711537   Nye County, P - Z; Ormsby County, A - Z; Storey County, A - Z; Washoe County, A - M
Microfilm- 1711538   Washoe County, N - Z; White Pine County, A - J
Microfilm- 1711539   White Pine County, K - Z
Microfilm- 2022391 item 4   Indians, Prisoners, Insane, In Hospitals, Late Registrants, A - Z

Nevada - Minorities
BeDunnah, Gary P. *A History of the Chinese in Nevada, 1855-1904, a Thesis.* Reno, Nev. : University of Nevada, 1966.
979.3 A1 no. 17 ,also on microfilm- 0940054 item 3

Rusco, Elmer R. *Good Time Coming? : Black Nevadans in the Nineteenth Century.* Westport, Conn. : Greenwood Press, c1975.
979.3 F2r

Eterovich, Adam S. *Yugoslavs in Nevada : 1859-1900, Croatians, Dalmatians, Montenegrins, Hercegovinians*. San Francisco : R and E Research Associates, c1973.
979.3 F2ye

Serb Federation Sloga Sub Assembly no. 99. *Members Record Book, Ely, Nevada, 1912-1916*. Salt Lake City : Filmed by the Genealogical Society of Utah, 1977.
Microfilm- 0982358 item 1
Microfilm of original manuscript. Text in Serbian.

Nevada - Minorities - Periodicals
The Basque Studies Program Newsletter. -- No. 1 (Nov. 1968)
973 F25bnv
Library has: nos. 1-25 (Nov 1968-May 1982), no. 26 (Nov 1982)-no. 27(May 1983), no. 29(June 1984)

Nevada - Names, Geographical
Carlson, Helen S. *Nevada Place Names : a Geographical Dictionary*. Reno, Nev. : University of Nevada Press, 1974.
979.3 E2c

Leigh, Rufus Wood. *Nevada Place Names : Their Origin and Significance*. Salt Lake City : Manufactured by Deseret News Press, c1964.
979.3 E2

Ward, Jill Anderson. *LDS Place Names Gazetteer*. [Salt Lake City] : Genealogical Library, The Church of Jesus Christ of Latter-day Saints, 1986.
289.3 W213, also on microfilm- 1059499 item 5
This gazetteer's intention is to identify the name of the LDS Church unit where that ancestor's membership records might be found" - Introd.

Nevada - Native races
Downs, James F. *The Two Worlds of the Washoe : an Indian Tribe of California and Nevada*. New York : Holt, Rinehart and Winston, c1966.
970.3 W279d

United States. Office of Indian Affairs. Utah Superintendency. *Records of the Utah Superintendency of Indian Affairs, 1853-1870.* Original records in The National Archives, Washington, D.C. US 5-100 (P 9713)Microcopy 834)
Microfilm- 1025139   Miscellaneous letters 1857-1870
Microfilm- 1025140   Miscellaneous records 1853-1870

Fowler, Don D. *Anthropology of the Numa : John Wesley Powell's manuscripts on the Numic peoples of western North America, 1868-1880.* Washington, D. C. : Smithsonian Institution Press, 1971.
970.1 F829a, also on microfilm- 0965792 item 7

Shutler, Richard. *The Pueblo Indian Occupation of the Southern Great Basin.* Ann Arbor, Michigan : University Microfilms, [1961?].
Microfilm- 1730826
No circulation to family history centers.

Hopkins, Sarah Winnemucca. *Life Among the Paiutes : Their Wrongs and Claims.* Ann Arbor, Mich. : Xerox University Microfilms, [197-?].
Microfilm- 0989498   item 1
No circulation to family history centers.

United States. Office of Indian Affairs. *Records of the Nevada Superintendency of Indian Affairs, 1869-1870.* Washington, D.C. : National Archives, 1970.
National Archives microfilm publications ; Microcopy 837.
The principal tribes living in Nevada were the Paiute, Washoe, and Shoshoni. The agencies were the Nevada   Agency serving Paiute and Washoe Indians and the South East Nevada Agency or Pi-Ute Agency serving Paiute Indians. The Walker River and Pyramid Lake Reservations also came under the jurisdiction of the Nevada Agency. Includes indexes and registers. These records include such matters as enforcement of treaties, annuities and other payments to Indians, farming, improvements, depredations, construction of buildings, purchase and transportation of supplies, conduct of employees, and accounts.
Microfilm- 1637276 Letters received, 1869-1870; Letters sent, 1869-1870, Miscellaneous records, 1869-1870; Account book of disbursements and receipts 1869-1870

Parker, Jimmy B. *Sanitary Record of Sick, Injured, Births, Deaths, etc. at Walker River Agency, Nevada, 1898 - 1909.* [Salt Lake City] : Genealogical Society, 1973.
970.1 A1 no.23, also on microfilm- 0928522   item 9

Alphabetical List of Paiute & Washoe Indian Allottees, Carson City Series & Public Domain Shoshones & Others of Elko series in Nevada. Q AREA 970.1 A1 no.5, also on microfilm- 1036782 item 10

Underhill, Ruth Murray. *The Northern Paiute Indians of California and Nevada.* Bureau of Indian Affairs, Branch of Education,1941. 970.3 P166u, also on microfilm- 1320771 item 12

United States. Bureau of Indian Affairs. *Indian Census Rolls, Bishop Agency, 1916-1926.* Washington, D.C. : The National Archives, 1965. Microfilm- 0573848
National Archives microfilm publications ; Microcopy 595. Originals in the National Archives in Washington, D.C. See also California Special, Carson, and Walker River under "Indian census roll, (Agency) ..." in Author/Title microfiche catalog. With: United States. Bureau of Indian Affairs / Indian census rolls, 1885-1940.
Includes information for the following:
1916: (Farrington), Mono Lake, Oasis, Bishop, Bodie, Big Pine, Lone Pine, Keeler, Queen, Round Valley, Paniment Valley, Darwin, Benton, Bridgeport, Olanche, Independence, Saline Valley, Lyda, Chalfant, Kaws, Lidy, Queen Station, Suda (all are mixed together).
1917: Offeen, Laws, Poleta, Ballarat, Dids (Lids), and all the places listed for 1916.
1918: Same as 1917.
1919: Whittier, Oakland, Mina (Nevada), Loraine, Zurich, and all the places listed for 1916-1917.
1920: Dyer, Coleville, Masonic, Death Valley, Tehatchapi, Isabella, Manzanar, Poleta, Saline, Deep Springs, Fish Springs, (a lot under the heading cannot locate), Sweetwater, North Fork, Rush Creek, Kernville, Los Angeles, Antelope, Mina, White Earth (Minn.), Queen, Aberdeen, Mt. Montgomery, Victorville, Daggert, Loraine, Boraine, Yerrington (Nevada) and all the places listed in 1918.
1921: Dyer (Nevada), Deep Springs, So. Antelope, Fresno, and all the places listed for 1920.
1922: Onyx, Poleta, and all the same places as listed in 1920. Includes information for the following:
1923: Weldon, Beatty (Nevada), Torrance, Little Lake and all the places listed for 1922.
1924: Lida (Nevada), Queen (Nevada), Queen Station (Nevada), Yerrington (Nevada), Caliente and all the places listed for 1923.
1925: Groveland, Brown, Hemet, Mindon (Nevada), El Centro, and all the places listed for 1924.
1926: Colton, Ryan, Verdi (Nevada), Salida, San Quinton, Weldon, San

Diego and all the places listed for 1925.
The following tribes are listed on these records:
1916: Paiute with some other tribes listed.
1917-1923: Paiute.
1924: Paiute, Shoshone, Monache.
1925: Paiute, Shoshone, Washoe, Monache.
1926: Paiute, Shoshone, Washoe, Monache.

United States. Bureau of Indian Affairs. *Indian Census Rolls, Fort McDermitt, 1910-1923.*
  Microfilm of originals in the National Archives in Washington, D.C.
  Some pages faded, bleeding through, etc. With: United States. Bureau of
  Indian Affairs / Indian census roll, 1885-1940. See also Carson and Reno
  under "Indian census roll, (Agency), ..." in Author/Title microfiche
  catalog. Includes the following: 1910: Fort McDermitt; 1911-1912: Quin
  River 1913-1923: Fort McDermitt
  Microfilm- 0576838 Fort McDermitt (Nevada) Paiute Indians 1910-1923
  [NOTE: 1910 Fort McDermitt. 1911-1912 Quinn River. 1913-1923 Fort
  McDermitt.]

United States. Bureau of Indian Affairs. Fort Hall Agency. *Student Records, 1946-1952.*
  Microfilm- 1030802
  Original records in the Federal Records Center, Seattle, Washington.
  Students come from Idaho, Oregon and Nevada. Also includes individual
  money ledgers, 1911-1927 and birth and death register, 1901-1907.

United States. Bureau of Indian Affairs. Nevada Agency. *Tribal roll for the Pyramid Lake Paiute tribe, Pyramid Lake Indian Reservation, Nevada.*
  Microfilm- 1036740 item 5

United States. Bureau of Indian Affairs. Walker River Agency. *Record of Employees, 1909-1926.*
  Microfilm- 0976980 item 3
  Microreproduction of original records at the Federal Archives and Records
  Center, San Bruno, California.

United States. Bureau of Indian Affairs. Walker River Agency. *Sanitary Record of Sick & etc., 1897-1910.*
  Microfilm- 0976980 item 4
  Microreproduction of original records at the Federal Archives and Records
  Center, San Bruno, California.

United States. Bureau of Indian Affairs. Western Shoshone Agency. *Record of Employees, 1883-1915.*
Microfilm- 0976980 item 5
Microreproduction of original records at the Federal Archives and Records Center, San Bruno, California.

United States. Bureau of Indian Affairs. *Indian Census Rolls, Fallon, 1909-1924.* Washington, D.C. : National Archives, 1965.
Originals in the National Archives in Washington, D.C. Some pages faded, bleeding through, etc. With: United States. Bureau of Indian Affairs / Indian census rolls, 1885-1940. See also Carson, Lovelocks, and Walker River under "Indian census roll, (Agency), ..." in Author/Title microfiche catalog. Includes the following: 1909-1913: Fallon 1914-1924: Fallon, Lovelock Indian Day School
Microfilm- 0575796 Fallon (Nevada) Paiute Indians, 1909-1924 [NOTE: 1909-1913 is for Fallon only. 1914-1924 is for Fallon and Lovelocks Indian Day School.]

United States. Bureau of Indian Affairs. *Indian Census Rolls, Carson, 1909-1939.* Washington, D.C. : National Archives, 1965.
Originals in the National Archives in Washington, D.C. With: United States. Bureau of Indian Affairs / Indian census rolls, 1885-1940. See also "Fallon, Fort McDermitt, Lovelocks , Nevada, Pyramid Lake, Reno and Walker River" under "Indian census roll, (Agency), ..." in Author/Title microfiche catalog. There is a letter of explanation and a map for 1909, but there is no census. The "scattered area" Indians of Nevada reside in the Northern part of the state, a great distance from the Carson Indian School. During 1927-1929 a separate census was made for each scattered colony, but in 1930 they were combined under the heading "Scattered Indians". In the 1937 census, if the person appeared on a different census roll for the previous year the name is abbreviated. The abbreviation and what it stands for are listed at the bottom of the census page involved. Includes information for the following:
1909: Letter of explanation and a map only
1925: Paiute; Fort McDermitt Reservation and Pyramid Lake Sub Agency
1926: Paiute; Fort McDermitt Reservation and Pyramid Lake Sub Agency
1927: Paiute; Fort McDermitt Sub Agency, Carson Agency (Beowawe, Carlin, Wells, Ruby Valley, East Gate, Austin (Nevada), Pine Valley, Palisade, Eureka, Deeth, Elko, Winnemucca, Battle Mountain, Ely, Pyramid Lake)
1928: Carson Agency (Dresslerville, Carson, Lovelock, Reno-Sparks, Austin, Wells, Pine Valley, Palisade, Carlin, Deeth, Ruby Valley, Winnemucca, Beowawe, Elko, Battle Mountain, Ely, East Gate, Eureka),

Fort McDermitt Sub Agency, Summit Lake Agency, Pyramid Lake Sub Agency

1929: Carson Agency (Austin, Battle Mountain, Beowawe (Shoshone and Paiutes), Carlin, Deeth, Dresslerville, Carson, Elko, East Gate, Ely, Eureka, Lovelock, Palisage, Pine Valley, Reno-Sparks Colony (Paiutes and Washoes), Wells, Ruby Valley (Shoshone), Winnemucca Indian Colony (Shoshone and Paiutes), Fort McDermitt, Nixon), Summit Lake Agency

1930: Carson Agency: Virginia City (Paiute), Virginia City (Public Domain), Carson Valley (Washoe), Carson (Shoshone), Palisade, Wells, Deeth (Allotments), Ruby Valley, Eureka, Carlin, Battle Mountain, Montello, Winnemucca (Paiute and Shoshone), Austin, Beowawe, Ely, Lovelock (Paiute), Elko, Reno-Sparks (Washoe and Paiute), Fort McDermit (Paiute), Pyramid Lake (Paiute), Summit Lake (Paiute). [NOTE: 1930 is mostly Shoshone unless otherwise stated.]

1931: Carson Jurisdiction: Austin (Shoshone), Battle Mountain (Shoshone), Beowawe (Shoshone), Carson Valley (Washoe), Elko (Shoshone), Ely (Shoshone), Fort McDermitt (Paiute), Lovelock (Paiute), Reno-Sparks (Washoe, Pauite), Carson jurisdiction scattered (Shoshone), Summit Lake Reservation (Paiute), Virginia City (Paiute), Winnemucca (Paiute, Shoshone)

1931: Carson Jurisdiction additions and deductions: Battle Mountain (Shoshone), Austin (Shoshone), Carson Valley (Washoe), Elko (Shoshone), Ely (Shoshone), Lovelock (Paiute), scattered area (Shoshone), Winnemucca (Shoshone, Paiute), Reno-Sparks (Washoe, Paiute), Fort McDermitt (Paiute), Summit Lake (Paiute) [NOTE: Additions and deductions are supplemental census rolls]

1926-1931: Deaths: Summit Lake (Paiute), Elko (Shoshone), Ely (Shoshone), Lovelock (Paiute), Scattered area (Shoshone), Reno-Sparks (Washoe, Paiute), Fort McDermitt (Paiute), Austin (Shoshone), Battle Mountain (Shoshone), Beowawe (Shoshone), Carson Valley (Washoe), Carlin (Paiute, Shoshone), Deeth (Shoshone), Wells (Shoshone), Ruby Valley (Shoshone, Paiute), Virginia City, Winnemucca (Paiute). [NOTE: not all years are recorded for each area.]

1926-1931: Births: Fort McDermitt (Paiute), Austin (Shoshone), Battle Mountain (Shoshone), Beowawe (Shoshone), Carson Valley (Paiute, Washoe), Elko (Shoshone), Ely (Shoshone), Lovelock (Paiute), Scattered area (Shoshone), Winnemucca (Paiute, Shoshone), Reno-Sparks (Paiute), Summit Lake (Paiute), Virginia City (Paiute), Palisade (Shoshone), Eureka (Shoshone), Ruby Valley (Shoshone), Deeth (Shoshone), Carlin (Shoshone). [NOTE: not all years are recorded for each area.]

1932: Austin (Shoshone, includes additions, deductions, deaths, births), Battle Mountain (Shoshone, includes additions and births), Beowawe

(Shoshone, includes additions), Carson Valley (Shoshone, Paiute, Washoe, includes deductions, additions, births, deaths), Elko (Shoshone, includes additions, births, deductions), Ely (Shoshone, includes additions, deductions, births, deaths), Fort McDermitt (Paiute, includes deductions, additions, births, deaths), Lovelock (Paiute, includes births, deaths), Reno-Sparks (Washoe, Paiute, includes additions, deductions, deaths), Scattered (Shoshone, includes deductions, additions, births, deaths), Summit Lake (Paiute, includes deaths, deductions), Virginia City (includes additions, deductions, deaths), Winnemucca (Paiute, Shoshone, includes births, deaths, deductions). [NOTE: additions, deductions, births and deaths are supplemental census rolls.]

1933: Pyramid Lake Reservation (Paiute); Carson Agency: Austin (Shoshone, includes deductions, additions, births, deaths), Battle Mountain (Shoshone, includes additions, deductions, births, deaths), Beowawe (Shoshone, includes births, deaths, deductions), Carson Valley (Paiute, Washoe, includes births, 1933 (cont.): additions, deaths), Elko (Shoshone, includes births, deaths, additions), Ely (Shoshone, includes births, deaths, deductions, additions), Fort McDermit Reservation (Paiute, includes births, additions, deaths, deductions), Lovelock (Paiute, includes births, deaths), Reno-Sparks (Paiute, Washoe, includes births, deaths), Scattered (Shoshone, includes births, deaths, additions), Summit Lake Reservation (Paiute, includes birth, death, addition, deductions), Virginia City (Paiute, includes births, additions), Winnemucca (Shoshone, Paiute, includes additions) [NOTE: Additions, deaths, births, deductions are part of the supplemental census rolls.]

1934: Carson Agency; Austin (Shoshone, includes deductions, births, deaths), Beowawe (Shoshone, includes births, deaths), Battle Mountain (Shoshone, includes births, deaths, deductions, additions), Carson Valley (Washoe, includes births, deaths, additions, deductions), Elko (Shoshone, includes births, deaths, additions, deductions), Ely (Shoshone, includes birth, deaths, additions, deductions), Fort McDermitt (Paiute, includes births, deaths), Lovelock (Paiute, includes births, deaths, additions, deductions), Pyramid Lake (Paiute, 1934 (cont.): includes births, additions, deaths, deductions), Carson Valley (Washoe, no names listed), Reno-Sparks (Washoe, Paiute, includes deaths, deductions, additions), scattered indians (Shoshone, includes births, deaths, additions, deductions), Summit Lake (Paiute, includes deaths), Virginia City (Paiute, includes births, deaths, additions), Winnemucca (Paiute, Shoshone, includes births, deaths, additions) [NOTE: Additions, deductions, births, deaths are part of the census supplemental rolls.]

1933-1934: Births; Austin, Battle Mountain, Beowawe, Carson Valley, Elko, Ely, Lovelock, Fort McDermit, Pyramid Lake, Reno-Sparks, Virginia City, Winnemucca, Scattered (Paiute, Shoshone, Washoe)

1933-1934: Deaths; Austin, Battle Mountain, Beowawe, Carson Valley, Elko, Ely, Lovelock, Fort McDermitt, Pyramid Lake, Summit Lake, Reno-Sparks, Virginia City, Winnemucca, Scattered (Paiute, Shoshone, Washoe)

1935: missing

1936: Bishop, California (supplemental roll); Fallon, Nevada (supplemental roll); Mason and Smith Valley, Nevada; McDermitt, Nevada (supplemental roll); Reno-Sparks, Nevada 1936 (cont.): (supplemental roll); Carson Valley (supplemental roll); Austin (supplemental roll); public domain area (Paiute, Shoshone, Washoe, (supplemental roll)); Pyramid Lake (supplemental roll); Summit Lake (supplemental roll); Walker River (supplemental roll)

1937: Carson Agency; Fallon Reservation (Paiute, Shoshone), Fort McDermitt (Paiute), Pyramid Lake (Paiute, Shoshone, Washoe), Summit Lake (Paiute), Walker River (Paiute) Non-reservation (Nevada); Esmeralda City (Paiute, Shoshone), Lincoln County (Paiute, Shoshone), Mineral County (Shoshone, Paiute), Nye County (Paiute, Shoshone), Churchill County (Paiute), Douglas County (Washoe), Ornesby County (Washoe), Fallon Town Colony (Paiute), Winnemucca Colony (Paiute), Mason Valley (Lyon County, Paiute), Humboldt County (Paiute), Smith Valley (Paiute), Yarington Colony (Paiute) Non-reservation (California); Inyo County (Shoshone), Indian Ranch (Shoshone), Death Valley (Shoshone, Paiute), Red Hill Colony (Paiute), Sunland Colony (Paiute), West Bishop Colony (Paiute), Mono County (Washoe, Paiute, Shoshone), Alpine County (Washoe), Fort Independence (Paiute) 1937: Non-reservation (Nevada) (cont.): Lyon County (Paiute), Lovelock Colony (Paiute), Pershing County (Paiute), Reno Colony (Paiute), Washoe County (Paiute), Elko County (Paiute, Shoshone), Eureka County (Shoshone), Lander County (Shoshone), White Pine County (Shoshone)

1936-1938: Births: Fallon (Paiute, Shoshone), Fort McDermitt (Paiute), Pyramid Lake (Paiute), Summit Lake (Paiute), Walker River (Paiute, Shoshone), Churchill County (Paiute), Lyon County (Paiute), Pershing County (Paiute), Washoe County (Paiute), Northwestern Nevada (Shoshone), Battle Mountain (Shoshone), Austin and Walsh Ranch (Shoshone), non-reservation (Shoshone), Washoe Area (Nevada), Fort Independence, Inyo County (Paiute), Mono County (Paiute), Humboldt County, Elko County, Lander County, White Pine County, Alpine County

1937-1939: Supplemental rolls: Fallon (Paiute, Shoshone) Fort McDermitt, Pyramid Lake, Walker River, non-reservation (Shoshone), Washoe area (Nevada), Inyo County (Paiute), Mono County, Southern Shoshone area, Humboldt County, Lyon County, Pershing County, Washoe County, Elko COunty, Eureka County, Lander County

1935-1938: Deaths: Fallon, Fort McDermitt, Pyramid Lake, Summit

Lake, Southern area (Carson Agency), Fort Independence (California), Washoe area (Nevada), Inyo County, Mono County, Elko County, Eureka County, White Pine County, Alpine County, Walker River, Churchill County, Humboldt County, Lyon County, Pershing County, Washoe County, Austin and Walsh Ranch, Battle Mountain, Northeastern area (Nevada).
Microfilm- 0573864 Indian census rolls, 1909, 1925-1930, Paiute, Shoshone, Washoe Indians
Microfilm- 0573865 Indian census rolls, 1931-1932, Paiute, Shoshoni, Washoe Indians
Microfilm- 0573866 Indian census rolls, 1933-1936, Paiute, Shoshone Washoe Indians
Microfilm- 0573867 Indian census rolls, 1927-1939, Paiute, Shoshone, Washoe, Digger Indians

Nevada - Native races - History
Hermann, Ruth. *The Paiutes of Pyramid Lake : a Narrative Concerning a Western Nevada Indian Tribe.* San Jose, Calif. : Harlan-Young Press.
970.3 P166h

Nevada - Newspapers
Lingenfelter, Richard E. *The Newspapers of Nevada, 1858-1958 : a History and Bibliography.* San Francisco, Calif. : John Howell-Books, 1964.
979.3 B3

Nevada - Newspapers - Bibliography
Western Newspapers on Microfilm.
979 A1 no. 4

Nevada - Newspapers - History
Nelson, Jack Adolph. *The Pioneer Press of the Great Basin.*
973 B3ne

Nevada - Notarial records - Indexes
Bell, Connie R. *Notary Record Book of James Abbott.* Salt Lake City : Filmed by the Genealogical Society,   1989.
Microfilm- 1597511 item 21
James Abbott, an early Mormon pioneer, kept a notary record of his dealing with a variety of people during his life in southern Utah and Nevada. This record is the index to the records he kept.

Nevada - Obituaries

Erwin, Patricia J. *Obituaries of Persons Born Pre-1900 and Early 1900's, Reno, Nevada Area & Various Localities and Family Bible Records.* Salt Lake City : Filmed by the Genealogical Society of Utah, 1993, 1995. Microfilm of photocopied newspaper obituary clippings, 1992-1995, and Bible records. 2 v. Collection of obituaries from newspapers of Nevada, California, Colorado, and Michigan. Family Bible records of DeWitt, Graham, Vail and Young families. Includes indexes of each section.
Microfilm- 1307672 item 10, Series 2
Microfilm- 1598297 item 4, Series 2 v.2

Erwin, Patricia J. *Obituaries of Persons Born pre-1900, Early 1900's, Nevada Sagebrush Members and family, Reno, Nevada Area and Various Localities.* Salt Lake City : Filmed by the Genealogical Society of Utah, 1994.
Microfilm- 1598226 item 9
Includes obituaries from Nevada, Reno Gazette Journal and other various newspapers.

Erwin, Patricia J. *Obituaries of Persons Born pre-1900 : Taken from Ohio, Michigan, Colorado, Kentucky, Nevada, and Other States.* Salt Lake City : Filmed by the Genealogical Society of Utah, 1992.
Microfilm- 1597926 item 13
Collection of obituaries taken from various sources on individuals born before 1900. Entries are taken from Nevada and Michigan newspapers are included in separate sections with individual indexes. These records were collected by members of the Daughters of the American Revolution chapters in these areas.

Card Catalog of Obituary Records Compiled from the Deseret News and Tribune, 1851 to June 1963. Salt Lake City : Filmed by the Genealogical Society of Utah, [1965?].
Microfilm of manuscript at the Church Historian's Office, Salt Lake City
Microfilm- 0321138 Aagaard, Andrew J. to Andrulakis, Mary Georgides
Microfilm- 0321139 Andrus, Abigail Jane to Barstow, William B.
Microfilm- 0321140 Bart Mabel W. to Birtwhistle, Dennis
Microfilm- 0321141 Bisaro, 1st Lt. Edmon to Bringman, John Martin Sr.
Microfilm- 0321142 Brink, Chas. to Bywrs, William
Microfilm- 0321143 C. T. C. Bro. Charles (Priest) to Christensen, Elvira.
Microfilm- 0321144 Christensen, Emelia J. to Coombs, Robert Alonza (Loonie)
Microfilm- 0321145 Coombs Robert Vance; Coombs, Ronald Clair to Davidson, Dirkje
Microfilm- 0321146 Davas, Ivan to Drysdale, William L.

Microfilm- 0321147	Duback, Edgar to Evans, Thomas
Microfilm- 0321148	Evans, Rudolph to Fredriksen, Laura Coates
Microfilm- 0321149	Free, Patriarch Absalom P. to Goodloe, Pvt. Harry R.
Microfilm- 0321150	Goodman (twins) to Halwegner, Mrs. Magelina
Microfilm- 0321151	Ham, Infant to Haxby, Ralph M.
Microfilm- 0321152	Hay, Ada Cunliffe to Holley, Wendie Lynn
Microfilm- 0321153	Holmgren, Mary Jensen to Izzedin, Yussof
Microfilm- 0321154	Jabbs, Pfc. Glenn William to Johnson, Kristen.
Microfilm- 0321155	Johnson, L. Eric to Kiepe, Elfriede Mayer
Microfilm- 0321156	Kier, Merle to Larson, Otto R.
Microfilm- 0321157	Larson, Pearl to Lowder Wm. H.
Microfilm- 0321158	Lowe, Infant to Mawson, William Oliver
Microfilm- 0321159	Max, Adolph to McEbroff, John Tauler
Microfilm- 0321160	Miaker, Mrs. Angeline L. to Mross, Justina
Microfilm- 0321161	Mucci, Giovanni to Noble, Joyce
Microfilm- 0321162	Noble, Kate Y. Wenner to Parissenti, Fioretto
Microfilm- 0321163	Park, Infant to Pettley, Kathleen
Microfilm- 0321164	Petty, Adella De Mills to Rapp, Melville B.
Microfilm- 0321165	Rapp, Sally Lorraine to Robinson, Duncan (Dee) E.
Microfilm- 0321166	Robinson, E. Chesley to Scermerhorn, Charles E.
Microfilm- 0321167	Schaad, Lena Albright to Simpson, Fred J.
Microfilm- 0321168	Simpson, G. S. to Spence William H.
Microfilm- 0321169	Spencer, Infant to Summerville, Vera Daxey Mrs.
Microfilm- 0321170	Summers, Abram to Thorsen, Lars Max.
Microfilm- 0321171	Thornton, Infant to Vybiral, Everal
Microfilm- 0321172	Waagen, Helen Berrett to Wezenaar Reinier
Microfilm- 0321173	Whaanga, Apikara to Wilson, John Jr.
Microfilm- 0321174	Wistisen, Iner Christian to Zysling, Paul.

Obituary Index File to the Salt Lake Tribune and Deseret News as of 31 December 1970. Salt Lake City : Church Historian's Office, 1971. Microfilm copy of card file at the Church Historical Department.

Microfilm- 0821636	Aacher - Andersen, Lorenzo
Microfilm- 0821637	Andersen, Louise J - Arnold, Mott
Microfilm- 0821638	Arnold, Odis D - Barber, Raymond
Microfilm- 0821639	Barber, Riley E - Beebe, James D
Microfilm- 0821640	Beebe, Jesse - Bircumshaw, Willard J
Microfilm- 0821641	Bird (Infant) - Bowen, Joseph L
Microfilm- 0821642	Bowen, Joseph T - Brown, Charlie
Microfilm- 0821643	Brown, Charlotte H - Burrows, Dee L
Microfilm- 0821644	Burrows, Earl - Carlson, Amelia B
Microfilm- 0821645	Carlson, Amelia C - Christensen, Alfred
Microfilm- 0821646	Christensen, Alfred - Cluff, Connie

Microfilm- 0821647	Cluff, Daisy M - Couchis, Katherine K
Microfilm- 0821648	Couchman, Arthur - Cushing, Ethel M
Microfilm- 0821649	Cushing, Eva G - Davis, Ann Lois
Microfilm- 0821650	Davis, Ann Louisa - Dickamore, William
Microfilm- 0821651	Dickard - Durrant, Michelle
Microfilm- 0821652	Durrant, Minnie - Epler, Minnie P
Microfilm- 0821653	Eppling - Ferrens
Microfilm- 0821654	Ferrero - Francis, Walter (Mrs.)
Microfilm- 0821655	Francis, Walter E - Geddes, Catherine
Microfilm- 0821656	Geddes, David - Gordon, Joseph B
Microfilm- 0821657	Gordon, Joseph N - Gunnel, Mary H
Microfilm- 0821658	Gunnell, Mary M - Hansen, Andrew Hagen
Microfilm- 0821659	Hansen, Andrew Hans - Harrop, Edwin
Microfilm- 0821660	Harrop, Ernest - Hendrickson, Ren (Mrs.)
Microfilm- 0821661	Hendrickson, Richard - Hofhine, Brighamine
Microfilm- 0821662	Hofhine, Edward - Hudson, Katherine M
Microfilm- 0821663	Hudson, Laurene - Jackson, Margaret A
Microfilm- 0821664	Jackson, Margaret J - Jenson, William
Microfilm- 0821665	Jentges - Jones, Cathryn A
Microfilm- 0821666	Jones, Cecelia - Kelly, Stephen
Microfilm- 0821667	Kelly, Steven - Koer, Henry H
Microfilm- 0821668	Koer, J W - Larter
Microfilm- 0821669	La Rue - Lindsay, Janet (Mrs.)
Microfilm- 0821670	Lindsay, Janet S - Lyon, Lucy
Microfilm- 0821671	Lyon, Luewella - Marx, Alvin
Microfilm- 0821672	Marx, Andrew - McGary, Barbara
Microfilm- 0821673	McGary, Edward - Miclea
Microfilm- 0821674	Midaugh - Moquist
Microfilm- 0821675	Mora - Nakken
Microfilm- 0821676	Nalden - Nielsen, Niels J
Microfilm- 0821677	Nielsen, Niels M - Ohman
Microfilm- 0821678	Ohmart - Packer, Durel P
Microfilm- 0821679	Packer, Edson W - Peck, Ronald D
Microfilm- 0821680	Peck, Ronald J - Pettingill, Keith W
Microfilm- 0821681	Pettingill, Merrell H - Preston, John C
Microfilm- 0821682	Preston, Katherine P - Record, James B
Microfilm- 0821683	Record, Wellic T - Ritchie, Martha B
Microfilm- 0821684	Ritchie, Mary E - Ross, Myrtle W
Microfilm- 0821685	Ross, Nancy A - Scardino, Nancy J
Microfilm- 0821686	Scarff, John W - Sheets, Iris P
Microfilm- 0821687	Sheets, John A - Small, Marion C
Microfilm- 0821688	Small, Mary A - Soffee, Mary C
Microfilm- 0821689	Soffee, Sarah B - Steffensen, Vern R

Microfilm- 0821690 Steffensen, Wayne E - Stuart, Simon D
Microfilm- 0821691 Stuart, Susan D - Taylor, Mabel O
Microfilm- 0821692 Taylor, Mae A - Thueson, Constant
Microfilm- 0821693 Thueson, Ellen - Ure, James J
Microfilm- 0821694 Ure, James W - Wallace, Guy W
Microfilm- 0821695 Wallace, Hamilton M - Welling, Judith O
Microfilm- 0821696 Welling, Lottie J - Wilkening, Henry F
Microfilm- 0821697 Wilkens, Arminla A - Winterrose, John W
Microfilm- 0821698 Winters, Alonzo R - Young, Alice N
Microfilm- 0821699 Young, Alice S - Zysling and includes some
miscellaneous A - M

Nevada - Officials and employees
Nevada State Directory. S.l. : s.n., 1975.
979.3 A1 no.25

Nevada - Periodicals
Northeastern Nevada Historical Society Quarterly.
979.31H25n
Holdings: Vol. 4 no. 3-4 (1974); v. 5 no. 1 & 4 (1974-1975); v. 6 no. 1-4
(1975-1976); v. 78 no. 3 (1978); v. 79 no. 1 & 4 (1979); v. 80 no. 2-4
(1980); v. 81 no. 1-4 (1981); v. 82 no. 1-2 (1982); v. 83 no. 2   (1983); v.
84 no. 2 & 4 (1984); v. 85 no. 1-4 (1985); v. 86 no. 2-4 (1986); v. 87 no.
1-4 (1987); v. 88 no. 1-4 (1988); v. 86 no. 2-4 (1986); v. 87 no. 1-4
(1987); v. 88 no. 1-4 (1988); v. 89 no. 1-4 (1989); v. 90 no. 1-4 (1990); v.
91 no. 1-4 (1991); v. 92 no. 1-4 (1992); v. 93 no. 1-4 (1994); v. 94 no.
1-4; v. 95 no. 1-2
ADDITIONAL FORMATS

Microfilm- 1698155 item 1-2	Vol. 4 no. 3-4	Winter-Spring 1974
Microfilm- 1698155 item 3	Vol. 5 no. 1	Summer 1974
Microfilm- 1698155 item 4	Vol. 5 no. 5	Spring 1975
Microfilm- 1698155 item 9	Vol. 78 no. 3	Summer 1978
Microfilm- 1698155 item 10	Vol. 79 no. 1	Winter 1979
Microfilm- 1698155 item 11	Vol. 79 no. 4	Fall 1979
Microfilm- 1698155 item 12-14	Vol. 80 no. 2-4	Spring-Fall 1980
Microfilm- 1698155 item 15-18	Vol. 81	1981
Microfilm- 1698155 item 19-20	Vol. 82 no. 1-2	Spring-Fall 1982
Microfilm- 1698155 item 21	Vol. 83 no. 2	Spring 1983
Microfilm- 1698155 item 22-23	Vol. 84 no. 2-4	Spring-Fall 1984
Microfilm- 1698155 item 24-27	Vol. 85	1985
Microfilm- 1698155 item 28-30	Vol. 86 no. 2-4	Spring-Fall 1986
Microfilm- 1698155 item 31-34	Vol. 87	1987
Microfilm- 1698155 item 35-38	Vol. 88	1988

Microfilm- 1698155 item 39-42	Vol. 89	1989
Microfilm- 1698155 item 43-46	Vol. 90	1990
Microfilm- 1698155 item 47-50	Vol. 91	1991
Microfilm- 1698155 item 51-54	Vol. 92	1992
Microfilm- 1698155 item 55-58	Vol. 93	1993
Microfilm- 1698155 item 59-62	Vol. 94	1994
Microfilm- 1698155 item 63-64	Vol. 95 no. 1-2	1995

ADDITIONAL COPIES- Another filming (filmed in reverse order):
Microfilm- 1698036 item 1-7   Vol. 4 no. 3-4; Vol. 5 no. 1, 4; Vol. 6 no. 1-3; Vol. 78 no.3
Another filming:
Microfilm- 1698058 item 1-24   Vol. 79 no. 1, 4; Vol. 80 no. 2-4; Vol. 81; Vol. 82 no. 1-2; Vol. 83; Vol. 84 no. 2, 4; Vol. 85 no. 2-4; Vol. 86 no. 2-4; Vol. 87 no. 1-3
Another filming (filmed in reverse order):
Microfilm- 1698036 item 26-30   Vol. 87 no. 4; Vol. 88
Another filming (filmed out of order):
Microfilm- 1698036 item 8-11   Vol. 89 no. 1-4
Another filming:
Microfilm- 1698036 item 12-20   Vol. 90; Vol. 91 no. 2-4; Vol. 92 no. 1-2
Another filming (filmed in reverse order):
Microfilm- 1698036 item 21-22   Vol. 92 no. 3-4
Another filming (filmed in reverse order):
Microfilm- 1698036 item 23-25   Vol. 93 no. 1-3

Nevada - Politics and government - Handbooks, manuals, etc.

Poulton, Helen J. *Nevada State Agencies : from Territory Through Statehood.*
Reno, Nev. : University of Nevada Press, c1964.
979.3 B4u v.5

Nevada - Postal and shipping guides

Gamett, James. *Nevada Post Offices : an Illustrated History.* Las Vegas, Nev. :
Nevada Publications, c1983.
979.3 E8g

Nevada - Postal and shipping guides - History

Harris, Robert P. *Nevada Postal History, 1861 to 1972.* Santa Cruz, Calif. :
Bonanza Press, 1973.
979.3 E8h

Nevada - Public records

United States. Department of the Interior. Appointment Division. *Interior Department Appointment Papers, Nevada, 1860-1907.* Washington : National Publications, 1976.

National Archives microfilm publications ; Microcopy 1033. Includes letters of application and recommendation, petitions, oaths of office, bonds, notices of dates of succession, applications for leaves of absence, resignations, removals, and materials regarding investigation of charges against officials.

Microfilm- 1695636	Surveyor General	1861-1907
Microfilm- 1695637	Land offices- Aurora, 1868-1873; Austin, 1867-1873; Belmont, 1867-1872; Carson City, 1861-1907; Elko, 1872-1874; Eureka, 1874-1893; Pioche, 1874-1877; Unspecified, 1860-1862	
Microfilm- 1695638	Indian agencies- Nevada, 1861-1907; Pyramid Lake, 1871-1907; South East Pi-Ute, 1870-1881; Walker River, 1871-1879; Western Shoshoni, 1876-1905	

Nevada - Schools - Directories

Anderson, Walter W. *State of Nevada Educational Directory and Information as to Certification of Teachers.*
979.3 A1 no.35
   Photocopy of original published: Carson City, Nevada : State Printing Office, 1928. p. 9-25.

Nevada - Societies - Directories

Steinheimer, Mrs. Frank M. *Daughters of the American Revolution, Nevada Society, 1958-1960 : no. 4*
979.3 A1 no.24

Nevada - Taxation - Bibliography

United States. Internal Revenue Service. *Internal Revenue Assessment Lists for the Territory of Nevada, 1863-1866.* Washington : National Archives and Records Service, 1980.
   National Archives microfilm publication ; Microcopy 779. Annual, monthly and special lists.

Microfilm- 1578506	District 1, Feb. 1863 - Nov. 1865
Microfilm- 1578507	District 1, Jan. - Dec. 1866

Federal Death Records of Nevada, June 1, 1869 to June 1, 1870.
979.3 A1 no. 34

Jensen, Edith Gunn. *Nevada Records.* Leandro, Calif. : [s.n., 190-?].
979.3 V2j ,also on microfilm 0962818 item 6

Birth Notices in Some Nevada Newspapers, 1961-1968. Salt Lake City :
Filmed by the Genealogical Society of Utah, 1986.
Microfilm- 1421597 item 1

Parkin, Nona. *Births, Marriages and Deaths, 1871-1879 : With Missing Dates
Published in the Nevada State Journal.*
979.3 A1 no.12, also on microfilm- 0962218 item 12

*Marriage Licenses and Marriage Notices in Miscellaneous Nevada
Newspapers, 1906-1968.* Salt Lake City : Filmed by the Genealogical
Society of Utah, 1986.
Microfilm- 1421646 item 6

Bell, Connie. *Materials Collected From Bank and Safe Deposit Boxes,
Unclaimed Property Division, Department of Commerce, State of Nevada :
June 30, 1986.* Salt Lake City : Filmed by the Genealogical Society of Utah,
1986.
Microfilm- 1421665 item 4
   Contains birth and death certificates, marriage licenses, divorce records
   and other court records, military records, taxation records, business
   records, church records, wills and other probate records, and deeds and
   other land records. Most of these records are Clark County and Las
   Vegas, Nevada, records. The land records are chiefly those of Lyon,
   Storey, and Washoe counties, Nevada. In addition there are records from
   many other states in the United States.

Nevada - Vital records - Indexes
Nevada Vital Statistics, Marriages by Name Index, 1968-1991. [S.l. : s.n.],
1992.
   Microfilm of records at the Office of Vital Statistics, Carson City, Nevada.
   Includes state of residence, marriage date and county where performed,
   county book and page number, instrument number and film number. No
   circulation to family history centers.
   Fiche- 6334402 A - Cogburn, Lawrence A (50 fiches)
   Fiche- 6334403 Cogburn, Lisa M. - Graves, Kathleen R. (50 fiches)
   Fiche- 6334404 Graves, Kathryn A. - Lee, Rhonda Rae (50 fiches)
   Fiche- 6334405 Lee, Rhone E. - Passanando, Joy (50 fiches)
   Fiche- 6334406 Passanando, Joy Dene - Starkey, Michael D (50 fiches)
   Fiche- 6334407 Starkey, Michael Dean - Z (43 fiches)

Parkin, Nona. *Births, Deaths and Miscellaneous Information : Gleaned From Round Mountain Nugget, 1908-1909.*
  979.3 A1 no. 9, also on microfilm- 0962517 item 4

Ostrander, Edna. *Index to Marriage Licenses and Marriage Notices in Miscellaneous Nevada Newspapers, 1906-1968.* Salt Lake City : Filmed by the Genealogical Society of Utah, 1986.
  Microfilm- 1421646 item 5

Nevada - Vital records - Inventories, registers, catalogs
Guide to Public Vital Statistics Records in Nevada. Prepared by the Nevada Historical Records Survey Project, division of community service programs, Work Projects Administration. Reno, Nev. : University of Nevada, Las Vegas, 1941.
  979.3 A1 no. 33, also on microfilm- 1697348 item 27

CHAPTER TWO

Churchill County

Churchill County is an original county, created by a Territorial Act approved on 25 November 1861. Churchill County is named after Fort Churchill, an early military post, which is within the present limits of Storey County. The fort was named in honor of an officer of the United States Army.

When Lander County was created on 19 December 1862, about one-third of the whole area of Churchill County was made part of the new county. An act of 20 February 1864 established the boundary line between Lyon and Churchill counties, a small cession to Lyon County. An act approved on 27 February 1869 ceded to Churchill County a triangular tract, from the southwest corner of Humboldt County. The same act established the boundary lines between Lyon and Churchill counties. An act of 5 March 1869 ceded a small triangular tract at the southeast corner of Churchill County to Nye County.

An act approved on 29 November 1861 attached Churchill county to Lyon County for county judicial and revenue purposes, including it in the Third Judicial District, and located its county seat at Buckland. On 19 February 1864 Churchill was made a county.

CHURCHES

FALLON
Adventist: Jehovah's Witnesses Hall, 2705 Schurz Hwy., Fallon, NV 89406
    Phone: 775 423-3547
Assemblies of God: Christian Life Center, 1435 Kaiser St., Fallon, NV 89406
    Phone: 775 423-6900
Baptist: First Baptist Church, 485 Tedford Lane, Fallon, NV 89406
    Phone: 775 423-3855
Westside Baptist Church, 1445 Lucas Road, Fallon, NV 89406
    Phone: 867-2772
Churches of Christ: Church of Christ, 20 Drumm Lane, PO Box 2217, Fallon, NV 89407 Phone: 775 423-6136
Christian Science: Christian Science Church, 447 Court St., Fallon, NV 89406
    Phone: 775 423-3319

Congregational: Country Church, 755 S. Crook Rd., Fallon, NV 89406
Phone: 775 423-3529
Episcopal: Holy Trinity Episcopal Church, 507 Churchill St., Fallon, NV
89406 Phone: 775 423-4745
Holiness: Church of the Nazarene, 1520 Grimes St., PO Box 485, Fallon, NV
Phone: 775 423-3427
Independent Fundamentalist: Silver Sage Bible Church: Silver Sage Bible
Church, 131 S. Maine St., Fallon, NV 89406 Phone: 775 423-7812
Latter-day Saints: Church of Jesus Christ Latter-day Saints, 750 W Richards
St., Fallon, NV 89406 Phone: 775 423-6990
Methodist: Epworth United Methodist Church, 280 E Stillwater Ave., Fallon,
NV 89406 Phone: 775 423-4714
Pentecostal: Calvary Full Gospel Church, PO Box 286, Fallon, NV 89407
Fallon Christian Temple, 96 N Broadway St., Fallon, NV 89406
Phone: 775 423-6360
Indian Chapel Pentecostal Church of God, Fall Indian Colony, Fallon, NV
89406 Phone: 775 423-2276
Roman Catholic: St. Patrick's Catholic Church, 850 W 4th St., Fallon, NV
89406 Phone: 775 423-2846
Seventh Day Adventist: Seventh Day Adventist Church, 755 Esmeralda St.,
Fallon, NV 89406 Phone: 775 423-3357
Southern Baptist: Fallon First Baptist Church, 900 S Taylor St., Fallon, NV
89406 Phone: 775 423-3590
St. James Missionary Baptist, 6727 Equinox Lane, Fallon, NV 89406
Phone: 775 867-3972

COURTHOUSE

Churchill County Courthouse
190 West First Street, Fallon, NV 89406-3309
Phone: 775 423-5136
Land records: County Recorder
Begin 1864, cost $1.00 per page. Public allowed access to records
Naturalization records: Court Clerk, transferred in August 1968 with Books of
Documents to the Federal Records Center, San Francisco, CA. Declaration of
Intention & Petition for Naturalization, Volumes 1-6.
When making inquiry refer to Fallon, Churchill County, NV Bin #56,
Accession No.69-A-608, Record Group No.21
Probate records: Court Clerk
Records begin 1904 - present. Fee: $1.00 per name searched. Copy costs:
$1.00 per page, no minimum

Vital records: County Recorder
  Marriage Certificates: 1864 to present, $1.00 per copy for genealogy, $7.00 certified copy. (Note: marriages are found in the county where the couple purchased the license.)

FUNERAL HOME

Austin, Matson & Smith Funeral Home
355 W. First St., Fallon, NV 89406
Phone: 775 423-2255

LIBRARIES

Churchill County Library
553 S. Maine St., Fallon, NV 89406-3387
Phone: 775 423-7581, Fax: 775 423-7766, E-mail: nmstark@clan.lib.nv.us
Founded: 1932
Hours: Monday through Friday: 9:00 a.m. to 6:00 p.m.
  Sat: 9:00 a.m. to 5:00 p.m.
Special Collections: Nevada history

Churchill County Museum Association, Museum & Archives
1050 S Maine St., Fallon, NV 89406
Phone: 775 423-3677
Subject interests: Local history
Collections: Books, manuscripts, maps, newspapers, photographs, oral histories (use on premises)

NEWSPAPERS

Lahontan Valley News, P.O. Box 1297, Fallon, NV 89407
Phone: 775 423-6041

Newspapers	City	UNLV Library has
The Ballot Box	Fallon	April 15, 1911 - June 28, 1913 (weekly- full run)
Churchill County Courier	Fallon	March 15, 1961- May 30, 1962 (weekly- full run)
Churchill County Eagle	Fallon	October 6, 1906 - Sept. 10, 1927 (weekly- full run)
Churchill County Standard	Fallon	March 5, 1908 - April 21, 1920 (weekly- full run)

Churchill News	White Plains	March 31, 1888
Churchill Standard	Fallon	Dec. 12, 1903 - Feb. 27, 1908 (weekly- full run)
CoOperative Colonist	Fallon	July 1916 - August-Sept. 1918 (monthly- full run)
Eagle Standard	Fallon	March 4, 1980 - Nov. 4, 1984
Fairview News	Fairview	March 3, 1906 - Feb. 15, 1908
Fallon Citizen	Fallon	January 3, 1963 - Nov. 2, 1967
Fallon Eagle	Fallon	Sept. 17, 1927 - June 25, 1949 (weekly- full run)
Fallon Eagle - Standard	Fallon	January 3, 1964 - Feb. 29, 1980 (weekly- 1958-)
Fallon Eagle Standard and Lahonton Valley News	Fallon	January 12 - September 28, 1985
Fallon Standard	Fallon	April 28, 1920 - Dec. 27, 1950 (weekly-1921-1958)
High View	Fallon	October 13, 1925 - May 26, 1926
Lahonton Valley News	Fallon	July 3, 1974 - January 4, 1985
Lahonton Valley News and Fallon Eagle Standard	Fallon	January 8, 1985 - date (weekly- full run)
Nevada Colony News	Fallon	April 1917
Western Nevada Dispatch	Fallon	January 2, 1986 - March 25, 1987
Wonder Mining News	Wonder	August 11, 1906 - Nov. 18, 1912 (weekly- full run)

FAMILY HISTORY LIBRARY (Salt Lake City, Utah) HOLDINGS

All microfilmed and microfiched records (unless restricted) are available to rent worldwide at branch Family History Centers and selected larger public and private libraries and societies.

Nevada, Churchill - Cemeteries
Parkin, Robert D. *Cemetery Records of Nevada : Churchill and Lander Counties.*
979.3 V3p, also on microfiche- 6088566

Nevada, Churchill - Census
Pompey, Sherman Lee. *Missourians in the 1870 Census Records of Churchill County, Nevada [and]... Douglas County, Nevada.*
979.35 X2p 1870, also on microfilm- 0823651

Nevada, Churchill - Census - 1862
Thompson, J. S. *Early Nevada Records : Certificates of Survey, Carson Valley, 1856; 1862 Census of Churchill County; 1864 Census of Nye County.* Salt Lake City : Filmed by the Genealogical Society of Utah, 1995.
Microfilm- 1598348 item 14
  Contents: List of names found on certificates in Carson Valley 1856 -- Alphabetical listing of 1862 census of Churchill County with name, age, gender, state of birth, occupation and residence -- Alphabetical list of names and age of those in Nye County census, 1864 -- List of names subscribed on 14 Feb 1863 at a meeting in Virginia City to organize the Democratic party in Nevada.

Nevada, Churchill - Genealogy - Periodicals
In Focus : Annual Journal of the Churchill County Museum Association.
Fallon, Nev. : The Association, 1987.
979.352 D35c   Library has: v. 1 (1987-1988).

Trails to Churchill County : Historical and Genealogical Society Quarterly.
Vol. 1, no. 1 (spring 1983)
979.352 H25t
  Library's holdings begin with: v. 1, no. 1 (spring 1983).

Nevada, Churchill - Military records - World War, 1914-1918
Banks, Raymond H. *The Banks Compilation of Birth Data of Men with Links to Churchill County, Nevada, who Were Born 1873-1900 : as Found in the Civilian Registration Cards.* L.D.S. microfilm series of World War I Selective Service draft registration cards. Salt Lake City : R.H. Banks, c1996
979.3 A1 no.47.
  An alphabetical listing by surname of men who completed civilian registration cards for their draft boards during 1917-1918. About 98% of men present in America and born 1873-1900 provided draft card information in 1917 or 1918. Aliens were required to register. Persons already in the military did not register. Includes name, date of birth, ethnic group, birth location or other information, and county or city draft board in the state where registered.

Nevada, Churchill - Vital records

Parkin, Nona. *Churchill County Records*. Salt Lake City : Filmed by the
Genealogical Society of Utah, 1997.
    Contents: v. 1. Birth records/notices; Cemetery census: Fairview
    Cemetery, Fallon Cemetery, Fort Church Cemetery, Hazen Cemetery,
    Wonder Cemetery; City directories: Fallon 1908-1909; Death
    records/obituaries: Church County death records 1889-1916, Obituaries
    from Church Standard 1904-1923; Obituaries from Fallon newspaper
    1923-1975, Stillwater 1969-1972, Wonder 1930; Family histories -- v. 2.
    Funeral home records: Austin Funeral Home, Fallon with index -- v. 3.
    Marriage records/notices: Churchill County marriage records 1903-1920;
    Marriage notices from newspapers 1894-1920; Pioneer families;
    Registered voters: Fairview 1906; Church records: Holy Trinity, Fallon,
    Nevada: Membership rolls 1906 and 1943, Baptisms, confirmations,
    communicants 1907-1933, marriages 1913-1940, burials 1917-1957.
    Includes index for funeral home records. Family histories include very
    brief biographies.
    Microfilm- 1598462 item 4-6   Vol. 1-3

Birth Records of Churchill County, Nevada.
    979.352 V21f, also on microfilm- 0874068 item 4

Nevada, Churchill, Fallon - Church records

Church of Jesus Christ of Latter-day Saints. Fallon Branch (Nevada). *Record
    of Members, 1920-1938*. Salt Lake City : Filmed by the Genealogical
    Society of Utah, 1954.
    Microfilm- 0001955 item 3   Record of members   1920-1938
    Photocopies not permitted except for direct line descendants. Remove all
    other data from photocopy.

Nevada, Churchill, Fallon - Directories

Parkin, Nona. *The Rawhide - Fallon Directory, Nevada, 1908-1909.*
    979.3 A1 no.13, also on microfilm- 0962913 item 5

Nevada, Churchill, Fallon - Vital records

Records of the Austin Funeral Home of Fallon, Nevada.
    979.352/F1 V3p, also on microfilm- 0874347 item 1

CHAPTER THREE

Clark County

Clark County was organized from Lincoln County in February 1909, when the Legislature passed the county division act. Las Vegas was the county seat, the bill taking effect 1 July 1909.

CEMETERIES

Boulder City

Boulder City Cemetery
Corner of Adams Blvd. & Utah St.
Records: City of Boulder City, Cemetery Clerk
401 California Avenue, Boulder City, NV 89005
Mailing address: P. O. Box 61350, Boulder City, NV 89006
Phone: 702 293-9292

Southern Nevada Veteran Memorial Cemetery
1900 Buchanan Blvd., Boulder City, NV 89005
Phone: 702 486-5920   Fax: 702 486-5923
Year of operation: 1990-present
Affiliations: State veteran cemetery
Records: Housed on-site

Henderson

Palm Cemetery
800 S. Highway, Henderson, NV 89015
Phone: 702 564-1888
Years of operation: 1964-present
Affiliations: Non-sectarian
Records: housed on-site; available for searches; call for appointment

<u>Las Vegas</u>

Bunker Eden Vale Memorial Park
1216 Las Vegas Blvd., Las Vegas, NV 89101
Phone: 702 388-7006   Fax: 702 388-7004
Years of operation: 1960-present
Affiliations: Non-sectarian
Records: Housed on-site; available for searches

Palm Cemetery
1600 S. Jones St., Las Vegas, NV 89115
Phone: 702 870-2100   Fax: 702 870-2248
Years of operation: 1988-present
Affiliations: Non-sectarian
Records: On-site; available for searches; make appointment.

Palm Cemetery
1325 N. Main St., Las Vegas, NV 89101
Phone: 702 382-1340   Fax: 702 382-6374
Years of operation: 1963-present
Affiliations: Non-sectarian
Records: Available for searches; call or write for appointment

Palm Cemetery
7600 S. Eastern Avenue, Las Vegas, NV 89123
Phone: 702 361-4040
Years of operation: 1972-present
Affiliations: Non-sectarian
Records: Housed on-site on computer; searches by appointment

Paradise Memorial Gardens
6200 S. Eastern Avenue, Las Vegas, NV 89119
Phone: 702 736-6200   Fax: 702 736-4524
Years of operation: 1964-present
Affiliations: Non-sectarian
Records: Housed on-site; available for searches
No appointment necessary; searches by office personnel.

Woodlawn Cemetery
1500 Las Vegas Blvd. North, Las Vegas, NV 89101
Phone: 702 386-6246

Moapa

Warm Springs Cemetery
P.O. Box 301, Moapa, NV 89025-0301
Phone: 702 864-2235   Fax: 702 864-2235
Years of operation: 1989-present
Affiliations: Non-sectarian
Records: Housed on-site; searches by office personnel
only. Telephone or written requests only

CHURCHES

BOULDER CITY
Baptist: Bethany Baptist Church: 210 Wyoming St., Boulder City, NV 89005
Phone: 702 293-1912
Churches of Christ: Church of Christ, 845 Cottonwood St., Boulder City, NV
89005 Phone: 702 293-4019
First Church of Christ, 1419 5th St., PO Box 926, Boulder City, NV 89005
Phone: 293-7740
Christian Science: First Church of Christ Scientist: 534 Nevada Hwy.,
Boulder City, NV 89005
Episcopal: St. Christopher's Episcopalian Church, 812 Arizona St.,
Boulder City, NV 89005 Phone: 702 293-4275
Latter-day Saints: Church of Jesus Christ Latter-day Saints, 606 Don Vicente
Dr., Boulder City, NV 89005 Phone: 702 293-2742
Church of Jesus Christ Latter-day Saints, 916 5th St., Boulder City, NV 89005
Lutheran: Christ Lutheran Church, 1401 5th St., Boulder City, NV 89005
Phone: 702 293-4332
Methodist: Grace Community Church, 1150 Wyoming St., Boulder City, NV
89005 Phone: 702 293-2018
Pentecostal: Foursquare Gospel Church, PO Box 215, Boulder City, NV
89006 Phone: 702 293-7773
Uncompromised Word Church, PO Box 62512, Boulder City, NV 89006
Protestant: Church of the Harvest, 1307 Darlene Way Apt. B3, Boulder City,
NV 89005
Roman Catholic: St. Andrews Catholic Church, 1399 San Felipe Dr.,
Boulder City, NV 89005 Phone 702 293-7500
Seventh Day Adventist: Seventh Day Adventist Church, PO Box 335,
Boulder City, NV 89005 Phone: 702 293-2841
Southern Baptist: First Baptist Church, 850 Ave. B, Boulder City, NV 89005
Phone: 702 293-1394
Unclassified: Pneumodynamics, 1324 Pinto Rd., Boulder City, NV 89005

GOODSPRINGS
Protestant: Sandy Valley Community Church, Sky Ranch Estates Box 450, Goodsprings, NV 89019
HENDERSON
Assemblies of God: Southwest Assembly of God, 711 Valle Verde Dr., Henderson, NV 89015 Phone: 702 565-8577
Green Valley Baptist Church, 270 Valle Verde Dr., Henderson, NV 89014 Phone: 702 434-1906
Churches of Christ: Church of Christ, 104 W. Victory Rd., Henderson, NV 89015 Phone: 702 565-8186
Church of Christ of Henderson, 131 E. King St., Henderson, NV 89015 Phone: 702 564-5959
Episcopal: St. Timothy's Episcopalian Church, 43 W. Pacific Ave., Henderson, NV 89015 Phone: 702 565-8033
Evangelical Lutheran: Christ the Servant Lutheran Church, 12 Commerce Center Dr., Henderson, NV Phone: 702 435-3634
Latter-day Saints: Second Ward, E Ocean Ave., Henderson, NV 89015 Phone: 702 565-0631
Third Ward, 173 Metropolitan Dr., Henderson, NV 89015 Phone: 702 565-9888
Lutheran: Green Valley Lutheran Church, 693 Valle Verde Dr., Henderson, NV 89014 Phone: 702 454-8979
Lutheran Church: Our Savior Lutheran Church, 59 Lynn Lane, PO Box 91449, Henderson, NV 89009 Phone: 702 565-9154
Methodist: First Henderson United Methodist Church, 609 E. Horizon Dr., Henderson, NV 89015 Phone: 702 565-6049
Pentecostal: Church of God of Prophecy, 416 Perlite Way, Henderson, NV 89015 Phone: 702 565-9379
Henderson Church of God, 519 N. Pueblo Blvd, Henderson, NV 89015
Presbyterian: Henderson Presbyterian Church, PO Box 91346, Henderson, NV 89009 Phone: 702 565-9684
Protestant: Neighborhood Church, 203 W. Basic Rd., Henderson, NV 89015 Phone: 702 565-9672
Roman Catholic: St. Thomas More Catholic Church, 130 N. Pecos Rd., Henderson, NV 89014
Southern Baptist: Henderson First Baptist Church, 240 S. Cholla St., Henderson, NV 89015 Phone: 702 565-6072
INDIAN SPRINGS
Later Day Saints: Indian Springs Latter-day Saints Church, Greata Lane, Indian Springs, NV 89018 Phone: 702 879-3691
Southern Baptist: Indian Springs First Baptist, PO Box 505, Indian Springs, NV 89018 Phone: 702 879-3691

JEAN
Later Day Saints: Latter-day Saints Church in Sandy Valley, Sandy Valley, Jean, NV 89019 Phone: 702 723-5225
LAS VEGAS
Adventist: Jehovah's Witnesses, 5546 W. Oakey Blvd, Las Vegas, NV 89102 Phone: 702 877-1172
Jehovah's Witnesses, 100 Shiloah Dr., Las Vegas, NV 89110 Phone: 702 452-4815
Jehovah's Witnesses, 5005 Donnie Ave., Las Vegas, NV 89130 Phone: 702 645-4590
Assemblies of God: Calvary Community Assembly of God, 3825 Melody Ln., Las Vegas, NV 89108
Full Gospel Church, 1580 Bledsoe Ln., Las Vegas, NV 89110 Phone: 702 453-4145
Mountain View Assembly of God, 3901 E. Bonanza Rd., Las Vegas, NV 89110 Phone: 702 452-8400
West Valley Assembly of God, 5825 W. Sahara Ave STE K., Las Vegas, NV 89102 Phone: 702 876-8338
Baptist: Bethany Baptist Church, 1229 W. Owens Ave., Las Vegas, NV 89106 Phone: 702 648-5665
Bethel Baptist Church, 400 W. Adams Ave., Las Vegas, NV 89106 Phone: 702 648-8663
Bible Baptist Church, 238 Sandy Ln., Las Vegas, NV 89115 Phone: 702 452-2622
Calvary Baptist Church, 317 Madison Ave., Las Vegas, NV 89106 Phone: 702 646-1559
Carver Baptist Church, 1221, N. J St., Las Vegas, NV 89106 Phone: 702 648-4111
Community Baptist Church, 220 N. 19th St., Las Vegas, NV 89101
Evergreen Baptist Church, 1915 Lexington St., Las Vegas, NV 89106 Phone: 702 647-3071
Fellowship Baptist Church, 6210 W. Cheyenne Ave., Las Vegas, NV 89108 Phone: 702 645-2415
First Korean Baptist Church, 440 W. Oakey Blvd, Las Vegas, NV 89102 Phone: 702 878-2444
Gateway Baptist Church, 1900 N. Gateway Rd., Las Vegas, NV 89115 Phone: 702 452-7111
Grace Immanuel Baptist Church, 805 W. Bartlett Ave., Las Vegas, NV 89106 Phone: 702 647-5797
Greater New Jerusalem Baptist Church, 1100 N. D St., Las Vegas, NV 89106 Phone: 702 648-8438
Greater St. James Baptist Church, 311 Madison Ave., Las Vegas, NV 89106 Phone: 702 646-4747

Harmony Regular Baptist Church, 1103 N. Nellis Blvd., Las Vegas, NV 89110
Phone: 702 438-2780

Homesite Baptist Church, 2413 Cedar Ave., Las Vegas, NV 89101
Phone: 702 384-2993

Iglesia Primera Bautista, 1490 E. University Ave., Las Vegas, NV 89119
Phone: 702 732-3385

Lakes Baptist Church, 8072 W. Sahara Ave. STE A, Las Vegas, NV 89117
Phone: 702 255-1335

Lamb Boulevard Missionary Baptist, 500 N. Lamb Blvd., Las Vegas, NV
89110 Phone: 702 452-9146

Liberty Baptist Church, 6501 E. Lake Mead Blvd., Las Vegas, NV 89115
Phone: 702 647-4522

Mount Calvary Baptist Church, 977 Hassell Ave., Las Vegas, NV 89106
Phone: 702 648-0665

Nellis Baptist Church, 4600 Las Vegas Blvd., Las Vegas, NV 89119
Phone: 702 643-8800

Oasis Regular Baptist Church, 3256 Aloha St., Las Vegas, NV 89121
Phone: 702 451-5694

Paradise Bible Baptist Church, 2525 Emerson Ave., Las Vegas, NV 89121
Phone: 702 732-8555

Paradise Valley Southern Baptist, 5424 Tamarus St., Las Vegas, NV 89119
Phone: 702 739-6400

Pleasant Grove Baptist Church, 1061 Hart Ave., Las Vegas, NV 89106
Phone: 702 648-1645

St. James Baptist Church, 316 Madison Ave:, Las Vegas, NV 89106

St. John Missionary Baptist Church, 1439 Lawry Ave., Las Vegas, NV 89106
Phone: 702 648-2382

Second Baptist Church, 500 Madison Ave., Las Vegas, NV 89106
Phone: 702 648-6155

Southern Nevada Baptist, 1482 E. University Ave., Las Vegas, NV 89119
Phone: 702 732-4171

True Love Missionary Baptist Church, 1941 N. H St., Las Vegas, NV 89106
Phone: 702 648-3603

Victory Baptist Church, PO Box 4037, Las Vegas, NV 89127
Phone: 702 648-2286

West Charleston Baptist Church, 6701 W. Charleston Blvd., Las Vegas, NV
89102 Phone: 702 878-5798

Buddhist: Kwan Um Sa, 2125 E. St. Louis Ave., Las Vegas, NV 89104
Phone: 702 457-6299

Las Vegas Buddist Sangha, 6341 O'bannon Dr., Las Vegas, NV 89102

Lian Hwa Temple, 905 North 21ˢᵗ St., Las Vegas, NV 89101

Nevada Buddist Association, 4189 S. Jones Blvd., Las Vegas, NV 89103
Phone: 702 252-7339

Nevada Nichiren Shoshu Temple: 120 Rancho Vista Dr., Las Vegas, NV 89106
Sung Bul Sa, 1900 E. Oakey Blvd., Las Vegas, NV 89104
  Phone: 702 641-6249
Vipassana Sitting Group, 5039 Andover Dr., Las Vegas, NV 89122
  Phone: 702 458-7648
Wat Buddhapavana Las Vegas, 3414 s. Sandhill Rd., Las Vegas, NV 89121
  Phone: 702 435-1504
Church of Christ: Central Christian Church, 3375 S. Mojave Rd., Las Vegas,
  NV Phone: 702 735-4004
Central Church of Christ, 3984 Schiff Dr., Las Vegas, NV 89103
  Phone: 702 871-1244
Charleston Heights Church of Christ, 3816 Vegas Dr., Las Vegas, NV 89106
  Phone: 702 648-4827
The Church of Las Vegas, 3388 S. Decatur Blvd No P, Las Vegas, NV 89102
  Phone: 702 876-3499
Church of Christ, 3240 N. Civic Center Dr., Las Vegas, NV 89114
  Phone: 702 649-3034
Church of Christ, State St., Las Vegas, NV 89109
Church of Christ, 2626 S. Highland Dr., Las Vegas, NV 89109
  Phone: 702 648-8283
First Christian Church, 101 S. Rancho Dr., Las Vegas, NV 89106
  Phone: 702 384-1544
Oakey Boulevard Church of Christ, 4000 W. Oakey Blvd., Las Vegas, NV
  89102 Phone: 702 877-9629
Second Christian Church, 940 W. Owens Ave., PO Box 5072, Las Vegas, NV
  89106 Phone: 702 646-1662
Southside Christian Church, 3070 Desmond Ave., Las Vegas, NV 89121
  Phone: 702 458-2731
Spring Valley Church of Christ, PO Box 26876, Las Vegas, NV 89126
Sunrise Church of Christ, PO Box 42091, Las Vegas, NV 89116
Valley Church of Christ, 4559 Mountain Vista St., Las Vegas, NV 89121
  Phone: 702 451-6932
Valley Church of Christ, 4775 Happy Valley Ave., Las Vegas, NV 89121
Christian Science: Christian Scientist Church, 1717 E. Charleston Blvd.,
  Las Vegas, NV 89104 Phone: 702 384-4155
First Christian Science Church, 300 S. 7th St., Las Vegas, NV 89101
  Phone: 702 384-3043
Congregational: Pilgrim Church of Christ, 1515 N. D St., Las Vegas, NV
  89106 Phone: 702 648-6504
Episcopal: All Saints Episcopalian Church, 4201 W. Washington Ave.,
  Las Vegas, NV 89107 Phone: 702 878-2373

Christ Episcopalian Church, 2000 S. Maryland Pky., Las Vegas, NV 89104
Phone: 702 735-7655
Emmanuel Episcopalian Church, 7246 Southpark Ct., Las Vegas, NV 89117
Phone: 702 871-6729
St. Luke's Episcopalian Church, PO Box 43720, Las Vegas, NV 89116
Phone: 702 642-4459
St. Matthew's Episcopalian Church, 4709 S. Nellis Blvd., Las Vegas, NV
89121 Phone: 702 451-2483
St. Thomas Episcopalian Church, 1579 Bledsoe Ln., Las Vegas, NV 89110
Phone: 702 452-1199
Evangelical Lutheran: Calvary Lutheran Church, 800 N. Bruce St.,
Las Vegas, NV 89101 Phone: 702 649-7788
Christ Lutheran Church, 111 N. Torrey Pines Dr., Las Vegas, NV 89107
Phone: 702 870-1421
Community Lutheran Church, 3720 E. Tropicana Ave., Las Vegas, NV 89121
Phone: 702 458-2241
Good Samaritan Lutheran Church, 6500 W. Flamingo Rd., Las Vegas, NV
89103 Phone: 702 873-3589
Holy Spiritual Lutheran Church, 6670 W. Cheyenne Ave., Las Vegas, NV
89108 Phone: 702 645-1777
The Lakes Lutheran Church, 3144 Clamdigger Lane, Las Vegas, NV 89117
Phone: 702 363-2515
Reformation Lutheran Church, 580 E. Saint Louis Ave. No 6, Las Vegas, NV
89104 Phone: 702 732-2052
St. Andrew Lutheran Church, 7824 Ramblewood Ave., Las Vegas, NV 89128
Phone: 702 255-1990
Holiness: Christian Alliance Church, 901 Stewart Ave., Las Vegas, NV 89101
Phone: 702 384-1950
Church of the Nazarene, 1769 E. Russell Rd., Las Vegas, NV 89119
Phone: 702 736-6681
Church of the Nazarene, 6219 W. Washington Ave., Las Vegas, NV 89107
Phone: 702 870-9911
Eleventh Street First Church of God, 318 S. 11th St., Las Vegas, NV 89101
Phone: 702 382-4838
First Church of God, 827 Balzar Ave., Las Vegas, NV 89106
Phone: 702 646-2824
Las Vegas Rescue Mission, PO Box 384, Las Vegas, NV 89125
Phone: 702 382-5924
The Salvation Army, PO Box 28369, Las Vegas, NV 89126
Phone: 702 382-4415
The Salvation Army, 2900 Palomino Ln., Las Vegas, NV 89107
Phone: 702 870-4430

Independent Fundamentalist: The Bible Way Fellowship, 1000 Garces Ave., Las Vegas, NV 89101

Grace Bible Church, 2457 N. Decatur Blvd., Las Vegas, NV 89108
Phone: 702 648-3570

Grace Bible Church of Las Vegas, 4504 Providence Ln., Las Vegas, NV 89107

Las Vegas Bible Church, 125 N. 14th St., Las Vegas, NV 89101
Phone: 702 385-3869

Las Vegas Evangelical Free Church, 1251 Robin St., Las Vegas, NV 89106
Phone: 702 648-1628

Living Word Church, 5720 Eugene Ave., Las Vegas, NV 89108
Phone: 702 648-9631

Upland Bible Church, 920 Upland Blvd, Las Vegas, NV 89107
Phone: 702 878-6291

Jewish: Congregation New Tamid, 2761 Emerson Ave., Las Vegas, NV 89121
Phone: 702 733-6292

Congregation Shaarei Tefilla, 1331 S. Maryland Pky., Las Vegas, NV 89104
Phone: 702 384-3565

Reformed Jewish Congregation, 2761 Emerson Ave., Las Vegas, NV 89121
Phone: 702 733-6292

Temple Beth Am, 6337 Moino St., PO Box 28879, Las Vegas, NV 89126
Phone: 702 645-8844

Temple Beth Sholom, 1600 E. Oakey Blvd, Las Vegas, NV 89104
Phone: 702 388-4438

Temple Emanuel, 4241 W. Charleston Blvd., Las Vegas, NV 89102
Phone: 702 870-1217

Latter-day Saints: Bishop Storehouse Las Vegas, 1438 Las Vegas Blvd., Las Vegas, NV 89101 Phone: 702 649-2909

Church of Jesus Christ Latter-day Saints, 2245 Lindell Rd., Las Vegas, NV 89102 Phone: 702 367-3548

Church of Jesus Christ Latter-day Saints, 5040 Champions Ave., Las Vegas, NV 89122 Phone: 702 431-2299

Church of Jesus Christ Latter-day Saints, 2068 N. Gateway Rd., Las Vegas, NV 89115 Phone: 702 642-5773

Church of Jesus Christ Latter-day Saints, 3200 Mustang St., Las Vegas, NV 89108 Phone: 702 645-0177

Church of Jesus Christ Latter-day Saints, 811 Sweeney Ave., Las Vegas, NV 89104 Phone: 702 384-3895

The Development Office, 1095 University Rd., Las Vegas, NV 89119
Phone: 702 736-4296

Las Vegas Church of Latter-day Saints, 5401 W. Oakey Blvd., Las Vegas, NV 89102 Phone: 702 871-7208

Las Vegas Eighteenth Ward, 2295 N. Walnut Rd., Las Vegas, NV 89115
Phone: 702 452-0279

Las Vegas Latter-day Saints Stake, PO Box 27055, Las Vegas, NV 89126
Phone: 702 871-4363
Las Vegas South Stake, 2245 Lindell Rd., Las Vegas, NV 89102
Phone: 702 878-0062
Las Vegas Thirty-First Ward, PO Box 27075, Las Vegas, NV 89126
Phone: 702 871-4363
Las Vegas Thirty-Seventh Ward, 5040 Champions Ave., Las Vegas, NV 89122
Phone: 702 452-3655
Las Vegas Thirty-Sixth Ward, 1251 Robin St., Las Vegas, NV 89106
Phone: 702 648-0749
Las Vegas Twelfth Ward, 2738 Potosi St., Las Vegas, NV 89102
Phone: 702 873-1115
Las Vegas Twenty-Second Ward, 5800 Cart Ave., Las Vegas, NV 89108
Phone: 702 648-5217
University Branch, 1095 University Rd., Las Vegas, NV 89119
Phone: 702 736-6709
Lutheran: Good Shepherd Lutheran Church, 301 S. Maryland Pky.,
Las Vegas, NV 89101 Phone: 702 384-6106
Lutheran Church: Mount Olive Lutheran Church, 3985 S. Sandhill Rd.,
Las Vegas, NV 89121 Phone: 702 451-1050
Mount Olive Lutheran Church, 3985 S. Sandhill Rd., Las Vegas, NV 89121
Phone: 702 451-1050
Mountain View Lutheran Church, 920 S. Decatur Blvd., Las Vegas, NV 89107
Phone: 702 878-7532
Redeemer Lutheran Church, 1730 N. Pecos Rd., Las Vegas, NV 89115
Phone: 702 642-7744
Metaphysical: Church of Universology, 3419 Thom Blvd., Las Vegas, NV
89130 Phone: 702 645-1799
Creative Life Community Church, 3310 S. Jones Blvd., Las Vegas, NV 89102
Phone: 702 367-0239
First Church Religious Science, 1420 E. Harmon Ave., Las Vegas, NV 89119
Phone: 739-8200
Paradise Metaphysical Center, 4618 Carriage Ln., Las Vegas, NV 89119
Spiritualist Desert Church, 1824 Winterwood Blvd., Las Vegas, NV 89122
Sunrise Community Church Religious Science, 3823 S. Maryland Pky.,
Apt P12, Las Vegas, NV 89119 Phone: 702 737-5219
Unity Church of the Desert, PO Box 4122, Las Vegas, NV 89116
Phone: 702 382-8688
Unity Church of the Desert, 1125 S. Maryland Pky., Las Vegas, NV 89104
Phone: 702 382-8688
Methodist: Advent United Methodist Church, 3460 N. Rancho Dr., Las Vegas,
NV 89130 Phone: 702 645-0447

Advent United Methodist Church, 2512 E. Oakey Blvd., Las Vegas, NV 89104
Phone: 702 457-4834

First United Methodist Church, 231 s. 3rd St., Las Vegas, NV 89101
Phone 702 382-9939

Griffith United Methodist Church, 1701 E. Oakey Blvd., Las Vegas, NV 89104
Phone: 702 382-7836

Sunrise Mount United Methodist Church, 4225 E. Sahara Ave., Las Vegas, NV
89104 Phone: 702 641-1994

Trinity United Methodist Church, 6151 W. Charleston Blvd., Las Vegas, NV
89102 Phone: 702 870-4749

University United Methodist Church, 4412 S. Maryland Pky., Las Vegas, NV
89102 Phone: 702 733-7155

Muslim: American Muslim Mission, 711 Morgan Ave., Las Vegas, NV 89106
Phone: 702 647-2757

Islamic Society of Nevada, 2280 Mohigan Way, Las Vegas, NV 89109

Masjid Muhammad, 1109 Wyatt, Las Vegas, NV 89106

Muhannad Mosque of Islam, 615 W. Van Buren Ave., Las Vegas, NV 89106
Phone: 702 648-5081

Muslim Students' Association of the University of Las Vegas, Park Student
Union, 4504 Maryland, Las Vegas, NV 89154

Orthodox: St. John the Baptist Church, 1229 Carson Ave., Las Vegas, NV
89101 Phone: 702 382-2750

St. Michael Antiochian Orthodox, 5719 Judson Ave., Las Vegas, NV 89115
Phone: 702 452-1299

St. Simeon Serbian Orthodox Church, PO Box 4221, Las Vegas, NV 89127
Phone: 702 367-7783

Pentecostal: Apostolic Church, 1675 Lindell Rd., Las Vegas, NV 89102
Phone: 702 878-8000

Calvary Chapel, 800 N. Rancho Dr., Las Vegas, NV 89106
Phone: 702 646-4626

Calvary Chapel Spring Valley, 3400 S. Jones Blvd No.23, Las Vegas, NV
89102 Phone: 702 362-9000

Calvary Foursquare Church, 2929 Cedar Ave., Las Vegas, NV 89101
Phone: 702 384-6960

Chapel of Lord Jesus, 1260 W. Bartlett Ave., Las Vegas, NV 89106
Phone: 702 648-0332

East Las Vegas Assembly, 6060 Boulder Hwy, Las Vegas, NV 89122
Phone: 702 456-9820

Echoes of Faith Church, 1401 E. Washington Ave., Las Vegas, NV 89101
Phone: 702 642-0011

Echoes of Faith Church, 3963 Bridle Ct., Las Vegas, NV 89121

Etz Hachaim Messianic Congregational, PO Box 85336, Las Vegas, NV 89185

Four Square Church, 318 S. 11th St., Las Vegas, NV 89101

Great Commission Ministries, 1911 N. H St., Las Vegas, NV 89106

Spanish Apostolic Church, 1401 Las Vegas Blvd N., Las Vegas, NV 89101
Phone: 702 382-3347

United Pentecostal Church, 4775 Happy Valley Ave., Las Vegas, NV 89121
Phone: 702 565-8234

Victory Bible Institute 601 Tiffany Ln., Las Vegas, NV 89101

Vineyard Christian Fellowship. PO Box 60056, Las Vegas, NV 89160
Phone: 702 322-0433

Word of Life Christian Center, 3900 W. Charleston Blvd, PO Box 28115,
Las Vegas, NV 89126 Phone: 702 870-1980

Pentecostal Church of God: Church of God in Christ, 1216 W. Adams Ave.,
Las Vegas, NV 89106 Phone: 702 646-5522

Church of God of Prophecy, 4780 Patterson Ave., Las Vegas, NV 89104
Phone: 702 438-7444

Church of God Trusted Fellowship, 2810 W. Charleston Blvd. No G-7,
Las Vegas, NV 89102

Ebenezer Church of God in Christ, 1072 W. Bartlett Ave., Las Vegas, NV
89106 Phone: 702 646-1503

Flamingo Boulevard Church of God, 1569 E. Flamingo Rd., Las Vegas, NV
89119

Friendship Church of God, 2249 W. Washington Ave., Las Vegas, NV 89106
Phone: 702 646-1361

Gateway to Heaven Church of God in Christ, 1425 Balzar Ave., Las Vegas,
NV 89106 Phone: 702 646-1185

Goodwill Church of God in Christ, 2080 La Salle St., Las Vegas, NV 89106

Goodwill Church of God in Christ, 976 Hassell Ave., Las Vegas, NV 89106
Phone: 702 648-9682

House of Holiness Church of God, 1216 Jefferson Ave., Las Vegas, NV 89106
Phone: 702 648-7937

Las Vegas Church of God, 4000 Spring Rd., Las Vegas, NV 89108
Phone: 702 648-3418

Las Vegas Church of God, 2212 Constantine Ave., Las Vegas, NV 89101,
Phone: 702 399-3552

Light House Church of God, 1021 N . H St., Las Vegas, NV 89106

Most High Church of God in Christ, 1641 N. L St., Las Vegas, NV 89106

Neway Church of God in Christ, 1305 N. D St., Las Vegas, NV 89106
Phone: 702 647-4645

North Church of God, 2520 Belmont St., Las Vegas, NV 89115

Power House Church of God, 909 W. Adams Ave., Las Vegas, NV 89106
Phone: 702 648-3142

Prayer House Church of God in Christ, 1026 Cunningham Dr., Las Vegas, NV
89106

St. Paul Church of God, 911 N. G. St., Las Vegas, NV 89106
Phone: 702 648-4230
Trinity Church of God in Christ, 305 Paul Ave., Las Vegas, NV 89106
Upper Room N. F St., Las Vegas, NV 89106 Phone: 702 648-6856
Presbyterian: Spring Meadows Presbyterian Church: PO Box 82225,
Las Vegas, NV 89180 Phone: 702 254-0570
First Presbyterian Church, 1515 W. Charleston Blvd., Las Vegas, NV 89102
Phone: 702 384-4554
Paradise Presbyterian, 3500 E. Harmon Ave., Las Vegas, NV 89121
Phone: 702 456-6918
Westminister Presbyterian Church, 4601 W. Lake Mead Blvd., Las Vegas, NV
89108 Phone: 702 648-8437
Protestant: Agape Love Center, 1018 E. Sahara Ave Ste B, Las Vegas, NV
89104 Phone: 702 731-9429
Bethel Korean Church, PO Box 42537, Las Vegas, NV 89116
Center for Spiritual Growth, 1709 Fontenelle St., Las Vegas, NV 89102
Christian Life Community Church, 900 Karen Ave., Las Vegas, NV 89109
Phone: 702 731-6965
Church at Las Vegas, 2917 Austin Ave., Las Vegas, NV 89107
City of Angeles Mission Church, 1350 E. Flamingo Rd., Las Vegas, NV 89119
El Bethel Ramah Temple, 820 W. Bonanza Rd., Las Vegas, NV 89106
Phone: 702 647-3771
Foundation Faith of God, 6209 Shadywood Dr., Las Vegas, NV 89102
Phone: 702 367-6808
Grapevine Fellowship, 1600 S. Nellis Blvd., Las Vegas, NV 89104
Phone: 702 431-8463
Harbor Christian Fellowship Church, 2675 S. Lamb Blvd., Las Vegas, NV
89121 Phone: 702 457-9300
Home of the Good Sheperd, 7000 N. Jones Blvd., Las Vegas, NV 89131
Las Vegas Friends Church, 3451 Middlebury Ave., Las Vegas, NV 89121
Las Vegas Valley Church, 5196 Sawyer Ave., Las Vegas, NV 89108
Meadows Christian Fellowship, 1725 S. Rainbow Blvd., Las Vegas, NV 89102
Phone: 702 254-1725
New Life Tabernacle Church, 2404 Stewart Ave., Las Vegas, NV 89101
New Testament Fellowship, 2162 Cascade St., Las Vegas, NV 89122
Pilgrim Rest Missionary, 1240 W. Adams Ave., Las Vegas, NV 89106
Phone: 702 648-5666
Prayer House New Covenant, 1341 Blankenship Ave., Las Vegas, NV 89106
Phone: 702 648-6309
St. Viator Youth Ministry, 4320 Channel 10 Dr., Las Vegas, NV 89119
Phone: 702 796-9400
Sunrise Congregation, 1881 N. Walnut Rd., Las Vegas, NV 89115
Phone: 702 453-1277

Teaching of Inner Christ, 3160 S. Valley View Blvd., Las Vegas, NV 89102
Phone: 702 367-8911

Trinity Life Center, 1000 E. Saint Louis Ave., Las Vegas, NV 89104
Phone: 702 734-2223

Vegas Valley Christ Church, 5515 Mountain Vista St., PO Box 12777,
Las Vegas, NV 89112 Phone: 702 451-9211

Roman Catholic: Catholic Church of St. Anne, 1901 S. Maryland Pky.,
Las Vegas, NV 89104 Phone: 702 735-0510

Christ the King Catholic, 4925 S. Torrey Pines Dr., Las Vegas, NV 89118
Phone: 702 871-1904

Holy Family Catholic Church, 4490 Mountain Vista St., Las Vegas, NV 89121
Phone: 702 458-2211

Our Lady of Ministry Sick and Aging, 3036 Alta Dr., Las Vegas, NV 89107
Phone: 702 878-2273

Our Lady of Victory Tradition, PO Box 72412, Las Vegas, NV 89170

Prince of Peace Catholic, 5485 E. Charleston Blvd., Las Vegas, NV 89122
Phone: 702 459-6776

St. Bridgets Catholic Church, 220 N. 14th St., Las Vegas, NV 89101
Phone: 702 384-3382

St. Francis De Sales Church, 1111 Michael Way, Las Vegas, NV 89108
Phone: 702 647-3440

St. James Catholic Church, 704 W. McWilliams Ave., Las Vegas, NV 89106

St. James the Apostle Church, 821 N. H St., Las Vegas, NV 89106
Phone: 702 648-6606

St. Joan of Arcs Catholic Church, 315 S. Casino Center, Las Vegas, NV 89101
Phone: 702 382-9909

St. Joseph Catholic Church, 7260 W. Sahara Ave., Las Vegas, NV 89117
Phone: 702 363-1902

St. Josephs Catholic Church, 816 Ogden Ave., Las Vegas, NV 89101
Phone: 384-6909

St. Mary the Virgin Catholic Church, 5083 Judson Ave., Las Vegas, NV 89115
Phone: 702 438-1960

St. Mary the Virgin Catholic Church, 1804 Theresa Ave., Las Vegas, NV
89101 Phone: 702 642-6287

St. Victors Catholic Church, 2461 E. Flamingo Rd., Las Vegas, NV 89121
Phone: 702 733-8323

Seventh Day Adventist: Highland Square Seventh Day Adventist Church,
3321 Winterhaven St., Las Vegas, NV 89108 Phone: 702 645-3295

Las Vegas Highland Square Seventh Day Adventist Church, 1702 N. J St.,
Las Vegas, NV 89106 Phone: 702 648-9898

Las Vegas Paradise Seventh Day Adventist Church, 1769 E. Russell Rd.,
Las Vegas, NV 89119 Phone: 702 435-7999

Las Vegas Spanish Seventh Day Adventist Church, 1200 n. Eastern Ave.,
Las Vegas, NV 89101 Phone: 702 642-2220
Seventh Day Adventist Church, 6001 W. Oakey Blvd, Las Vegas, NV 89102
Phone: 702 871-0814
Tenth Street Seventh Day Adventist Church, 1701 E. Oakey Blvd., Las Vegas,
NV 89104
Southern Baptist: Desert Hills Baptist Church, 4401 S. Nellis Blvd.,
Las Vegas, NV 89121 Phone: 702 451-2100
Frontier Baptist Church, 3919 Savoy Ct., Las Vegas, NV 89115
Phone: 702 644-1116
Lone Mountain Baptist Church, 7450 W. Craig Rd., Las Vegas, NV 89129
Phone: 702 877-2861
Paradise Baptist Church, 1712 Leslie Ave., Las Vegas, NV 89101
Phone: 702 457-9300
Redrock Baptist Church, 5500 Alta Dr., Las Vegas, NV 89107
Phone: 702 870-9198
Sunnyside Baptist Church, 1980 Saylor Way, Las Vegas, NV 89108
Sunrise southern Baptist Church, 1780 Betty Ln., Las Vegas, NV 89115
Phone: 702 452-8599
Twin Lakes Baptist Church, 5700 Vegas Dr., Las Vegas, NV 89108
Phone: 702 648-5864
West Oakey Baptist Church, 4400 W. Oakey Blvd., Las Vegas, NV 89102
Phone: 702 878-6991
Unclassified: Church of Scientology, 1100 S. 10th St., Las Vegas, NV 89104
Phone: 702 731-1500
Church of Scientology of Nevada, 846 E. Sahara Ave., Las Vegas, NV 89104
Phone: 702 731-1500
Las Vegas Fellowship, 4765 Brussells St., Las Vegas, NV 89119
Phone: 702 736-2207
Metropolitian Community Church, 1119 S. Main St., Las Vegas, NV 89104
Phone: 702 384-2325
St. Paul Universal Church, PO Box 14661, Las Vegas, NV 89114
Unification Church, 105 Woodley St., Las Vegas, NV 89106
Phone: 702 383-0609
MESQUITE
Latter-day Saints: Church of Jesus Christ Latter-day Saints, General Delivery,
Mesquite, NV 89024 Phone: 702 346-5252
NORTH LAS VEGAS
African Methodist: First African Methodist Episcopal Church,
2450 Revere St. North Las Vegas, NV 89030 Phone: 702 649-1774
Baptist: Bible Baptist Church, PO Box 4335, North Las Vegas, NV 89036
Phone: 702 452-2622

Calvary Baptist Church, PO Box 3248, North Las Vegas, NV 89036
Phone: 702 646-1559
Cheyenne Avenue Community Church, 2828 E. Cheyenne Ave.,
North Las Vegas, NV 89030 Phone: 702 643-1523
Community College Baptist Church, 3459 E. Cheyenne Ave., North Las Vegas,
NV 89030 Phone: 702 642-8776
First Baptist Church, 2828 E. Cheyenne Ave., North Las Vegas, NV 89030
Phone: 702 643-1523
Gateway Baptist Church, PO Box 3807, North Las Vegas, NV 89036
Phone: 702 452-7111
Grace Imanuel Baptist Church, 1404 Helen Ave., North Las Vegas, NV 89030
Greater Faith Baptist Church, 2736 Chamberlain Ln., North Las Vegas, NV
89030 Phone: 702 647-4110
Nellis Baptist Church, 4600 Vegas Blvd. North, North Las Vegas, NV 89115
Phone: 702 643-8800
Valley Baptist Church, 2844 Civic Center Dr., North Las Vegas, NV 89030
Phone: 702 642-6357
Churches of God: Church of Christ, 2450 Revere St., North Las Vegas, NV
89030 Phone: 702 642-3141
Church of Christ, 2800 Dogwood Ave., North Las Vegas, NV 89030
Phone: 702 642-3687
Las Vegas Church of Christ, 3240 Civic Center Dr No.B, Las Vegas, NV
89030 Phone: 702 362-2615
Martin Luther King Drive Church of Christ, 2626 Martin L King Blvd.,
North Las Vegas, NV 89030 Phone: 702 648-8283
Northside Church of Christ, 2424 McCarran St., North Las Vegas, NV 89030
Phone: 702 642-3141
Latter-day Saints: Church of Jesus Christ Latter-day Saints, 2272 Crestline
Loop, North Las Vegas, NV 89030 Phone: 702 642-9789
Las Vegas Fourth Ward, Lola Ave and White, North Las Vegas, NV 89030
Phone: 702 642-1011
Methodist: Wesley United Methodist Church, 2727 Civic Center Dr.,
North Las Vegas, NV 89030 Phone: 702 642-0243
Zion United Methodist Church, 2108 Revere St., North Las Vegas, NV 89030
Phone: 702 648-7806
Pentecostal: Emmanuel Deliverance Temple, 2417 North St., North Las Vegas,
NV 89030 Phone: 702 648-0041
Golden Valley Apostolic, PO Box 3189, North Las Vegas, NV 89036
Phone: 702 649-2884
Holy Ghost Temple Apostolic, 2624 Clayton St., North Las Vegas, NV 89030
Phone: 702 646-0805
Pentecostal Church of God: Angelic Church of God in Christ,
3329 Coleman St., North Las Vegas, NV 89030 Phone: 702 648-4695

Belmont Street Church of God, 2540 Belmont St., North Las Vegas, NV 89030

Church of God North Las Vegas, 2520 Belmont St., North Las Vegas, NV 89030 Phone: 702 399-3633

Ebenezer Church of God in Christ, 2009 Jeffery Ave., North Las Vegas, NV 89030

First Church of God, 2109 Baltzar Ave., North Las Vegas, NV 89030 Phone: 702 646-2824

Iglesia De Dios, 2540 Belmont St., North Las Vegas, NV 89030 Phone: 702 642-4023

The Most High Church of God Christ, 2717 York Ave., North Las Vegas, NV 89030 Phone: 702 646-9721

St. John Church of God in Christ, 2301 Comstock Dr., North Las Vegas, NV 89030 Phone: 702 647-7393

St. Paul Church of God in Christ, 1882 Renada Cir., North Las Vegas, NV 89030

Vegas View Church of God in Christ, 415 Beth Cir., North Las Vegas, NV 89030

Vegas View Church of God in Christ, 1906 Gider St., North Las Vegas, NV 89030 Phone; 702 642-6211

Roman Catholic: St. Christopher Catholic Church, 1840 N. Bruce St., North Las Vegas, NV 89030 Phone: 702 642-1154

Southern Baptist: Calvary Baptist Church, 1600 E. Cartier Ave., North Las Vegas, NV 89030 Phone: 702 649-2644

College Park Baptist Church, 2101 E. Owens Ave., North Las Vegas, NV 89030 Phone: 702 642-5921

Palestine Baptist Church, PO Box 3206, North Las Vegas, NV 89030 Phone: 702 438-3992

OVERTON

Protestant: Calvary Community Church, PO Box 602, Overton, NV 89040 Phone: 702 397-8028

PRIMM (STATELINE)

Jewish: Jewish Congregation, PO Box 5099, Primm, NV 89449

Protestant: Harvestime Church, Hwy 50 and Kingbury Gr., Primm, NV 89449 Phone: 702 588-5446

Southern Baptist: Tahoe Douglas Baptist Church, PO Box 6598, Primm, NV 89449 Phone: 702 588-3827

SEARCHLIGHT

Protestant: Searchlight Community Church, PO Box 732, Searchlight, NV 89046 Phone: 702 297-1505

COURTHOUSE

Clark County Courthouse
500 S. Grand Central Parkway, P. O. Box 551510, Las Vegas, NV 89155-1510
Phone: 702 455-4336
County Recorder- http://www.co.clerk.nv.us/recorder/recindex.htm
County Clerk- http://www.co.clerk.nv.us/clerk/clerkidx.htm
Land records: County Recorder, from 1909
Marriages: 1909 to present, County Recorder, applications $3.00, certificates $7.00
http://www.co.clerk.nv.us/recorder/mar_disc.htm- this site is a new marriage database, it lists Clark county marriages 1984 through the present. It lists name, spouse, marriage date and certificate number.

Clark County District Health Department
625 Shadow Lane, Las Vegas, NV 89101
P.O. Box 4426 Las Vegas, NV 89127
Phone: 702 383-1223
Birth: 1970 to present, $11.00
Death: 1975 to present, $8.00
Birth & death records not open to public, search by vital records staff- $5.00
No viewing of Birth Certificates
Viewing of Death Certificates $5.00-no writing of information in presence of Vital Records staff.

Clark County Clerk
601 N. Pecos Rd., Las Vegas, NV 89101
Phone: 702 455-2590
Probate records: County Clerk
Probate Search Service: $1.00 per year per name. Copy costs: $1.00 per page, $3.00 for certification, no minimum
Divorce Decrees: County Clerk, Family Court (attention: certificates)
1909 to present, $1.00 per year searched, plus $6.00 per record- Not open to public, search staff

Clark County Clerk Marriage Bureau
200 South Third St., 1st floor, P.O. Box 551601, Las Vegas, NV 89155-1601
Phone: 702 455-4416
Marriage license/application: $4.00 certified copy, $1.00 plain copy
Fee is $1.00 per year per name of couple

FUNERAL HOMES

Henderson

Palm Mortuary
800 South Boulder Highway, Henderson, NV 89015
Phone: 702 564-1888

Las Vegas

Bunker Mortuary & Memorial Park
925 Las Vegas Blvd., Las Vegas, NV 89101
Phone: 702 385-1441

Davis Funeral Home
2127 West Charleston Blvd., Las Vegas, NV 89102
Phone: 702 383-2900

Davis Funeral Home North
310 Foremaster, Las Vegas, NV 89101
Phone: 702 384-7600

Davis Paradise Valley Funeral Home
6200 S. Eastern Avenue, Las Vegas, NV 89119
Phone: 702 736-6200

Desert Memorial
1111 Las Vegas Blvd. N-Ste 6, Las Vegas, NV 89101
Phone: 702 382-1000

Forest Lawn Mortuary
2300 Patrick Lane, Las Vegas, NV 89119
Phone: 702 262-2232

Palm Downtown Mortuary
1325 N. Main Street, Las Vegas, NV 89101
Phone: 702 382-1340

Palm Redrock Mortuary
1600 South Jones, Las Vegas, NV 89102
Phone: 702 870-2100

Palm Summerlin Mortuary
7400 W. Cheyenne, Las Vegas, NV 89129
Phone: 702 656-3311

Palm Valley View Mortuary
7600 South Eastern, Las Vegas, NV 89123
Phone: 702 361-4040

Universal Funeral Home, Inc.
2200 E. Patrick Lane, Las Vegas, NV 89119
Phone: 702 262-2230

West Las Vegas Memorial Chapel (black)
615 West Van Buren Avenue, Las Vegas, NV 89106
Phone: 702 647-1000

Logandale

Metcalf Mortuary
5090 N. Hwy 169, Logandale, NV 89021
Phone: 702 398-3600

LIBRARIES

Boulder City

Boulder City Library
813 Arizona St., Boulder City, NV 89005-2697
Phone: 702 293-1281   Fax: 702 293-0239   E-mail: duncan@nevada.edu
Founded 1933

Hours: Monday through Thursday: 9:00 a.m. to 8:30 p.m., Friday: 9:00 a.m. to
5:00 p.m., Saturday: 11:00 a.m. to 4:00 p.m., Sunday (except summers):
1:00 p.m. to 4:00 p.m.
Subject Interests: Local history

Boulder City Family History Library
906 5th St., Boulder City, NV 89005
Phone: 702 293-3304

Henderson

Henderson District Public Library
280 Water St., Henderson, NV 89015
Phone: 702 565-8402 Fax: 702 565-8832 E-mail: landauzuki@earthlink.net
Hours: Monday through Thursday: 9:00 a.m. to 9:00 p.m., Friday & Saturday:
9:00 a.m. to 5:00 p.m., Sunday: noon to 4:00 p.m.
Branches:
Malcolm Branch Library, 80 N. Pecos Ave., Henderson, NV 89014
Phone: 702 263-7522
Fax: 702 263-7402; E-mail: hdmalcolm@earthlink.net
Hours: Monday through Thursday: 9:00 a.m. to 8:00 p.m., Friday &
Saturday: 9:00 a.m. to 5:00 p.m., Sunday: 12:00 noon to 4:00 p.m.
Pittman Branch Library, 1640 Price St., Henderson, NV 89015;
Phone: 702 565-5816
Hours: Tuesday through Thursday: 2:00 p.m. to 6:00 p.m., Saturday: 9:00
a.m. to 1:00 p.m.

Las Vegas

Las Vegas-Clark County Library District
833 Las Vegas Blvd, North, Las Vegas, NV 89101
Phone: 702 382-3493 Fax: 702 382-1280 E-mail: genen@lvccld.lib.nv.us
Internet:http://www.lvccld.lib.nv.us
Founded: 1966
Hours:Monday through Thursday: 9:00 a.m. to 9:00 p.m., Friday & Saturday:
9:00 a.m. to 5:00 p.m., Sunday: 12:00 noon to 5:00 p.m.
Blue Diamond Branch, P.O. Box 40, Blue Diamond, NV 89004
Phone: 702 875-4295; Fax: 702 875-4095
E-mail: tammyd@lvccld.lib.nv.us
Hours: Tuesday & Wednesday: 2:00 p.m. to 7:00 p.m., Thursday: 1:00 p.m.
to 8:00 p.m., Saturday: 9:00 a.m. to 12:00

Bunkerville Branch, P.O. Box 7208, Bunkerville, NV 89007
Phone: 702 346-5238; Fax: 702 346-5784
E-mail: carolynl@lvccld.lib.nv.us
Hours: Monday: 4:00 p.m. to 8:00 p.m., Tuesday through Thursday: 1:00
p.m. to 5:00 p.m., Saturday: 9:00 a.m. to 1:00 p.m.

Clark County (Las Vegas Public Library), 1401 E Flamingo Rd, Las Vegas, NV 89119
Phone: 702 733-7810; Fax: 702 733-1173; E-mail: montih@lvccld.lib.nv.us
Hours: Monday through Thursday: 9:00 a.m. to 9:00 p.m., Friday & Saturday: 9:00 a.m. to 5:00 p.m., Sunday: 1:00 p.m. to 5:00 p.m.
Nevada newspaper indexes:
  Las Vegas Review Journal, 1972-currently being updated
  Las Vegas Sun, 1972-currently being updated

Enterprise Library, 25 E. Shelbourne Ave., Las Vegas, NV 89123;
Phone: 269-3000; Fax: 702 269-8030
E-mail: judithg@lvccld.lib.nv.us

Goodsprings Branch, P.O. Box 667, Goodsprings, NV 89019;
Phone: 702 874-1366; Fax: 702 874-1335
Hours: Monday through Thursday: 3:00 p.m. to 7:00 p.m., Saturday; 10:00 a.m. to 2:00 p.m.

Green Valley, 2797 N Green Valley, Henderson, NV 89015;
Phone: 702 435-1840; Fax: 702 435-3481
E-mail: sallyf@lvccld.lib.nv.us
Hours: Monday through Thursday: 9:00 a.m. to 9:00 p.m., Friday & Saturday: 9:00 a.m. to 5:00 p.m., Sunday: 1:00 p.m. to 5:00 p.m.

Indian Springs Branch, P.O. Box 628, Indian Springs, NV 89018;
Phone: 702 879-3845; Fax: 702 879-5227
Hours: Tuesday through Thursday: 11:00 a.m.' to 7:00 p.m., Saturday: 9:00 a.m. to 3:00 p.m.

Laughlin Library, 3100 S Needles Hwy No 100, Laughlin, NV 89029;
Phone: 702 298-1081
Fax: 702 298-3940; E-mail: joycep@lvccld.lib.nv.us
Hours: Monday, Wednesday & Thursday: 9:00 a.m. to 6:00 p.m., Tuesday: 9:00 a.m. to 9:00 p.m.,
Friday & Saturday: 9:00 a.m. to 5:00 p.m., Sunday: 1:00 p.m. to 5:00 p.m.

Mesquite Library, P.O. Box 549, Mesquite, NV 89024;
Phone: 702 346-5224; Fax: 702 346-5788
E-mail: geraldz@lvccld.lib.nv.us
Hours: Monday & Wednesday: 12:00 noon to 8:00 p.m., Tuesday & Thursday: 10:00 a.m. to 6:00 p.m., Friday & Saturday: 9:00 a.m. to 5:00 p.m.

Moapa Town Library, P.O. Box 250, Moapa, NV 89025;
Phone: 702 864-2438; Fax: 702 864-2467
E-mail: lynw@lvccld.lib.nv.us
Hours: Tuesday & Thursday: 1:00 p.m. to 5:00 p.m., Thursday: 12:00 noon to 8:00 p.m., Saturday: 9:00 a.m. to 1:00 p.m.

Moapa Valley, 350 Hwy. 169, P.O. Box 397, Overton, NV 89040;
Phone: 702 397-2690; Fax: 702 397-2698
E-mail: toniap@lvccld.lib.nv.us
Hours: Tuesday & Thursday: 12:00 noon to 8:00 p.m., Friday & Saturday:
9:00 a.m. to 5:00 p.m.

Mount Charleston, HCR 38, Box 269, Mount Charleston, NV 89124;
Phone: 702 872-5585
Fax: 702 872:5631; E-mail: sandyg@lvccld.lib.nv.us
Hours: Monday & Tuesday: 12:00 noon to 8:00 p.m., Wednesday &
Thursday: 12:00 noon to 5:00 p.m., Saturday: 9:00 a.m. to 3:00

Rainbow, 3510 N. Buffalo, Las Vegas, NV 89128; Phone: 702 243-7323;
Fax: 702 243-7000
E-mail: janer@lvccld.lib.nv.us
Hours: Monday through Thursday: 9:00 a.m. to 9:00 p.m., Friday &
Saturday: 9:00 a.m. to 5:00 p.m., Sunday: 1:00 p.m. to 5:00 p.m.

Saraha West, 9002 W. Sahara Ave., Las Vegas, NV 89117;
Phone: 702 228-1940; Fax 702 228-1943
E-mail: annla@lvccld.lib.nv.us
Hours: Monday through Thursday: 9:00 a.m. to 9:00 p.m., Friday &
Saturday: 9:00 a.m. to 5:00 p.m., Sunday: 1:00 p.m. to 5:00 p.m.

Sandy Valley Branch, HCR 31, Box 377, Sandy Valley, NV 89109;
Phone: 702 723-5333
Fax: 702 723-1010; E-mail: gwend@lvccld.lib.nv.us
Hours: Monday, Tuesday & Thursday: 1:00 p.m. to 5:00 p.m., Wednesday:
5:00 p.m. to 9:00 p.m., Saturday: 1:00 p.m. to 5:00 p.m.

Searchlight Branch, P.O. Box 98, Searchlight, NV 89046;
Phone: 702 297-1442; Fax: 702 297-1782
Hours: Tuesday & Wednesday: 1:00 p.m. to 6:00 p.m., Thursday: 1:00 p.m.
to 7:00 p.m., Saturday: 9:00 a.m. to 1:00 p.m.

Spring Valley, 4280 S. Jones Blvd., Las Vegas, NV 89103;
Phone: 702 368-4411; Fax: 702 368-2586
E-mail: 702 laurag@lvccld.lib.nv.us
Hours: Monday through Thursday: 9:00 a.m. to 9:00 p.m., Friday &
Saturday: 9:00 a.m. to 5:00 p.m., Sunday: 1:00 p.m. to 5:00 p.m.

Summerlin Library, 1771 Inner Circle Dr., Las Vegas, NV 89101;
Phone: 702 256-5111; Fax: 702 256-7228
E-mail: richardl@lvccld.lib.nv.us
Hours: Monday through Thursday: 9:00 a.m. to 9:00 p.m., Friday &
Saturday: 9:00 a.m. to 5:00 p.m., Sunday: 1:00 p.m. to 5:00 p.m.

Sunrise, 5400 Harris Ave., Las Vegas, NV 89110; Phone: 702 453-1104;
  Fax: 702 438-2296
  E-mail: beryla@lvccld.lib.nv.us
  Hours: Monday through Thursday: 9:00 a.m. to 9:00 p.m., Friday &
  Saturday: 9:00 a.m. to 5:00 p.m., Sunday: 1:00 p.m. to 5:00 p.m.
West Charleston Heights Library, 6301 W.Charleston Blvd., Las Vegas, NV
  89102; Phone: 702 878-3682
  Fax: 702 877-0620; E-mail: mariec@lvccld.lib.nv.us
  Hours: Monday through Thursday: 9:00 a.m. to 9:00 p.m., Friday &
  Saturday: 9:00 a.m. to 5:00 p.m., Sunday: 12:00 noon to 5:00 p.m.
West Las Vegas, 951E Lake Mead Blvd., Las Vegas, NV 89106;
  Phone: 702 647-2117; Fax: 702 646-5664
  E-mail: kellyr@lvccld.lib.nv.us
  Hours: Monday through Thursday: 9:00 a.m. to 9:00 p.m., Friday &
  Saturday: 9:00 a.m. to 5:00 p.m., Sunday: 1:00 p.m. to 5:00 p.m.
Whitney Library, 5175 E. Tropicana Ave., Las Vegas, NV 89122;
  Phone: 702 454-4575; Fax: 702 454-3161
  E-mail: barbc@lvccld.lib.nv.us
  Hours: Monday through Thursday: 9:00 a.m. to 9:00 p.m., Friday &
  Saturday: 9:00 a.m. to 5:00 p.m., Sunday: 1:00 p.m. to 5:00 p.m.

Las Vegas Family History Center
509 S. Ninth Street, Las Vegas, NV 89101
Phone: 702 382-9695 Fax: 702 382-1597
Founded: 1966
Special Collections: Local Histories (Nevada); state and county histories (US &
  Canada)

Nevada State Museum and Historical Society- Cahlan Library
700 Twin Lakes, Lorenzi Park, State Mail Complex, Las Vegas, NV 89107
Phone: 702 486-5205 Fax: 702 486-5172
Founded: 1982

University of Nevada, Las Vegas
James R. Dickinson Library, 4505 Maryland Pkwy., Las Vegas, NV
  89154-0001
Phone: 702 895-3286 Fax: 702 895-1207 Internet:
http://www.nscee.edu/unlv/libraries/libhome/html
Founded: 1957

North Las Vegas

North Las Vegas Library District
2300 Civic Center Dr., Las Vegas, NV 89030
Phone: 702 649-2363 Fax: 702 649-2576
Founded: 1962
Hours: Monday: 9:00 a.m. to 6:00 p.m., Tuesday through Thursday: 9:00 a.m.
to 9:00 p.m., Friday & Saturday: 9:00 a.m. to 6:00 p.m.
Special collections: Kiel Ranch Collection; Nevada Collection

NEWSPAPERS

Las Vegas

Las Vegas Review Journal
1111 W. Bonanza Rd., Las Vegas, NV 89106
Phone: 702 383-0211 Internet: http://www.lvrj.com

Las Vegas Sun
P.O. Box 4275, Las Vegas, NV 89127
Phone: 702 385-3111 Internet: http://www.lvrjsun.com

Newspapers	City	UNLV Library has
Argus (Las Vegas)	Las Vegas	September 1926; February 1927
Basic Bombardier	Henderson	May 7, 1943 - Nov. 17, 1944 (semimonthly- full run)
Big Job- Basic Magnesium Newsletter	Henderson	June 26, 1942 - April 22, 1943 (? - full run)
Boulder City Age	Las Vegas	May 14 & 24, 1932; Aug. 1, 1933
Boulder City Daily News	Boulder City	November 18, 1946 - Jan. 30, 1948 (daily- full run)
Boulder City News (1940)	Boulder City	January 2, 1941 - Nov. 15, 1946 (daily- full run)
Boulder City News (1948)	Boulder City	February 4, 1948 - date (weekly- full run)
Bullseye	North Las Vegas	January 4, 1974 - date
Clark County Review	Las Vegas	Sept. 18, 1909 - Feb. 24, 1922 (weekly- full run)
Daily Desert Sun	Las Vegas	September 21 - December 4, 1931
Daily Fax	Las Vegas	August 23, 1965 - Feb. 4, 1966

Daily Fax and
Commercial News   Las Vegas   February 7, 1966 - April 30, 1970
Democratic News   Las Vegas   December 1971 - April 1972
Desert Scorpion   Boulder City   January 30 - March 27, 1943
Eldorado Canyon Miner Nelson   April 20, 1917
Goodsprings Gazette   Goodsprings   July 29, 1916 - May 21, 1921
    (weekly- full run)
Henderson Home News Henderson   January 4, 1951 - date
    (weekly - full run)
Lake Mead Monitor   Logandale   October 4, 1979 - June 25, 1981
Las Vegas Age   Las Vegas   August 19, 1905 - Nov. 30, 1947
    (varies - full run)
    (Index *Las Vegas Age*, 1905-1940 at Nevada Museum and Historical
    Society, Las Vegas, NV)
Las Vegas Bullet   Las Vegas   Dec. 30, 1987 - July 26, 1989
Las Vegas Evening Review   Las Vegas   January 28 - July 19, 1929
    (triweekly - full run)
Las Vegas Evening & Journal Las Vegas   July 20, 1929 - June 22, 1931
    (daily - full run)
Las Vegas Evening
Review Journal   Las Vegas   June 23, 1931 - Dec. 11, 1941
    (daily - full run)
    (Index *Las Vegas Evening Review Journal*, 1930-1958-currently being
    updated-at Nevada Museum and Historical Society, Las Vegas, NV)
Las Vegas Evening Review
Journal (1943)   Las Vegas   December 2, 1943 - June 11, 1945
Las Vegas Evening Review
Journal & Boulder City Journal Las Vegas   December 12, 1941 - Dec. 1, 1943
Las Vegas Evening Review
Journal & Boulder City Journal
(1945)   Las Vegas   June 12, 1945 - April 9, 1949
Las Vegas Free Press   Las Vegas   January 1970 - Nov. 24, 1971
    (weekly- full run)
Las Vegas Israelite   Las Vegas   June 17, 1966 - date
    (weekly- 1965 to date)
Las Vegas Israelite of Nevada Las Vegas   January 29, 1965 - June 10, 1966
Las Vegas Journal   Las Vegas   April 5, 1929
Las Vegas Morning Sun   Las Vegas   July 1, 1950 - December 31, 1951
Las Vegas Morning Tribune Las Vegas   Nov. 21, 1943 - Dec. 14, 1945
Las Vegas News   Las Vegas   January 23 - March 20, 1941
Las Vegas Review   Las Vegas   March 3, 1922 - Jan. 25, 1929
    (triweekly- full run)
Las Vegas Review Journal   Las Vegas   April 10, 1949 - date

(daily - full run)
(Index *Las Vegas Review Journal*, 1972-currently being updated- at Las Vegas Public Library)

Las Vegas Sun	Las Vegas	January 1, 1952 - date

(daily- 1950 - date)
(Index *Las Vegas Sun*, 1972-currently being updated-at Las Vegas Public Library)

Las Vegas Times	Las Vegas	April 1, 1905 November 3, 1906
		(weekly- full run)
Las Vegas Times (1932)	Las Vegas	July 18 & 25, 1932
Las Vegas Today	North Las Vegas April 6 - June 25, 1975;	
		April 19, 1983 - June 11, 1984
Las Vegas Tribune	Las Vegas	April 2 -November 14, 1943
		(weekly- full run)
Las Vegas Tribune and		
Henderson Herald	Las Vegas	July 5 & 12, 1946
		(weekly- full run)
Las Vegas Voice	Las Vegas	January 2, 1964 - August 7, 1980
		(weekly- ?)
Laughlin Gambler	Laughlin	August 1, 1984 - date
Moapa Valley Herald	Overton	January 10, 1976 - Mar. 26, 1980
Nellis Century	North Las Vegas November 15, 1963; April 17,	
		1969 - December 21, 1973
Nevada Business News	Las Vegas	June 1973 - September 1974
Nevada Citizen (Las Vegas)	Las Vegas	April 17, 1954 - Feb. 18, 1956
Nevada Legal News	Las Vegas	May 1, 1970 - date
Nevada Veteran	Las Vegas	April 17 - 30, 1946 (weekly- ?)
Nevso News	Las Vegas	October 11 - December 17, 1954
North Las Vegas Valley Times North Las Vegas Nov. 13, 1973 - June 18, 1974		
North Las Vegas Valley Times &		
Moapa- Virgin Valley Times North Las Vegas Nov. 5, 1964 - Nov. 9, 1973		
North Las Vegas Valley Times-		
News & Moapa-Virgin Valley		
Times	North Las Vegas January 2 - November 2, 1964	
Oak	Logandale	July 1920
Outlook	Las Vegas	April 19, 1952
Rebel Yell	Las Vegas	April 20, 1955 - Nov. 16, 1970
Rebel Yells	Las Vegas	May 23, 1968
Searchlight	Searchlight	June 26, 1903 - October 19, 1906
		(weekly- 1902-06)
Searchlight Bulletin	Searchlight	October 26 1906 - Dec. 27, 1912
		(weekly- 1906-13)
Sibert Scorpion	Boulder City	November 1, 1941 - Jan. 16, 1943

UNLV Yell	Las Vegas	August 28, 1980 - July 8, 1982
Valley Herald	Overton	April 2, 1980 - June 25, 1981
Valley Herald and Lake		
Mead Monitor	Overton	July 2, 1981 - July 30, 1987
Valley Times (North Las Vegas) North Las Vegas June 21, 1974 - June 2, 1984		
Vegas Visitor	Las Vegas	May 1, 1969 - date
Vegas Voice	Las Vegas	March 15, 1981 - Nov. 20, 1982
Veteran's Journal	Las Vegas	May, June and August 1971
Western Business News	Las Vegas	December 1974 - August 1975
What's Hapening	Las Vegas	September 1975 - February 1976
Yell	Las Vegas	December 11, 1970 - May 8, 1980

FAMILY HISTORY LIBRARY (Salt Lake City, Utah) HOLDINGS

All microfilmed and microfiched records (unless restricted) are available to rent worldwide at branch Family History Centers and selected larger public and private libraries and societies.

Nevada, Clark - Cemeteries

Nevada Cemetery Records. Salt Lake City : Filmed by the Genealogical
Society of Utah, 1971.
Microfilm- 0869278 item 3
Microfilm of original records in the D.A.R. Library in Washington, D.C.
Contents: Clark County cemetery records -- Lone Mountain Cemetery
records (Carson City, Nevada) -- Old mining town records.

Parkin, Nona. *Clark County Records.* Salt Lake City : Filmed by the
Genealogical Society of Utah, 1996.
Microfilm- 1598461 item 5.
Includes cemetery census: Bunkerville, Good Springs, Kaolin, Nelson,
Las Vegas (Military section at Woodlawn Cemetery), Mesquite,
Searchlite, St. Thomas; Death records/obituaries: Caliente 1918-1956, Las
Vegas 1931-1943, Mesquite 1948-1975, Searchlite 1932-1947; Pioneer
families; Church records: Caliente Catholic Church 1908-1923, Las Vegas
Episcopal Church 1905-1944.

Leavitt, Ethel. *Bunkerville Cemetery Row & Plot Layout, Clark County,
Nevada, as of 7 November, 1994*
979.3 A1 no.43

Nevada Cemetery Records. Salt Lake City : Filmed by the Genealogical
Society of Utah, 1971.
Microfilm- 0869278 item 3
Microfilm of original records in the D.A.R. Library in Washington, D.C.
Contents: Clark County cemetery records -- Lone Mountain Cemetery
records (Carson City, Nevada) -- Old mining town records.

Nevada, Clark - Genealogy - Periodicals
The Name Tracer. -- Vol. 1, no. 1 (May-June 1967) Las Vegas : Las Vegas
Genealogical Library, 1967.
979.313 B2n
Library has: Vol. nos. 1-4, Vol. 2, nos. 2,4, (problems on numbering),
Vol. 2, nos. 1-6 (problems on numbering), Vol. 3, nos. 1-4-
Also on microfiche.
Microfiche- 6049192   Vol. 1 no. 1-4 (1 fiche)
Microfiche- 6049193   Vol. 2 no. 1-6 (1 fiche)
Microfiche- 6049194   Vol. 3 no. 1-4 (1 fiche)
Microfiche- 6049195   Vol. 4 no. 1-4 (1 fiche)
Microfiche- 6049196   Vol. 5 no. 1-4 (1 fiche)
Microfiche- 6049197   Vol. 6 no. 1-4 (1 fiche)
Microfiche- 6049198   Vol. 7 no. 1-4 (1 fiche)

The Prospector : publication of the Clark County Nevada Genealogical
Society, Las Vegas, Nevada. Vol. 1, no. 1. Las Vegas, Nevada : The Society,
[1981].
979.313 D25p
Library's holdings begin with v. 6, no. 4.

Nevada, Clark - History
Hafner, Arabell Lee. *100 Years on the Muddy.* Springville, Utah : Art City
Pub. Co., 1967.
979.313 H2h, also on microfiche- 6051187

Nevada, Clark - Military records - World War, 1914-1918
Banks, Raymond H. *The Banks Compilation of Birth Data of Men with Links
to Clark County, Nevada, Who Were Born 1873-1900.* : as found in the
civilian registration cards L.D.S. microfilm series of World War I Selective
Service draft registration cards. Salt Lake City : R.H. Banks, c1996.
979.3 A1 no.48
An alphabetical listing by surname of men who completed civilian
registration cards for their draft boards during 1917-1918. About 98% of
men present in America and born 1873-1900 provided draft card
information in 1917 or 1918. Aliens were required to register. Persons

already in the military did not register. Includes name, date of birth, ethnic group, birth location or other information, and county or city draft board in the state where registered.

Nevada, Clark - Obituaries

Moapa Valley, Overton, and St. Thomas News : Clippings Taken From the Las Vegas Age, 1909-1931. Salt Lake City : Filmed by the Genealogical Society of Utah, 1985.
Microfilm- 1035780 item 4
> Contains obituaries, vital records, church history, and notices concerning activities of many persons residing in the Moapa Valley area of Clark County, Nevada.

Nevada, Clark - Obituaries - Indexes

Ostrander, Edna. *Index to Moapa Valley, Overton, and St. Thomas News : Clippings Taken From the Las Vegas Age, 1909-1931.* Salt Lake City : Filmed by the Genealogical Society of Utah, 1985.
Microfilm- 1035780 item 3

Nevada, Clark - Vital records

Bell, Connie. *Materials Collected From Bank and Safe Deposit Boxes, Unclaimed Property Division, Department of Commerce, State of Nevada : June 30, 1986.* Salt Lake City : Filmed by the Genealogical Society of Utah, 1986.
Microfilm- 1421665 item 4
> Includes a surname index. Contains birth and death certificates, marriage licenses, divorce records and other court records, military records, taxation records, business records, church records, wills and other probate records, and deeds and other land records. Most of these records are Clark County and Las Vegas, Nevada, records. The land records are chiefly those of Lyon, Storey, and Washoe counties, Nevada. In addition there are records from many other states in the United States.

Birth Notices in Clark County, Nevada, Newspapers, 1911-1968. Salt Lake City : Filmed by the Genealogical Society of Utah, 1987.
Microfilm- 1421795 item 5-8

Clark County (Nevada). County Recorder. *Marriages, 1928-1949; Index 1909-1951.* Salt Lake City : Filmed by the Genealogical Society of Utah, 1993.
> Includes index containing both bride and groom surnames.

| Microfilm- 1870106 | Index, A-Z | 4 Aug. 1910- 7 May 1940 |
| | Index, A-L | 15 May 1940-26 Dec. 1940 |

Microfilm- 1870107	Index, M-Z	15 May 1940-26 Dec. 1940
	Index, A-Z	26 Dec. 1940- 1 Apr. 1942
Microfilm- 1870108	Index, A-Z	13 Apr. 1942-17 July 1944
	Index, A-M	17 July 1944-26 Sep. 1944
Microfilm- 1870109	Index, M-Z	26 Sep. 1944-25 June 1945
	Index, A-Z	25 June 1945-13 June 1946
	Index, A-F	13 June 1946-28 Oct. 1946
Microfilm- 1870110	Index, M-Z	29 July 1946-29 Oct. 1946
	Index, A-Z	14 Nov. 1946-13 Aug. 1947
	Index, A-N	4 Sep. 1947- 2 Jan. 1948
Microfilm- 1870234	Index, O-Z	28 Aug. 1947- 2 Jan. 1948
	Index, A-Z	16 Jan. 1948-20 Apr. 1949
Microfilm- 1870235	Index, A-Z	25 Apr. 1949-11 Sep. 1950
	Index, A-K	18 Sep. 1950- 2 Feb. 1951
Microfilm- 1870236	Index, K-Z	30 Oct. 1950-19 Feb. 1951

Marriage certificates:

	Vol. 1-4 (p. 1-397)	24 Dec. 1928-29 Dec. 1934
Microfilm- 1870237	Vol. 4 (p. 397-end)	29 Dec. 1934-20 Mar. 1937
	Vol. 5-7	20 Mar. 1935-21 July 1937
	Vol. 8 (p. 1-173)	21 July 1937-19 Oct. 1937
Microfilm- 1870238	Vol. 8 (p. 173-end)	19 Oct. 1937-22 Mar. 1938
	Vol. 9-10	18 Mar. 1938-22 May 1939
	Vol. 11 (p. 1-447)	22 May 1939- 4 Oct. 1939
Microfilm- 1870239	Vol. 11 (p. 447-end)	4 Oct. 1939- 4 Oct. 1939
	Vol. 12-14	4 Oct. 1939-10 June 1940
	Vol. 15 (p. 1-208)	10 June 1940-26 June 1940
Microfilm- 1870240	Vol. 15 (p.203-end)	26 June 1940-26 July 1940
	Vol. 16-18	26 July 1940-27 Nov. 1940
Microfilm- 1870408	Vol. 19-21	27 Nov. 1940-23 Apr. 1941
	Vol. 22 (p. 1-287)	23 Apr. 1941-27 May 1941
Microfilm- 1870409	Vol. 22 (p.287-end)	27 May 1941-27 May 1941
	Vol. 23-25	27 May 1941- 4 Sep. 1941
Microfilm- 1870410	Vol. 26-28	4 Sep 1941- 4 Dec. 1941
	Vol. 29 (p. 1-309)	4 Dec. 1941-29 Dec. 1941
Microfilm- 1870411	Vol. 29 (p.309-end)	29 Dec. 1941-29 Dec. 1941
	Vol. 30-32	29 Dec. 1941-13 Apr. 1942
Microfilm- 1870412	Vol. 33	13 Apr. 1942-16 July 1942
	Vol. 36 (p. 1-293)	16 July 1942-12 Aug. 1942
Microfilm- 1870413	Vol. 36 (p. 293-end)	12 Aug. 1942-31 Aug. 1942
	Vol. 37-39	31 Aug. 1942-14 Dec. 1942
	Vol. 40 (p. 1-41)	14 Dec. 1942-21 Dec. 1942

Microfilm- 1870414	Vol. 40 (p. 41-end) 21 Dec. 1942- 2 Mar. 1943
	Vol. 41-42 2 Mar. 1943- 2 Aug. 1943
	Vol. 43 (p. 1-309) 2 Aug. 1943-21 Sep. 1943
Microfilm- 1870415	Vol. 43 (p. 309-end)21 Sep. 1943-26 Oct. 1943
	Vol. 44-46 26 Oct. 1943-11 Aug. 1944
Microfilm- 1870416	Vol. 47-49 11 Aug. 1944- 1 May 1945
	Vol. 50 (p. 1-265) 1 May 1945-25 June 1945
Microfilm- 1870417	Vol. 50 (p. 264-end)26 June 1945-24 July 1945
	Vol. 51-53 24 July 1945-31 Dec. 1945
Microfilm- 1870590	Vol. 54-56 31 Dec. 1945-22 Apr. 1946
	Vol. 57 (p. 1-281) 22 Apr. 1946-10 May 1946
Microfilm- 1870591	Vol. 57 (p. 281-end)10 May 1946- 6 June 1946
	Vol. 58-59 29 May 1946-29 July 1946
	Vol. 60 (p. 1-135) 29 July 1946- 5 Sep. 1946
Microfilm- 1870592	Vol. 61-62 5 Sep. 1946-14 Nov. 1946
	Vol. 63 (p. 1-435) 14 Nov. 1946- 9 Dec. 1946
Microfilm- 1870593	Vol. 63 (p. 435-end) 9 Dec. 1946-18 Dec. 1946
	Vol. 64-66 18 Dec. 1946-28 Mar. 1947
	Vol. 67 (p. 1-217) 28 Mar. 1947-17 Apr. 1947
Microfilm- 1870594	Vol. 67 (p. 217-end)17 Apr. 1947- 8 May 1947
	Vol. 68-70 8 May 1947-21 Aug. 1947
Microfilm- 1870595	Vol. 71 21 Aug. 1947-19 Sep. 1947
Microfilm- 1851618	Vol. 72 24 Sep. 1947- 9 Oct. 1947
	Vol. 73 (p. 1-331) 9 Oct. 1947-22 Oct. 1947
Microfilm- 1851703	Vol. 73 (p. 331-end) 9 Oct. 1947-22 Oct. 1947
	Vol. 74-75 6 Nov. 1947-18 Dec. 1947
Microfilm- 1851704	Vol. 76-77 18 Dec. 1947-11 Mar. 1948
	Vol. 78 (p. 1-260) 11 Mar. 1948-28 Mar. 1948
Microfilm- 1851705	Vol. 78 (p. 260-end)28 Mar. 1948-26 Apr. 1948
	Vol. 79 26 Apr. 1948- 6 June 1948
	Vol. 80 (p. 1-468) 8 June 1948- 8 July 1948
Microfilm- 1851706	Vol. 80 (p. 468-end)8 July 1948-19 July 1948
	Vol. 81-82 19 July 1948-20 Oct. 1948
	Vol. 83 (p. 1-156) 20 Oct. 1948-23 Oct. 1948
Microfilm- 1851707	Vol. 83 (p. 156-end)23 Oct. 1948- 8 Dec. 1948
	Vol. 84 8 Dec. 1948- 2 Feb. 1949
	Vol. 85 (p. 1-406) 2 Feb. 1949-31 Mar. 1949
Microfilm- 1851789	Vol. 85 (p. 406-end) 31 Mar. 1949-16 May 1949
	Vol. 86-87 16 May 1949- 5 Dec. 1949
Microfilm- 1851790	Vol. 88-89 5 Dec. 1949-30 June 1950
	Vol. 90 (p. 1-296) 30 June 1950- 7 Aug. 1950

Clark County 91

Microfilm- 1851791	Vol. 90 (p. 296-end) 7 Aug. 1950-20 Sep. 1950
	Vol. 91-92 29 Sep. 1950- 2 Apr. 1951
Microfilm- 1877701	Vol. 93-94 2 Apr. 1951- 9 Jul. 1951
Microfilm- 1877702	Vol. 95-96 16 Oct. 1951-23 Apr. 1952
	Vol. 97 (p. 1-201) 23 Apr. 1952-26 May 1952
Microfilm- 1877703	Vol. 97 (p. 201-end)26 May 1952-21 July 1952
	Vol. 98 21 July 1952-20 Oct. 1952
	Vol. 99 (p.1-369) 21 Oct. 1952- 6 Dec. 1952
Microfilm- 1877704	Vol. 99 (p. 369-end)6 Dec. 1952- 7 Jan. 1953
	Vol. 100-101 7 Jan. 1952-10 June 1953
	Vol. 102 (p. 1-134) 10 June 1953-19 June 1953
Microfilm- 1877705	Vol. 102 (p. 134-end)19 June 1953-24 Aug. 1953
	Vol. 103-104 24 Aug. 1953-31 Dec. 1953
Microfilm- 1877706	Vol. 105 25 Dec. 1953-16 Feb. 1954

Nevada, Clark, Boulder City - Cemeteries
Greene, Diane E. *Boulder City Cemetery, Boulder City, Nevada*. Boulder City,
Nevada. : Silver State Chapter, DAR, 1993.
979.313/B1 V3g, also on microfilm- 1750737 item 18

Greene, Diane E. *Southern Nevada Veterans Memorial Cemetery, Boulder
City, Nevada : April 1990- February 1995*. Boulder City, Nevada. : D. E.
Greene, 1995.
979.313/B1 V3gs, also on microfilm- 2055149 item 3

Nevada, Clark, Boulder City - Church records
Church of Jesus Christ of Latter-day Saints. Boulder City Ward (Nevada).
*Record of Members, 1932-1941; Annual Genealogical Report, Form E,
1932- 1948*. Salt Lake City : Filmed by the Genealogical Society of Utah,
1951.
Microfilm of originals in the LDS Church Archives, Salt Lake City.
Microfilm- 0014894 item 1   Record of members 1932-1941
Microfilm- 0014894 item 2   Form E   1932-1948
   Photocopies not permitted except for direct line descendants. Remove all
other data from photocopy.

Nevada, Clark, Bunkerville - Cemeteries
Cemetery records, Bunkerville and Overton, Nevada. *Card file of Cemetery
Information.*Salt Lake City : Filmed by the Genealogical Society of Utah,
1989.
Microfilm- 1597556 item 12

Nevada, Clark, Bunkerville - Notarial records
Abbott, Jas. S. *Notary Record Book, 12 November 1934 to 5 September 1944, of Jas. S. Abbott, Notary and Postmaster of Bunkerville, Clark County, Nevada.* Salt Lake City : Filmed by the Genealogical Society of Utah, 1987.
Microfilm- 1421753- item 4

Nevada, Clark, Henderson - Church records
Church of Jesus Christ of Latter-day Saints. Henderson Ward (Nevada). *Annual Genealogical Report, Form E, 1943-1948.* Salt Lake City : Filmed by the Genealogical Society of Utah, 1951.
Microfilm of original records in the LDS Church Archives, Salt Lake City. Henderson Ward, created in 1946, was formerly known as the Basic Branch and the B.M.I. Branch.
Microfilm- 0014902   Form E   1943-1948

Nevada, Clark, Henderson - Directories
R. L. Polk and Company. *Polk's Henderson and Boulder City (Clark County, Nevada) City Directory : including Pittman.* Kansas City, Mo. : R. L. Polk & Co., [190-?] decade uncertain.
979.313 E4p

Nevada, Clark, Las Vegas - Biography - Indexes
Barentsen, Ada Ruth. *Index to We Were 49rs.* Salt Lake City : Filmed by the Genealogical Society of Utah, 1993.
Microfilm- 1598077 item 5

Murdock, Lorna D. *Index to Ghosts of Humboldt Region by Dave Basso.* Salt Lake City : Filmed by the Genealogical Society of Utah, 1993.
Microfilm- 1598077 item 4

Murdock, Lorna D. *Index to Who Are the Women of Las Vegas, 1984.* Salt Lake City : Filmed by the Genealogical Society of Utah, 1993.
Microfilm- 1598077 item 1

Nevada, Clark, Las Vegas - Cemeteries
Woodlawn Cemetery Records, Las Vegas, Clark County, Nevada : A to Cleandeohe (?). Salt Lake City : Filmed by the Genealogical Society of Utah, 1985.
Microfilm- 1035781 item 1

Nevada, Clark, Las Vegas - Church records

Church of Jesus Christ of Latter-day Saints. Las Vegas 1st Ward (Nevada).
*Record of Members, 1922-1942;Annual Genealogical Report, Form E,
1922- 1948.* Salt Lake City : Filmed by the Genealogical Society of Utah,
1951.
Microfilm- 0014907 item 1   Record of members 1922-1942
Microfilm- 0014907 item 2   Form E   1922-1948

Church of Jesus Christ of Latter-day Saints. Las Vegas 2nd Ward (Nevada).
Annual Genealogical Report, Form E, 1940-1948. Salt Lake City : Filmed
by the Genealogical Society of Utah, 1951.
Microfilm of original records in the LDS Church Archives, Salt Lake City.
Las Vegas 2nd Ward, created in 1944, was formerly known as the Las
Vegas North Ward.
Microfilm- 0014908   Form E   1940-1948

Nevada, Clark, Las Vegas - Church records - Indexes

Murdock, Lorna D. *Index to First United Methodist Church of Las Vegas,
Nevada.* Salt Lake City : Filmed by the Genealogical Society of Utah, 1993.
Microfilm- 1598077 item 3

Nevada, Clark, Las Vegas - Directories

Las Vegas, Nevada Telephone Directory, 1931. Las Vegas, Nev. : Southern
Nevada Telephone, [1931?].
979.3 A1 no.32, also on microfilm- 1320994 item 9

*Telephone Directory, Las Vegas, Boulder City, Overton and and Moapa
Valley, 1937-1938.* Salt Lake City : Filmed by the Genealogical Society of
Utah, 1990.
Microfilm- 1320969 item 8

*Las Vegas, Nevada City and Telephone Directory, 1934 : an Alphabetical List
of Residents, Professional Men and Business Firms, City Officials,
Churches, Lodges and Miscellaneous Organizations, a Classified Business
Directory, Street Guide and Numerical Phone Guide.* Compiled and
published by Western Directory Co. Salt Lake City : Filmed by the
Genealogical Society of Utah, 1990.
Microfilm- 1320969 item 11

Nevada, Clark, Las Vegas - History

Roske, Ralph J. *Las Vegas : a Desert Paradise.* Tulsa, Okla. : Continental
Heritage Press, c1986.
Q AREA 979.3135 H2r

Paher, Stanley W. *Las Vegas : as it Began, as it Grew.* Las Vegas : Nevada
Publications, c1971.
979.3135 H2p

Nevada, Clark, Las Vegas - History - Indexes
Murdock, Lorna D. *Index to Nevada Ghost Towns and Mining Camps.* Salt
Lake City : Filmed by the Genealogical Society of Utah, 1993.
Microfilm- 1598077 item 2

Nevada, Clark, Las Vegas - Obituaries
Chico Enterprise Obituaries, 1993-1994. Salt Lake City : Filmed by the
Genealogical Society of Utah, 1995.
Microfilm- 1698208 item 16
> Also includes obituaries from the Red Bluff Daily News; the Las Vegas
> Review-Journal; the Phoenix Gazette.

Kelly, Jacqueline Strobel. *Micellaneous [sic] Obituaries.* Salt Lake City :
Filmed by the Genealogical Society of Utah, 1988.
Microfilm- 1421878 item 2
> Includes, The Herald (Fillmore, California), 1985; The Big Bear Life, &
> The Grizzley (Big Bear Valley, California), 1980; Las Vegas, Nevada,
> 1979; Santa Barbara News-Press (California), 1974, 1979; Santa Ynez
> Valley News (Santa Ynez, California), 1979; Los Angeles Times
> (California), 1979; The Poughkeepsie Journal (Poughkeepsie, New York),
> 1981.

Las Vegas Family History Center (Las Vegas, Nevada). *Index to Las Vegas
Age [newspaper] deaths, 1909-1930.* Salt Lake City : Filmed by the
Genealogical Society of Utah, 1988.
Microfilm- 1421865 item 10

*Moapa Valley, Overton, and St. Thomas news : Clippings Taken from the Las
Vegas Age, 1909-1931.* Salt Lake City : Filmed by the Genealogical Society
of Utah, 1985.
Microfilm- 1035780 item 4
> Contains obituaries, vital records, church history, and notices concerning
> activities of many persons residing in the Moapa Valley area of Clark
> County, Nevada.

Nevada, Clark, Las Vegas - Societies
Children of the American Revolution. John Ashley Society, Las Vegas, Nevada, 1960-1961.
979.3 A1 no.37
Includes Society officers, membership directory, and programs for 1960-1961.

Nevada, Clark, Las Vegas - Vital records
Bell, Connie R. *Index to Las Vegas Age [newspaper] Births, 1909-1931.* Salt Lake City : Filmed by the Genealogical Society of Utah, 1988.
Microfilm- 1421865 item 9
Collection of newspaper birth announcements published in the Las Vegas Age between 1909-1931.

Nevada, Clark, Logandale - Church records
Church of Jesus Christ of Latter-day Saints. Logandale Ward (Nevada).
Annual Genealogical Report, Form E, 1922-1948. Salt Lake City : Filmed by the Genealogical Society of Utah, 1951.
Microfilm of original records in the LDS Church Archives, Salt Lake City.
Microfilm- 0014905 Form E 1922-1948

Nevada, Clark, Mesquite - Church records
Church of Jesus Christ of Latter-day Saints. Mesquite Ward (Nevada). *Record of Members, 1901-1941; Annual Genealogical Report, Form E, 1907- 1948.* Salt Lake City : Filmed by the Genealogical Society of Utah, 1951.
Microfilm of original records in the LDS Church Archives, Salt Lake City.
Mesquite Ward, created in 1880, was disbanded between 1882 and 1901.
The Form E includes reports from the St. George and Moapa Stakes.
Microfilm- 0014912 item 1-2   Record of members 1901-1941
Microfilm- 0014912 item 3   Form E 1907-1948

Nevada, Clark, Overton - Cemeteries
West, Carl R. *Overton Cemetary.*
Map- Scale [1:168]. 1 in. to 14 feet.
979.313/O1 V3o

Nevada, Clark, Overton - Church records
Church of Jesus Christ of Latter-day Saints. Overton Ward (Nevada). *Record of Members, 1884-1941; Annual Genealogical Report, Form E, 1907- 1948.* Salt Lake City : Filmed by the Genealogical Society of Utah, 1951.
Microfilm of original records in the LDS Church Archives, Salt Lake City. Some pages lacking. The Form E includes reports from the St. George and Moapa Stakes.

Microfilm- 0014913 item 1   Record of members 1884-1941
Microfilm- 0014913 item 2   Form E 1907-1948

Nevada, Clark, Searchlight - Cemeteries
Perry, Leland M. *Bulloch Family Cemetery.* Salt Lake City : Filmed by the Genealogical Society of Utah, 1983.
Microfiche- 6018280

Nevada, Clark, St. Thomas - Church records
Church of Jesus Christ of Latter-day Saints. St. Thomas Ward (Nevada). *Record of Members, 1865-1933; Annual Genealogical Report, Form E, 1909-1932.* Salt Lake City : Filmed by the Genealogical Society of Utah, 1951.
Microfilm of original records in the LDS Church Archives, Salt Lake City. Indexed in the Early Church Information File at the main library only. St. Thomas Ward, created in 1908, was formerly known as St. Thomas Branch and was a local unit of the Muddy Mission and the St. George and Moapa Stakes. The Form E includes reports from the St. George and Moapa Stakes.

Microfilm- 0014924 item 1-3   Record of members 1865-1870, 1908-1933
Microfilm- 0014924 item 4   Form E 1909-1932

SOCIETIES

Clark County Nevada Genealogical Society
P. O. Box 1929, Las Vegas, NV 89125-1929
Phone: 702 458-5540   Voice Mail: 702 225-5838   Fax: 702 258-4099   E-
Founded: 1967
Publication: Quarterly, *The Prospector*
Mail: ccngs@juno.com
Web site: www.lvrj.com/communitylink/ccngs/

CHAPTER FOUR

Douglas County

Douglas is one of the nine counties created by the Territorial Legislature on 25 November 1861, when Nevada was first subdivided into minor divisions. In 1859 it was part of Millard County, Utah, and later Carson County, Nevada.

Douglas County was named in honor of Stephen A. Douglas, of Illinois.

CEMETERY

Eastside Memorial Park
1600 Buckeye Rd., Minden, NV 89423
Phone: 775 782-2215   Fax: 775 782-2216
Years of operation: 1986?-present
Affiliations: Private cemetery
Records: Housed on-site; searches by appointment

CHURCHES
GARDNERVILLE
Adventist: Jehovah's Witness, Sorensen Lane, Gardnerville, NV 89410
   Phone: 775 265-5481
Assemblies of God: Calvary Assembly of God, PO Box 2459, Gardnerville, NV 89410
Christian Churches of Christ: Mountain View Church of Christ, PO Box 904, Gardnerville, NV 89410 Phone: 775 782-5231
Holiness: Carson Valley Church of the Nazarene, PO Box 160, Gardnerville, NV 89410 Phone: 775 782-4495
Latter-day Saints: Church of Jesus Christ of Latter-day Saints, Gardnerville, NV 89410 Phone: 775 782-4234
Lutheran Church: Trinity Lutheran Church, 1480 Douglas Ave., Gardnerville, NV 89410 Phone: 775 782-8153
Methodist: Carson Valley United Methodist, PO Box 278, Gardnerville, NV 89410 Phone: 775 782-2011
Coleville United Methodist Church, PO Box 278, Gardnerville, NV 89410
Smith Valley United Methodist, PO Box 278, Gardnerville, NV 89410

Coleville United Methodist Church, PO Box 278, Gardnerville, NV 89410

Smith Valley United Methodist, PO Box 278, Gardnerville, NV 89410

Pentecostal: Pentecostal Church of God, Mitch and S. River Rd., Gardnerville, NV 89410

Protestant: Genoa Community Church, PO Box 904, Gardnerville, NV 89410

Roman Catholic: St. Gall Catholic Church, 1343 Centerville Lane, Gardnerville, NV 89410 Phone: 775 782-2852

Southern Baptist: Gardnerville First Baptist Church, PO Box 576, Gardnerville, NV 89410 Phone: 775 782-5513

GLENBROOK

Episcopal: St. John's Episcopalian Church, US Hwy 50, Glenbrook, NV 89413 Phone: 775 882-8460

Latter-day Saints: Latter-day Saints Church South Lake Tahoe, PO Box 137, Glenbrook, NV 89413 Phone: 541-9677

MINDEN

Baptist: First Baptist Church, Hwy 88 and 395, Minden, NV 89423 Phone: 775 782-5513

Episcopal: Coventry Cross Episcopalian Church, PO Box 518, Minden, NV 89423 Phone: 775 782-4161

Latter-day Saints: Church of Jesus Christ Christ Latter-day Saints, PO Box 221, Minden, NV 89423

ZEPHYR COVE

Metaphysical: Lake Tahoe Religious Science Church, PO Box 1519, Zephyr Cove, NV 89448 Phone: 775 541-1624

COURTHOUSE

Douglas County Courthouse
P.O. Box 218, Minden, NV 89423-0218
Phone: 775 782-9026 or 775 782-9027, Recorder's Office
Land records: from 1855 to present, Recorder's Office
  Copies: $1.00 per page, $3.00 for certification per document
Probate records: County Clerk
Vital records: from 1855 to present, Recorder's Office
  Copies: $1.00 per page, $3.00 for certification

LIBRARIES

Minden

Douglas County Public Library
1625 Library Lane, P.O. Box 337, Minden, NV 89423
Phone: 775 782-9841   Fax: 775 782-6766   E-mail: jklouch@clan.lib.nv.us

Founded: 1967
Hours: Monday: 11:00 a.m. to 8:00 p.m., Tuesday through Thursday: 9:00 a.m.
 to 8:00 p.m. Friday & Saturday: 9:00 a.m. to 6:00 p.m.
Special collections: Carson Valley History (Van Sickle Collection)
Newspaper Index: *Carson Valley News*, 1875-1900
Branch
Lake Tahoe Branch Library, P.O. Box 10979, Zephyr Cove, NV 89448;
Phone: 775 588-6411
 Fax: 775 588-6464; E-mail: pstimmen@clan.lib.nv.us
 Hours: Tuesday through Saturday: 11:00 a.m. to 6:00 p.m.

NEWSPAPERS

Newspapers	City	UNLV Library has
Air Age News	Gardnerville	January 1, 1966 - Feb. 27, 1967 (monthly- 1966-68)
Bugle	Genoa	June 1888
Carson Valley News	Genoa	Feb. 29, 1875 - July 16, 1880 (weekly - full run)
(Index *Carson Valley News*, 1875-1900 at Douglas County Library, Minden, NV)		
Courier	Gardnerville	June 9, 1899 - April 1, 1904 (weekly - full run)
Courier	Genoa	May 5 - June 1899
Douglas County Banner	Genoa	October 7 - December 23, 1865 (weekly - full run)
Gardnerville Record	Gardnerville	July 12, 1898 - July 4, 1902 (weekly - 1898-1904)
Genoa Courier	Genoa	August 1, 1884 - April 17, 1885 (weekly - 1880-89)
Genoa Courier (1898)	Genoa	March 18, 1898 - April 28, 1899
Genoa Journal	Genoa	April 10, 1880 (weekly - 1880-1881)
Genoa Weekly Courier	Genoa	Jan. 7, 1881 - July 25, 1994 (weekly - 1880-1889)
Genoa Weekly Courier	Genoa	April 24, 1885 - March 11, 1898
Minden Times	Minden	June 19, 1936 - Dec. 25, 1942
Nevadan Lutheran	Gardnerville	June 10, 1918
Nevada Prohibitionist	Genoa	April 1, 1889
Record	Gardnerville	July 11, 1902 - March 4, 1904
Record - Courier	Gardnerville	April 8, 1904 - date (weekly - full run)

Territorial Enterprise	Genoa	January 1, 1859 - August 4, 1860;
(Genoa)	July 20, 1861	(weekly - 1858-1860)

SOCIETIES

Carson Valley Historical Society
P. O. Box 957, Minden, NV 89412
Phone: 775 782-2738
Collections: Books, manuscripts, maps, photographs

FAMILY HISTORY LIBRARY (Salt Lake City, Utah) HOLDINGS

All microfilmed and microfiched records (unless restricted) are available to rent worldwide at branch Family History Centers and selected larger public and private libraries and societies.

Nevada, Douglas - Archives and libraries - Inventories, registers, catalogs
Inventory of the County Archives of Nevada, no. 03, Douglas County (Minden).
Prepared by the Historical Records Survey, Division of Women's and
Professional Projects, Works Progress Administration. Reno, Nev.
Historical Records Survey, 1937.
979.359 A3i, also on microfiche- 6100362

Nevada, Douglas - Cemeteries
Inscriptions from Cemeteries in Douglas County, Nevada.
979.359 V3i
A project of the Young Women of the Carson Valley First Ward. Includes indexes. Contains inscriptions from Mottsville Cemetery and from another larger cemetery that may be either the Genoa Cemetery or the Gardnerville Cemetery.

Parkin, Nona. *Douglas County Records.* Salt Lake City : Filmed by the Genealogical Society of Utah, 1997.
Microfilm- 1598455 item 1
Microfilm of typescript and ms. (1 v., various pagings) in the Nona Parkin collection: Nevada Historical Research, at Reno, Nevada Stake Family History Center, Reno, Nevada. Emigration and immigration records (called pioneer families) which were prepared from Early day family questionnaires, include name, birth place and date, arrival place and date, place of residence in Nevada, method of travel, route traveled, and brief biography. Other information taken from newspapers and county records. Contents: Birth records/notices; Cemetery census: Gardnerville, Genoa, Jacks Valley, Mottsville; Death records/obituaries: Douglas County

records 1878-1893, Newspaper notices 1865-1918, Newspaper obituaries [for] Gardnerville and surrounding area 1922-1983, Genoa 1929-1982, Jacks Valley and Mottsville 1929-1975; Marriage records/notices: Douglas County records 1873-1919, Newspaper notices 1868-1916.

Nevada, Douglas - Census - 1862

Nevada Territorial Census, 1862, Douglas County. Markleeville, Calif. : Alpine County Museum, 1993.
979.3 A1 no.40

Nevada, Douglas - Military records - World War, 1914-1918

Banks, Raymond H. *The Banks Compilation of Birth Data of Men with Links to Douglas County, Nevada, who were Born 1873-1900 : as Found in the Civilian Registration Cards.* L.D.S. microfilm series of World War I Selective Service draft registration cards.
979.3 A1 no.49

An alphabetical listing by surname of men who completed civilian registration cards for their draft boards during 1917-1918. About 98% of men present in America and born 1873-1900 provided draft card information in 1917 or 1918. Aliens were required to register. Persons already in the military did not register. Includes name, date of birth, ethnic group, birth location or other information, and county or city draft board in the state where registered.

Nevada, Douglas - Vital records

Douglas County (Nevada). County Clerk. *Affidavit of Application for Marriage Licenses, 1919-1949.* Salt Lake City : Filmed by the Genealogical Society of Utah, 1993.

Microfilm- 1902086	Vol. 1-3 (no. 1-2103)	25 Aug 1919-20 Sep 1937
Microfilm- 1902087	Vol. 3-6 (2103-4321)	20 Sep 1937- 7 Jun 1941
Microfilm- 1902088	Vol. 6-9 (4321-6546)	7 June 1941-16 Feb 1943
Microfilm- 1902089	Vol. 9-12 (6546-8812)	16 Feb 1943-12 Nov 1946
Microfilm- 1902090	Vol. 12-15 (8813-11019)	13 Nov 1946-26 Jun 1948
Microfilm- 1902091	Vol. 15-17 (11020-13055)	28 Jun 1948-31 Dec 1949
Microfilm- 1902092	Vol. 18-19 (13057-14605)	1 Jan 1950-30 Jun 1951

Douglas County (Nevada). Recorder. *Birth Records, 1887-1982; Index 1887-1919.* Salt Lake City : Filmed by the Genealogical Society of Utah, 1993.
Includes index, and indexes at beginning of volumes.

Microfilm- 1901973 item 1-2 Index to births   28 Jul 1887- 2 Jan 1911
    Recorded certificates   28 Jul 1887- 2 Jan 1919
Microfilm- 1901974 item 1
    Recorded certificates   5 Feb 1919- 5 Feb 1923
Microfilm- 1901973 item 3
    Duplicate cert., v. 1   17 Aug 1911- 2 Apr 1923
Microfilm- 1901974 item 2
    Duplicate cert., v. 2   4 Apr 1923- 3 Jun 1982

Douglas County (Nevada). Recorder. *Burial and Death Records, 1887-1978; Index 1887-1923.* Salt Lake City Filmed by the Genealogical Society of Utah, 1993.
Includes index, and indexes at beginning of volumes.
Microfilm- 1901974 item 3-6
    Index of burials   1887-1923
    Burial certs., v. A   7 Jul 1887-12 Apr 1923
    Burial permits   14 Jul 1911-14 Dec 1933
    Dup. certs. of death and burial permits 25 Jan 1934- 3 Oct 1978

Douglas County (Nevada). Recorder. *Marriage Records, 1862-1951.* Salt Lake City : Filmed by the Genealogical Society of Utah, 1993.
Includes indexes at beginning of volumes.
Microfilm- 1901975
    Marriages, v. 1-A   11 Feb 1862-10 Dec 1872
    Marriages, v. A-E   24 Apr 1887-24 Jun 1940
    Marriages, v. F (1-239)   25 Jun 1940-15 Jun 1941
Microfilm- 1901976 Marr. v. F (p.239-end) 14 Jun 1941-17 Jul 1941
    Marriages, v. G-I   17 Jul 1941-17 May 1947
    Marr. v. J (p.1-285)   17 May 1947-26 Dec 1947
Microfilm- 1901977 Marr. v. J (p.286-end)26 Dec 1947-14 Jun 1948
    Marriages, v. K-L   14 Jun 1948- 8 Feb 1951

Jensen, Edith Gunn. *Nevada Records.*
979.3 V2j, also on microfilm- 0962818 item 6
Vol. 5. Douglas County, Nevada. Includes index.

Nevada, Douglas, Genoa - Cemeteries
Genoa, Douglas Co., Nevada, Cemetery Census Taken 1964. Salt Lake City :
   Filmed by the Genealogical Society of Utah, 1987.
   Microfilm- 1421794 item 9

Nevada, Douglas, Genoa - Cemeteries - Indexes
Hall, Norma. *Index to Genoa, Douglas Co., Nevada, Cemetery Census Taken*
   1964. Salt Lake City : Filmed by the Genealogical Society of Utah, 1987.
   Microfilm- 1421794 item 10
   Much of the early part of the cemetery is gone.

Nevada, Douglas, Glenbrook - Cemeteries
Landre, Lowell Henry. *Farewells Along the Great Bonanza Road : Graves and*
   Burials on the South Shore of Lake Tahoe. South Lake Tahoe, CA : L.H.
   Landre, 1994.
   979.441/S1 V3
   The Happy Homestead Cemetery inscriptions are arranged in two sections:
   alphabetical order by surname; chronological order by date of burial.
   Includes inscriptions from Old Al Tahoe Cemetery, Glenbrook Cemetery
   (Nevada), and Happy Homestead Cemetery.

Nevada, Douglas, Minden - Emigration and immigration
Let's Go to America : the Path of Emigrants from Eastern Westphalia to the
   USA. Lohne, Germany : Hermann Brackmann Kg, [1986?].   973 W2 g
   This book documents the emigration of nearly 2000 people during the
   nineteenth century from the areas of Lohne and Bad Oeynhausen to
   Washington, Clinton, Monroe, and Douglas counties in Illinois. Includes
   index.

CHAPTER FIVE

Elko County

Elko County was formed by legislative acts from 1869 to 1875 and at the latter date was given its present boundaries. It was created out of Lander County, later another portion was taken from Lander County and given to Elko County. The last act of the Legislature gave a portion of the southwestern corner of the County to Eureka County.

CEMETERY

Burns Memorial Gardens
Burns Rd. & Fairgrounds Rd., Elko, NV 89801
Phone: 775 738-5111

CHURCHES

CARLIN
Assemblies of God: Calvary Temple Assembly of God, PO Box 647, Carlin, NV 89822
Latter-day Saints: Church of Jesus Christ Latter-day Saints, Hwy. 20, Carlin, NV 89822 Phone: 775 754-6210
Methodist: Carlin United Methodist Church, PO Box 246, Carlin, NV 89822 Phone: 775 754-6439
Roman Catholic: Sacred Heart Catholic Church, PO Box 235, Carlin, NV 89822 Phone: 775 754-6425
Southern Baptist: Carlin First Baptist Church, PO Box 642, Carlin, NV 89822 Phone: 775 754-6753
Crescent Valley Baptist Church, PO Box 55, Carlin, NV 89822 Phone: 775 468-0217
ELKO
Adventist: Jehovah's Witnesses Hall, 585 Sage St., Elko, NV 89801 Phone: 775 738-5241
Assemblies of God: First Assembly of God, 424 S. 7th St., Elko, NV 89801 Phone: 775 738-5605
Baptist: Community Baptist Church, Elko, NV 89801
Christian Church of Christ: Church of Christ, 1225 6th, PO Box 296, Elko, NV 89803

Holiness: Church of the Nazarene, 740 W. Sage St., Elko, NV 89801
Phone: 775 738-3263

Independent: Ruby Mountain Bible Church, 475 Diamondback Dr., Elko, NV
89801 Phone: 775 753-6700

Latter-day Saints: Church of Jesus Christ Latter-day Saints, Elko, NV 89801
Phone: 775 753-6288

Lutheran Church: St. Mark Lutheran Church, 277 Willow St., Elko, NV
89801 Phone: 775 738-5436

Pentecostal: Elko Indian Chapel, 1695 Indian V. W. Heights, PO Box 1659,
Elko, NV 89803 Phone: 775 738-6044

Presbyterian Church: First Presbyterian Church, 1559 Sewell Dr.,
PO Box 609, Elko, NV 89803 Phone: 775 738-3430

Seventh Day Adventist: Elko Seventh Day Adventist Church, 373 W. Fir St.,
Elko, NV 89801 Phone: 775 738-7860

Southern Baptist: Calvary Baptist Church, 521 Walnut St., Elko, NV 89801
Phone: 775 738-6840

JIGGS

Latter-day Saints: Elko Nevada Stake Ranch, S. Fork, Jiggs, NV 89801
Phone: 775 744-4292

LAMOILLE

Presbyterian: Lamoille Presbyterian, Lamoille, NV 89828
Phone: 775 753-6714

OWYHEE

Assemblies of God: Assembly of God Indian Church, PO Box 8, Owyhee, NV
89832 Phone: 775 757-2622

Presbyterian: Owyhee Presbyterian Church, PO Box 68, Owyhee, NV 89832
Phone: 775 757-3295

WELLS

Assemblies of God: Christian Fellowship, PO Box 17, Wells, NV 89835
Phone: 775 752-3628

Baptist: First Baptist Church, PO Box 344, Wells, NV 89835
Phone: 775 752-3815

Christian Churches of Christ: Church of Christ, 1st and Lake St., Wells, NV
89835 Phone: 775 752-3763

Episcopal: St. Barnabas Episcopalian Church, PO Box 93, Wells, NV 89835
St. Barnabas Episcopalian Church, PO Box 266, Wells, NV 89835

Latter-day Saints: Church of Jesus Christ Latter-day Saints, 1st Lake, Wells,
NV 89835 Phone: 775 752-3763

Presbyterian: Wells Presbyterian Church, PO Box 251, Wells, NV 89835

Roman Catholic: St. Thomas Aquinas Catholic Church, PO Box 371, Wells,
NV 89835 Phone: 775 752-3400

COURTHOUSE

Elko County Courthouse
571 Idaho Street, Elko, NV 89801-3770
Phone: 775 738-6526, County Recorder; 775 738-3044, County Clerk
Land records: 1869 to present, Recorder's Office, Room 103
Naturalization records: old up to ca 1985, Clerk's Office, Third Floor
Probate records: late 1800's to present, Clerk's Office
    Probate search service: $1.00 per year per name
    Copy cost: $1.00 per page; certification $3.00 per document, no minimum
Vital records: Recorder's Office
    Marriage: 1869 to present
    Birth and death: 1887 to 1915 (approx.)
    Vital records search service: no charge if approximate dates are furnished

FUNERAL HOMES

Burns Funeral Home, Inc
Burns & Fairground, Elko, NV 89801
Phone: 775 738-5111

LIBRARIES

Elko County Library
720 Court St., Elko, NV 89801-3397
Phone: 775 738-3066   Fax: 775 738-8262   E-mail: klmaster@clan.lib.nv.us
Founded: 1926
Hours: Monday through Thursday: 9:00 a.m. to 8:00 p.m., Friday & Saturday:
    9:00 a.m. to 5:00 p.m.
Austin Library, Austin, NV 89310; Phone: 775 964-2428
    Hours: Monday: 1:00 p.m. to 5:00 p.m., Wednesday: 1:00 p.m. to 6:00 p.m.,
    Friday: 2:00 p.m. to 5:00 p.m.
Battle Mountain Library, Battle Mountain, NV 89820; Phone: 775 635-2534
    Hours: Monday: 11:00 a.m. to 5:00 p.m., Tuesday: 12:00 noon to 6:00 p.m.,
    Wednesday: 2:00 p.m. to 6:00 p.m., Thursday: 4:00 p.m. to 8:00 p.m.,
    Friday: 12:00 noon to 4:00 p.m., Saturday: 10:00 a.m. to 2:00 p.m.
Beowawe Library, Beowawe, NV 89821; Phone: 775 468-2103
    E-mail: jblandru@clan.lib.nv.us
    Hours: Monday: 10:00 a.m. to 2:30 p.m., Thursday: 1:00 p.m. to 5:30 p.m.

Carlin Library, Carlin, NV 89822; Phone: 775 754-6766
E-mail: hmfetter@clan.lib.nv.us
Hours: Tuesday & Thursday: 11:00 a.m. to 5:00 p.m., Wednesday: 4:00 p.m.
to 8:00 p.m., Friday: 1:00 p.m. to 5:00 p.m., Saturday: 10:00 a.m. to 2:00
p.m.
Cresent Valley Branch Library, HC 66 Unit 1 box 3. Beowawe, NV 89821;
Phone: 775 468-0249
E-mail: jblandru@clan.lib.nv.us
Hours: Tuesday & Wednesday: 10:00 a.m. to 2:30 p.m.
Eureka Library, P.O. Box 293, Eureka, NV 89316; Phone: 775 237-5307
Hours: Monday & Wednesday: 12:00 noon to 5:00 p.m., Tuesday &
Thursday: 1:00 p.m. to 5:00 p.m., Friday: 12:00 noon to 4:00 p.m.
Tuscarora Library, Tuscarora, NV 89834; Phone: 775 756-6597
Hours: Monday through Friday: 8:00 a.m. to 2:00 p.m.
Wells Library, P.O. Box 691, Wells, NV 89835; Phone: 775 752-3856;
E-mail: elarsen@clan.lib.nv.us
Hours: Monday, Tuesday, Wednesday, Friday: 11:00 to 5:00 p.m., Thursday:
1:00 p.m. to 5:00 p.m. & 7:00 p.m. to 9:00 p.m.
West Wendover Library, P.O. Box 2350, West Wendover, NV 89883;
Phone: 775 664-2510
E-mail: crloncar@clan.lib.nv.us
Hours: Monday & Wednesday: 12:00 noon to 6:00 p.m., Tuesday: 1:00 p.m.
to 5:00 p.m. & 6:00 p.m. to 8:00 p.m., Thursday & Friday: 12:00 noon to
5:00 p.m.

NEWSPAPERS

Free Press
3720 Idaho St., Elko, NV 89801
Phone: 775 738-3118   Fax: 775 738-2215

Newspapers	City	UNLV Library has
Business Talks	Tuscarota	October 30 & November 21, 1908
Carlin Courier	Carlin	May 7 - August 4, 1976
Commonwealth	Carlin	Sept. 14, 1910 - Feb. 21, 1912 (weekly - 1909-1912)
Commonwealth	Deeth	March 6, 1912 - Oct. 28, 1914 (weekly - 1909-1914)
Contract Miner	Contract	June 4, 1914; February 4, 1915; April 1915
Daily Argonaut	Elko	December 21, 1897 - Feb. 6, 1899 (daily- full run)

Daily Elko Independent	Elko	August 17, 1875 - August 3, 1882 (daily- 1875-87?)
Daily Free Press	Elko	February 17, 1908
Daily Free Press (1911)	Elko	March 16, 1911 - April 16, 1919
Daily Independent (1885)	Elko	July 1, 1885 - March 29, 1915 (daily- full run)
Elko Chronicle	Elko	June 5 - December 4, 1870
Elko Daily Free Press	Elko	June 15, 1931 - date

(Index *Elko Daily Free Press*, 1883-1994-currently being updated- at Northeastern Nevada Museum, Elko, NV)

Elko Enterprise	Elko	December 1, 1916 - Feb. 9, 1917 (weekly - full run)
Elko Free Press	Elko	February 9, 1909 - Mar. 15, 1991
Elko Free Press (1919)	Elko	April 18, 1919 - June 12, 1931
Elko Free Press, Weekly Edition	Elko	March 5, 1909 - March 14, 1913
Elko Independent	Elko	June 19, 1869 - May 25, 1872 (weekly - full run)
Elko Independent (1915)	Elko	March 30, 1915 - March 12, 1964
Elko Independent (1965)	Elko	January 7, 1965 - date

(Index *Elko Independent*, 1869-1994-currently being updated-at Northeastern Nevada Museum, Elko, NV)

Elko Post	Elko	Sep. 8, 1877 - Aug. 28, 1880
Elko Weekly Post	Elko	Sept. 11, 1875 - Sept. 1, 1877 (daily- full run)
Elko Weekly Post	Elko	Sept. 4, 1880 - April 30, 1881 (daily- full run)
Free Press	Elko	January 5, 1883 - Feb. 14, 1908
Gold Circle Miner	Midas	April 11, 1908 (weekly - 1908-?)
Gold Circle News	Midas	June 20 & September 26, 1908 (weekly - full run)
Gold Circle Porcupine	Midas	May 20, 1914 (weekly - full run)
Gold Creek News	Gold Creek	Dec. 24, 1896 - Dec. 10, 1897 (weekly - full run)
Metropolis Chronicle	Metropolis	Sep. 15, 1911 - Apr. 15, 1913 (semi-weekly - full run)
Mining Review	Tuscarora	October 24 - December 30, 1877 (daily- full run)
Mountain City Mall	Mountain City	May 19, 1938 - Feb. 23, 1939 (weekly - full run)
Mountain City Messenger	Mountain City	September 1, 1933
Mountain City Times	Mountain City	January 21 - May 13, 1898 (weekly - full run)

Nevada Democrat (Carlin) Carlin		February 23 & April 13, 1917 (weekly- full run)
Nevada Silver Tidings	Elko	January 2, 1897 - July 15, 1899 (weekly- 1895-1899)
Nevada State Herald	Wells	Mar. 19, 1897 - April 14, 1933 (weekly- 1897-1937)
Progress	Wells	Sep. 15, 1983 - April 19, 1984
Progress (1986)	Wells	Sep. 12, 1986 - Jan. 10, 1989
Telegram	Elko	June 2, 1909
Times Review	Tuscarora	Sep. 25, 1880 - April 7, 1883
Tuscarora Mining News	Tuscarora	September 21, October 26 & Dec. 7, 1907
Tuscarora Times and Mining Review	Tuscarora	April 9, 1883 - Dec. 31, 1886
Tuscarora Times Review	Tuscarora	January 3, 1887 - Dec. 26, 1903 (daily- 1878-1905)
Weekly Elko Independent	Elko	June 1, 1872 - January 23, 1887 (weekly - full run)
Weekly Elko Independent	Elko	March 19, - December 31, 1964
Weekly Independent	Elko	Jan. 30, 1887 - Dec. 11, 1914 (weekly - 1887-1919?)
Wells Progress	Wells	June 26, 1936 - Sep. 8, 1983 (weekly - 1937- date)
Wells Progress (1984)	Wells	May 2, 1984 - Sep. 11, 1986
Wells Progress (1989)	Wells	January 24 - August 29, 1989
Western Home Builder	Carlin	June 6, 1914 - Nov. 23, 1916 (weekly - full run)

SOCIETIES

Northeastern Nevada Historical Society, Research Library
1515 Idaho St., Elko, NV 89801
Phone: 775 738-3418 Fax: 775 778-9318
Founded: 1968
Special Collections: Area newspaper collection (1869-present)
Nevada newspaper indexes:
  Elko Daily Free Press, 1883-1994-currently being updated
  Elko Independent, 1869-1994-currently being updated

FAMILY HISTORY LIBRARY (Salt Lake City, Utah) HOLDINGS

All microfilmed and microfiched records (unless restricted) are available to rent worldwide at branch Family History Centers and selected larger public and private libraries and societies.

Nevada, Elko - Archives and libraries - Inventories, registers, catalogs
Inventory of the County Archives of Nevada, no. 04, Elko County (Elko).
Prepared by the Historical Records Survey, Division of Women's and Professional Projects, Works Progress Administration. Reno, Nev. : Historical Records Survey, 1938
979.316 A3i, also on microfiche- 6100348

Nevada, Elko - Cemeteries
Parkin, Nona. *Elko County Records, 1863-1938.* Salt Lake City : Filmed by the Genealogical Society of Utah, 1997.
V. 1. Birth records/notices, Elko County records, 1869-1889; Record of births, Dr. A. C. Olmsted, 1897-1914; Cemetery census: Carlin, Clover Valley, Elko, Lamoille Valley, Metropolis, Montrell and Tecoma, small cemeteries, Starr Valley, Tuscarora, and Wells -- v. 2. Death records/obituaries: Elko County, records, 1887-1917; Elko County death notices, 1864-1914; Newspaper notices, 1869-1922; Newspaper obiuaries for Jackpot & Jarbridge, 1923-1977; Newspaper obituaries for Metropolis, Montello, Owyhee, 1931-1983; Newspaper obituaries for Tuscarora & Wells, 1943-1982 -- v. 3. Funeral home records: Burns Mortuary, 1941-1972; Jurors called for duty: Elko County, 1887; Marriage record/notices: Elko County records, 1869-1889; Elko County records, 1870-1938 (male); Elko County records, 1879-1938 (female) -- v. 4. Pioneer families; Registered voters; Church records: St. Luke's Episopal Church, Clover Valley, 1907 and St. Barnabos Mission, Wells, 1932; and Elko Church (Catholic or Episcopal?).
Microfilm- 1598453 item 6   Vol. 1
Microfilm- 1598454 item 1-3   Vol. 2-4

Nevada, Elko - History
Patterson, Edna B. *This Land Was Ours : an In-depth Study of a Frontier Community.* Springville, Utah : Art City Pub. Co., c1973.
979.316 H2p
A history of the Lamoille area of Elko County, Nevada. Includes biographical sketches.

Bowen, Marshall E. *Utah People in the Nevada Desert : Homestead and Community on a Twentieth Century Farmers' Frontier.* Logan, Utah : Utah State University Press, c1994.
979.316 H2b

> Between 1909 and 1915, two groups of migrants settled and began to farm railroad and public lands in eastern deserts near Wells, Nevada. One group, mostly Mormons, the other mainly non-Mormon, first generation Irish and German Americans from urban Salt Lake City, established the four small communities of Metropolis, Afton, Tobar Flat, and Independence Valley.

Nevada, Elko - Military records - World War, 1914-1918

Banks, Raymond H. *The Banks Compilation of Birth Data of Men with Links to Elko County, Nevada, Who were born 1873-1900 : as Found in the Civilian Registration Cards.* L.D.S. microfilm series of World War I Selective Service draft registration cards. Salt Lake City : R.H. Banks, c1996
979.3 A1 no.46

> An alphabetical listing by surname of men who completed civilian registration cards for their draft boards during 19 17-1918 about 98 % of men present in America and born 1873-1900 provided draft card information in 1917 or 1918. Aliens were required to register. Persons already in the military did not register. Includes name, date of birth, ethnic group, birth location or other information, and county or city draft board in the state where registered.

Nevada, Elko - Vital records

Elko County (Nevada). County Recorder. *Marriage Records, 1869-1951; Index 1869-1955.*

Microfilm- 1888134 item 4	Index, grooms	1869-1949	
Microfilm- 1888135 item 2	Index, grooms	1950-1955	
Microfilm- 1888135 item 3	Index, grooms	1950-1955	
Microfilm- 1888135 item 1	Index, brides	1869-1949	
Microfilm- 1888135 item 3	Index, brides	1950-1955	
Microfilm- 1888136	Licenses and certificates, v. 1	1869-1884	
	Certificates, v. 2-4	1884-1934	
	Certificates, v. 5 (p. 1-347)	1934-1939	
Microfilm- 1888137	Certificates, v. 5 (p. 347-end)	1939-1941	
	Certificates, v. 6-7	1941-1947	
	Certificates, v. 8 (p. 1-113)	1947-1948	
Microfilm- 1888138	Certificates, v. 8 (p. 113-end)	1947-1948	
	Certificates, v. 9-10	1948-1951	

Elko County (Nevada). County Clerk. *Marriage Licenses, 1886-1951.*
Microfilm of records at Elko County courthouse, Elko, Nevada.

Microfilm- 1943268	Licenses, A - S	1886-1931
Microfilm- 1943269	Licenses, S - Z	1886-1931
	Licenses, no. 1-1100	1931-1936
Microfilm- 1943270	Licenses, no. 1101-4845	1936-1944
Microfilm- 1943271	Licenses, no. 4846-8700	1944-1947
Microfilm- 1943272	Licences, no. 8701-12525	1947-1949
Microfilm- 1943273	Licenses, no. 12526-16265	1949-1951

Parkin, Nona. *Elko County Records, 1863-1938.*
Contents: v. 1. Birth records/notices, Elko County records, 1869-1889; Record of births, Dr. A. C. Olmsted, 1897-1914; Cemetery census: Carlin, Clover Valley, Elko, Lamoille Valley, Metropolis, Montrell and Tecoma, small cemeteries, Starr Valley, Tuscarora, and Wells -- v. 2. Death records/obituaries: Elko County, records, 1887-1917; Elko County death notices, 1864-1914; Newspaper notices, 1869-1922; Newspaper obiuaries for Jackpot & Jarbridge, 1923-1977; Newspaper obituaries for Metropolis, Montello, Owyhee, 1931-1983; Newspaper obituaries for Tuscarora & Wells, 1943-1982 -- v. 3. Funeral home records: Burns Mortuary, 1941-1972; Jurors called for duty: Elko County, 1887; Marriage record/notices: Elko County records, 1869-1889; Elko County records, 1870-1938 (male); Elko County records, 1879-1938 (female) -- v. 4. Pioneer families; Registered voters; Church records: St. Luke's Episopal Church, Clover Valley, 1907 and St. Barnabos Mission, Wells, 1932; and Elko Church (Catholic or Episcopal?).

Microfilm- 1598453 item 6   Vol. 1
Microfilm- 1598454 item 1-3   Vol. 2-4

Elko County (Nevada). County Recorder. *Birth and Death Records, 1887-1917.* Salt Lake City : Filmed by the Genealogical Society of Utah, 1993.

Microfilm- 1888133	Index, births, v. 1	1887-1939
	Index, deaths, v. 1	1887-1917
	Birth and death certificates, v. 1	1887-1901
	Birth certificates, v. 2-3	1899-1915
Microfilm- 1888134 item 1-3	Birth certificates, v. 3	1907-1917
	Death certificates, v. 2-3	1907-1917

Nevada, Elko, Carlin - Church records
Church of Jesus Christ of Latter-day Saints. Carlin Branch (Nevada). *Record of Members, 1925-1937*. Salt Lake City : Filmed by the Genealogical Society of Utah, 1954.
Carlin Branch was a unit of the California Mission from 1923-1937, when it was re-named Carlin Ward and incorporated into the Nevada Stake. Includes index.
Microfilm- 0001955 item 1-2   Record of members   1925-1937
Photocopies not permitted except for direct line descendants. Remove all other data from photocopy.

Nevada, Elko, Charleston - Church records
Church of Jesus Christ of Latter-day Saints. Charleston Ward (Nevada). *Annual Genealogical Report, Form E, 1947-1948*. Salt Lake City : Filmed by the Genealogical Society of Utah, 1951.
Microfilm- 0014906   Form E   1947-1948
Photocopies not permitted except for direct line descendants. Remove all other data from photocopy.

Nevada, Elko, Deeth - History
Scott, Doris Black. *Deeth, Nevada*. San Bruno, Calif. : D. Scott, 1955.
979.3. A1 no.46
Includes biography of families in Deeth.

Nevada, Elko, Elko - Church records
Church of Jesus Christ of Latter-day Saints. Elko Branch (Nevada). *Record of Members, 1922-1937*. Salt Lake City : Filmed by the Genealogical Society of Utah, 1955.
Microfilm- 0002036 item 3   Record of members   1922-1937
Photocopies not permitted except for direct line descendants. Remove all other data from photocopy.

Church of Jesus Christ of Latter-day Saints. Elko Ward (Nevada). *Record of Members, 1937-1941; Annual Genealogical Report, Form E, 1937- 1948*. Salt Lake City : Filmed by the Genealogical Society of Utah, 1951.
Microfilm- 0014900 item 1   Record of members   1937-1941
Microfilm- 0014900 item 2   Form E   1937-1948
Photocopies not permitted except for direct line descendants. Remove all other data from photocopy.

First Presbyterian Church (Elko, Nevada). *Church Records, 1870-1920.* Salt Lake City : Filmed by the Genealogical Society of Utah, 1981.
Microfilm of original records at the Presbyterian Historical Society in Philadelphia, Pennsylvania.
Microfilm- 1310561 item 1
    Session minutes   1870-1920
    List of elders and deacons; By-laws; Members, 1893
    Communicants; Baptisms, 1871-1914; Marriages, 1871-1911,
        Deaths, 1873-1912

Nevada, Elko, Elko - Directories
R. L. Polk and Company. *Elko, Elko County, City Directory.* Monterey Park, Calif. : R.L. Polk, 1969.
  979.316/E1 E4p

Nevada, Elko, Elko - Obituaries
Elko Independent, 1970-1972, Elko, Elko, Nevada. Salt Lake City : Filmed by the Genealogical Society of Utah, 1987.
Microfilm- 1421750 item 4
    Microreproduction of photocopied newspaper obituaries. Includes obituaries from the Elko Independent.
Microfilm- 1421750 item 6   Index to Elko Independent, 1970-1972, Elko, Elko, Nevada

Nevada, Elko, Metropolis - Church records
Church of Jesus Christ of Latter-day Saints. Metropolis Ward (Nevada).
Record of Members, 1912-1941; Annual Genealogical Report, Form E, 1912- 1948. Salt Lake City : Filmed by the Genealogical Society of Utah, 1951.
    Microfilm of original records in the LDS Church Archives, Salt Lake City.
    The Form E includes reports from North Weber Stake.
Microfilm- 0014910 item 1-2   Record of members 1912-1941
Microfilm- 0014910 item 3   Form E   1912-1948

Nevada, Elko, Montello - Cemeteries
Cemetery Records, Montello, Elko County, Nevada. Compiled by the Genealogical Committee of the L.D.S. Church. Salt Lake City : Filmed by the Genealogical Society of Utah, 1956.
Microfilm- 0002112 item 2

Nevada, Elko, Montello - Church records
Church of Jesus Christ of Latter-day Saints. Montello Ward (Nevada). *Record of Members, 1930-1941: Annual Genealogical Report, Form E, 1930- 1947.*
Salt Lake City : Filmed by the Genealogical Society of Utah, 1951
Microfilm of original records in the LDS Church Archives, Salt Lake City.
Microfilm- 0014911 item 1   Record of members 1930-1941
Microfilm- 0014911 item 2   Form E   1930-1947

Nevada, Elko, Ruby - Church records
Church of Jesus Christ of Latter-day Saints. Ruby Branch (Nevada). Church Archives, Salt Lake City. Ruby Branch created in 1914 and discontinued in 1920, was a local unit of the North Weber and Nevada Stakes. The Form E includes reports from the North Weber Stake.
Microfilm- 0014919 item 1   Record of members 1914-1919
Microfilm- 0014919 item 2   Form E   1915

Nevada, Elko, Wells - Cemeteries
Dyer, Heather Noel. *Wells Cemetery.*
979.316 V3d, also on microfilm- 1697746 item 10

Martin, Phyllis J. *Wells, Nevada Cemetery.*
979.3 A1 no.31

Starr Valley Cemetery Records, Wells, Elko County, Nevada. Salt Lake City : Filmed by the Genealogical Society of Utah, 1956.
Microfilm- 0002112 item 4

Nevada, Elko, Wells - Church records
Church of Jesus Christ of Latter-day Saints. Wells Ward (Nevada). *Record of Members, 1928-1946; Annual Genealogical Report, Form E, 1928- 1948.*
Salt Lake City : Filmed by the Genealogical Society of Utah, 1951.
Microfilm- 0014926
Wells Ward, created in 1937, was formerly known as Wells Branch and was a local unit of the Nevada and Humboldt Stakes.

Nevada, Elko, Wells - Vital records
Burns Mortuary (Wells, Nevada). *Death Records, 1863-1954.* Salt Lake City : Filmed by the Genealogical Society of Utah, 1956.
Microfilm- 0002112 item 3

CHAPTER SIX

Esmeralda County

Esmeralda County was one of the nine original counties into which the Territory of Nevada was divided.

Esmeralda is the Spanish word for emerald. J. M. Corey christened a mining district Esmeralda Mining District, and Corey may have had in mind some beauty who answered to that musical word, as it is a common name for girls with green eyes. Esmeralda soon became the popular word for a territorial empire.

COURTHOUSE

Esmeralda County Courthouse
P.O. Box 547, Goldfield, NV 89013-0547
Phone: 775 485-6337 County Recorder; 775 485-6367 County Clerk
Land records: County Recorder
Probate records: County Clerk
Naturalization records: County Clerk

LIBRARIES

Dyer

Fish Lake Library
P.O. Box 105, Dyer, NV 89010
Phone: 775 572-3311   E-mail: mlhunter@clan.lib.nv.us
Hours: Wednesday, Thursday, Friday: 9:00 a.m. to 4:00 p.m., Saturday: 9:00
    a.m. to 1:00 p.m.
Subject Interests: Nevada local history

Goldfield

Goldfield Public Library
P.O. Box 430, Goldfield, NV 89013
Phone: 775 485-3236   Fax: 775 485-3236   E-mail: dcshimp@clan.lib.nv.us
Founded: 1976
Hours: Tuesday, Wednesday, Thursday: 10:15 a.m. to 6:00 p.m.

Silverpeak Branch Library, P.O. Box 128, Silverpeak, NV 89047;
Phone: 775: 937-2215; Fax: 775 937-2215
Hours: Tuesday: 8:00 a.m. to 5:00 p.m., Wednesday: 12:00 noon to 8:00
p.m., Thursday: 10:00 a.m. to 6:00 p.m.

NEWSPAPERS

Newspapers	City	UNLV Library has
Blair Press	Blair	January 4, 1908 - June 17, 1910 (weekly - 1906-10)
Borax Miner	Columbus	October 18, 1873; February 20, 1875 - September 15, 1877 (weekly - 1873-78)
Columbia Topics	Columbia	October 14, 1908 - June 4, 1909 (weekly - full run)
Divide City Times	Divide City	March 29 - April 19, 1919 (weekly - 1919-20?)
Gilbert Record	Gilbert	February 21, 1925 - May 8, 1926 NEWSPAPERS(weekly - full run)
Goldfield Chronicle	Goldfield	January 24, 1907 - Feb. 27, 1909 (weekly - 1906-09)
Goldfield Daily News Evening Edition	Goldfield	March 9, 1909 - March 18, 1911 (daily - full run)
Goldfield Daily Sun	Goldfield	February 2, 1905 - Sep. 22, 1906
Goldfield Daily Tribune	Goldfield	Sep. 24, 1906 - Mar. 29, 1930 (daily - full run)
Goldfield Enterprise: Goldfield & Esmeralda County News	Goldfield	February 1 - November 1958
Goldfield Gossip	Goldfield	October 1906 - September 1907 (weekly - full run)
Goldfield Magazine	Goldfield	April 10, 1907
Goldfield News	Goldfield	April 29, 1904 - Dec. 31, 1910 (weekly - full run)
Goldfield News and Beatty Bulletin	Goldfield	June 13, 1947 - Dec. 28, 1956
Goldfield News and Weekly Tribune	Goldfield	January 10, 1914 - June 6, 1947
Goldfield News Annual Edition	Goldfield	1905 - 1906; 1906 - 1907
Goldfield Post	Goldfield	May 25, 1912
Goldfield Review	Columbia	June 29, 1905 - March 9, 1907

Goldfield Review	Goldfield	April 20, 1907 - Feb. 13, 1909 (weekly - full run)
Goldfield Vigilant	Goldfield	January 30, 1905 (weekly - full run)
Hornsilver Herald	Hornsilver	May 9 - September 12, 1908 (weekly - full run)
Nevada Mining Bulletin	Goldfield	December 1906
Nevada Mining News	Goldfield	June 14, 1906
Nevada Workman	Goldfield	September 7, 1907
Palmetto Herald	Palmetto	March 9 & 16, June 1, 1906 (weekly - full run)
Silver Peak Post	Silver Peak	June 6, 1906 (weekly)
Sporting Bulletin	Goldfield	August 29, 1906
Weekly Market Letter	Goldfield	August 19, 1904

SOCIETIES
Goldfield Historical Society
P.O. Box 178, 115 Columbia St., Goldfield, NV 89013
Phone: 775 485-6365   Fax: 775 485-3542

FAMILY HISTORY LIBRARY (Salt Lake City, Utah) HOLDINGS

All microfilmed and microfiched records (unless restricted) are available to rent worldwide at branch Family History Centers and selected larger public and private libraries and societies.

Nevada, Esmeralda - Cemeteries
Parkin, Nona. *Esmeralda County Records.*
    Contents: v. 1. Cemetery census: Index to Goldfield Cemetery; Goldfield
    Cemetery -- v. 2. Death records/obituaries: Esmeralda County death
    notices from newspapers 1864-1920, Goldfield newspaper obituaries
    1922-1983, Newspaper notices 1864-1920; Marriage records/notices:
    Newspaper notices 1875-1916; Tax assessment records: Esmeralda
    County assessment roll 1864. Includes index.
Microfilm- 1598448 item 5-6   Vol. 1-2

Nevada, Esmeralda - Court records
Esmeralda (Nevada). County Recorder. *Attachments Index, 1864-1916.*
Microfilm- 1862944 item 5
    Alphabetical list of plaintiff, defendant and date.

Nevada, Esmeralda - Funeral homes
Nevada. State Board of Health. *Funeral Registers, 1906-1937.*
Microfilm of records at Esmeralda County Courthouse, Goldfield, Nevada.
Includes indexes at beginning of volumes. Includes some copies of death
certificates.
Microfilm- 1862584 item 2-4   Vol. 1 Death certificates Jun 1906-Oct 1907
     Vol. 2   Funeral record   Nov 1907-Dec 1913
     Vol. 3   Funeral record   Dec 1913-Nov 1925 (p. 1-463)
Microfilm- 1862658 item 1-5
     Vol. 3   Funeral record   Oct 1924-Jul 1937
     Vol. 4   Funeral record   Nov 1937-May 1963
         Financial records   Jun 1906-Jul 1907
         Financial records   Jul 1907-Dec 1912
         Funeral record   Dec 1916-Sep 1937

Nevada, Esmeralda - History
Aston, M. B. *History of Esmeralda County, Nevada.* Seattle, Wash. : Shorey
Book Store, 1968.
979.3 A1 no. 22

Nevada, Esmeralda - Land and property
Esmeralda (Nevada). County Recorder. *Combined Book of Miscellaneous
Contracts, Agreements, Leases, Assignments.*
Microfilm- 1862944 item 6-9   Index, v. 1-4   1907-1923
 Miscellaneous contracts, assignments, leases, mortgages, liens releases,
 power of attorneys, assignment of mortgages, agreements, etc.
Microfilm- 1863091   Index, v. 5-6   1923-1933
     Vol. 1   May 1907-Sep 1909
     Vol. 2 (p. 1-413)   Aug 1907-May 1908
Microfilm- 1863251   Vol. 2 (413-end)-v. 5 (1-327) May 1908-Jan 1911
Microfilm- 1863252   Vol. 5 (327-end)-v. 9   Jan 1911-Jun 1923
Microfilm- 1863253 item 1-3   Vol. 10-12   Aug 1916-Jun 1923

Esmeralda (Nevada). County Recorder.
Microfilm- 1862944 item 2-4
 Contracts and agreements, 1863-1907; attachments, 1864-1916.
 Index, contracts & agreements, 1863-1907; Contracts & agreements, v. A,
 Aug 1863-Aug 1907 Contracts & agreements, v. B, Jan 1882-May 1907;
 Contracts & agreements, v. A, Aug 1863-Aug 1907; Attachments,
 alphabetical list, 1864-1916

Esmeralda (Nevada). County Recorder. *Deeds, 1871-1908.*
Microfilm- 1862659 item 4-5

Index to deeds, v. A	Oct 1863-Oct 1868
Index to deeds, v. B (part)	Mar 1871-Feb 1904

Microfilm- 1862660

Index to deeds, v. B (part)	Feb 1904-Mar 1904
Deeds, v. A	Sep 1863-Apr 1864
Deeds, v. B (p. 1-604)	Sep 1863-May 1865

Microfilm- 1862661

Deeds, v. B (p. 604-end)	May 1865-Aug 1866
Deeds, v. C	May 1863-Jul 1868
Deeds and conveyances, v. DAug 1866-Nov 1876	
Deeds, v. E (p. 1-137)	Oct 1866-Jan 1868

Microfilm- 1862662

Deeds, v. E (p. 137-end)	Jan 1868-Nov 1873
Deeds, v. F	Nov 1868-Jun 1879
Deeds, v. G (p. 1-507)	Dec 1873-Jun 1878

Microfilm- 1862764

Deeds, v. G (p. 507-end)	Jun 1878-Jan 1879
Deeds, v. H	Nov 1866-Sep 1878
Deeds, v. I	Jul 1876-Jul 1880
Deeds, v. J	Jun 1878-Aug 1880
Deeds, v. K (p. 1-37)	Apr 1879-Apr 1880

Microfilm- 1862765

Deeds, v, K (p. 37-end)	Apr 1880-Sep 1881
Deeds, v. L	Apr 1879-Jan 1882
Deeds, v. M	May 1880-Aug 1881
Deeds, v. N (p. 1-307)	May 1881-Mar 1882

Microfilm- 1862766

Deeds, v. N (p. 307-end)	May 1882-Oct 1892
Deeds, v. O	Dec 1880-Apr 1883
Deeds, v. P	
Nov 1881-Jun 1885	

Microfilm- 1862767

Deeds, v. Q-S (p. 1-421)	Oct 1882-Jan 1886

(Waranty deed, land patents, Sheriff's deeds, administrator's deeds, U.S. patents)

Microfilm- 1862768

Deeds, v. S (p. 421-end)	Jan 1886-Apr 1886
Deeds, v. T-U (p. 1-193)	Apr 1886-Dec 1890
Deeds, v. V (p. 1-193)	Jan 1886-Dec 1890

(land patents, conveyance of real estate sold for non-payment of state and county taxes, homestead certificates)

122 Nevada Guide to Genealogical Records

Microfilm- 1862769
  Deeds, v. V (p. 193-end)   Dec 1890-Mar 1907
  Deeds, v. W-X   Aug 1892-Mar 1908
  (patents, estates, executors deeds, tax deeds, conveyances and
  sales)

Esmeralda (Nevada). County Recorder. *Homesteads, 1863-1908; Index 1863-1908.*
Microfilm- 1862914 item 1-2   Index   1863-1911

Esmeralda (Nevada). County Recorder. *Mining Locations, 1863-1892; Index 1866-1904.*
Microfilm- 1862914 item 3-8
        Index v. A   1866-1904
        Vol. A-B (p. 1-204)   Nov 1863-Jun 1881
Microfilm- 1862915
        Vol. B (p. 204-end)   Jun 1881-Oct 1904
        Vol. C-E (p. 1-279)   Aug-1883-May 1892
Microfilm- 1862916
        Vol. E (p. 279-end)-v. F-G   Nov 1863-Aug 1907

Esmeralda (Nevada). County Recorder. *Mortgages, 1863-1916; Index 1863-1909.*
Microfilm- 1862917 item 1   Index, mortgages   1863-1909
Microfilm- 1862942 item 3   Index, chattel mortgages 1888-1906
Microfilm- 1862943 item 3   Index, liens   1863-1907
Microfilm- 1862943 item 5-6 Index, assignments of mortgages 1864-1905
        Index, powers of attorney   1863-1907
Microfilm- 1862917 item 2-4
        Mortgages, v. A-C (p. 1-275)   Aug 1863-Jul 1880
        Mortgages, v. B   Jan 1878-May 1906
        Mortgages, v. C (p. 1-275)   Mar 1881-Jan 1875

Microfilm- 1862942 item 1-2
        Mortgages, v. C (p. 275-end)   Jan 1875-Aug 1907
        Mortgages, v. D   Jun 1887-Aug 1907
Microfilm- 1862942 item 4-5
        Chattel mortgages, v. A   1888-1916
        Premption claims, v. A   Apr 1863-Mar 1883
Microfilm- 1862943 item 1-2
        Premption claims, v. B   1879-1907
        Premption claims, v. C   1883-1907
Microfilm- 1862943 item 4   Leases, v. A   1863-1907

Microfilm- 1862943 item 7-8
    Powers of attorney, v. A   Sep 1863-Aug 1882
    Powers of attorney, v. B   May 1880-Feb 1889 (p. 1-159)
Microfilm- 1862944 item 1
    Powers of attorney, v. B   Feb 1889-Apr 1907 (p. 159-end)

Esmeralda (Nevada). County Recorder. *Official Records of Indentures, Mining Claims, Quit Claims, Homesteads, Deeds, etc., 1923-1955.*
Microfilm- 1863253 item 4-5 Vol. 3-3A (p. 1-131) Jun 1923-Jun 1928
Microfilm- 1863254   Vol. 3A (p. 131-end)   Jun 1928-Apr 1935
                Vol. 3B-v. 3D (p. 1-95)   Apr 1935-Jul 1947
Microfilm- 1863255   Vol. 3D (p. 95-end)   Jul 1947-Apr 1950
                Vol. 4-v. 4A   Jun 1923-Oct 1956
Microfilm- 1863366   Vol. 5-v. 5A   Jun 1923-Jan 1955

Nevada, Esmeralda - Military records - World War, 1914-1918

Banks, Raymond H. *The Banks Compilation of Birth Data of Men with Links to Esmeralda County, Nevada, Who Were Born 1873-1900 : as Found in the Civilian Registration cards.* L.D.S. microfilm series of World War I Selective Service draft registration cards.
979.3 A1 no.50
    An alphabetical listing by surname of men who completed civilian registration cards for their draft boards during 1917-1918. About 98% of men present in America and born 1873-1900 provided draft card information in 1917 or 1918. Aliens were required to register. Persons already in the military did not register. Includes name, date of birth, ethnic group, birth location or other information, and county or city draft board in the state where registered.

Nevada, Esmeralda - Vital records

Esmeralda (Nevada). County Recorder. *Marriages and Miscellaneous Records.*
    Includes indexes at beginning of volumes. Includes marriages, certificate of sales, official appointments, trustee oaths, rites of restitution, release of attachments, estate bonds,   passports, and homestead decrees.
Microfilm- 1862658 item 6-7   Index   1863-1907
                Vol. A (p. 1-103)   Dec 1863-Jul 1872
    Certificates of marriages, certificates of sales, official appointments, trustee oaths, rite of restitutions, release of attachments, estate bonds, and homestead decrees.
Microfilm- 1862659 item 1-3   Vol. A (p. 103-end) Jul 1872-1883
                Vol. B   1881-1907

Caution notices, marriages licenses, proof of labor, estates, mortgages, notarial bonds, bill of sales, incorporations, co-partnerships.

Vol. C   Feb 1983-Jun 1908
Passports, bond estates, service certificates, bill of sales, water claims, marriage certificates, deeds, notice of forfeitures.

Esmeralda (Nevada). County Clerk. *Marriage Licenses, 1871-1992.*

Microfilm- 1863390 item 14	
Register of licenses	Mar 1871-Apr 1892
Microfilm- 1863365 item 1-2	
Register of licenses	1898-1992
Microfilm- 1863365 item 3-4	
Licenses	11 Jun 1898-22 May 1911
Microfilm- 1863390 item 1-13	
License applications	1 Jun 1911-18 Mar 1956
Microfilm- 1863390 item 14-15	
License applications	6 Nov 1871-8 Jan 1874

Nevada. State Board of Health. *Births and Deaths, 1887-1992.*

Microfilm- 1862583 item 1	
Index, births, deaths	Oct 15 1887-Apr 28 1978
Microfilm- 1862582	
Births, v. A & deaths	May 1887-Aug 1908
Microfilm- 1862583 item 2-3	
Births, v. B	Oct 01 1924-Sep 28 1945
Affidavits of births	Mar 01 1909-May 21 1962
Microfilm- 1862583 item 4-8	
Death records	Mar 1904-Feb 11 1909
Death cert., v. 2-3	Aug 08-Jan 19 1911
Burial transits	Jul 4 1986-June 17 1992
Death certificates	Aug 3 1907-Dec 27 1916
Death cert. v. 4	May 1923-Oct 16 1932 (p. 1-89)
Microfilm- 1862584 item 1	
Death cert. v. 4	Nov 4 1932-Aug 27 1969 (p. 89-end)

Nevada. Esmeralda. Aurora - History

Ransom, Jay Ellis. *Aurora was Brawling Rival to Virginia City During Heyday of Gold Boom Days.*
979.3 A1 no. 2, also on microfilm- 0924689 item 16
Newspaper article on Aurora, Nevada taken from Sacrament Bee, 1964.

CHAPTER SEVEN

Eureka County

Up until 1 March 1873, Eureka County was part of Lander County. By an Act approved 2 Mar 1881, a small strip was detached from White Pine County and added to Eureka County.

In September of 1864 a prospecting party from Austin, including W. O. Arnold found a species of rock different from any other they had previously seen. When they put pieces of the rocks into their campfire, it melted into a flow of metal. They exclaimed, "Eureka!" They located their claims and organized a district under that name.

CHURCHES

EUREKA
Baptist: Diamond Valley Baptist Church, Rte. 1, Box 16, Eureka, NV 89316
   Phone: 775 237-5596
Episcopal: St. James Episcopalian Church, Ely St., Eureka, NV 89316
Latter-day Saints: Latter-day Saints Church in Eureka, PO Box 533, Eureka, NV 89316 Phone: 775 237-5543
Protestant: St. James Church, PO Box 351, Eureka, NV 89316
Roman Catholic: St. Brendans Catholic Church, PO Box 305, Eureka, NV 89316

COURTHOUSE

Eureka County Courthouse
P. O. Box 677, Eureka, NV 89316-0677
Phone: 775 237-5262
Land records: From September 1873, County Recorder
Naturalization records: from 1873 through the 1940s, County Clerk
Probate records: From 1873; copies $1.00 per page, County Clerk
Vital records: From August 1887, County Recorder

NEWSPAPERS

Newspapers	City	UNLV Library has
Eureka Daily Leader	Eureka	June 25, 1878 - October 1, 1881 (daily 1878-1885)
Eureka Daily Republican	Eureka	January 8, 1877 - June 24, 1878 (daily - full run)
Eureka Daily Sentinel	Eureka	May 23, 1871 - October 2, 1887 (1870-1889)
Eureka Evening Leader	Eureka	October 3, 1881 - May 16, 1885
Eureka High School Enterprise	Eureka	November 21, 1896
Eureka Miner	Eureka	June 11, 1971 - March 16, 1973 (weekly - full run)
Eureka Sentinel	Eureka	Nov. 12, 1870 - May 20, 1871
Eureka Sentinel (1885)	Eureka	November 14, 1885 - Oct. 1, 1887
Eureka Sentinel (1902)	Eureka	January 18, 1902 - date (weekly - to date)
Eureka Tri-Weekly Standard	Eureka	August 6, 1885 - Sep. 15, 1886
Eureka Weekly Sentinel	Eureka	August 30, Sep. 6 & 27, 1879
Eureka Weekly Sentinel	Eureka	October 8, 1887 - Jan. 11, 1902
Mining News	Ruby Hill	October 30, 1880 - Jan. 22, 1881
Republican Press	Eureka	November 30, 1884 - May 9, 1885
Ruby Hill Mining News	Ruby Hill	October 1, 1883 - Nov. 3, 1884 (weekly - 1880-84)
Ruby Hill Mining Report	Ruby Hill	August 7 & 14, 1879
Eureka Hill Weekly Mining Report	Ruby Hill	August 29, 1881 - Sep. 17, 1883
Safford Express	Palisade	June 2 & 9, 1883
Silver Plume	Eureka	July 4 - September 1, 1877

SOCIETY

Eureka County Historical Society
P. O. Box 178, Eureka, NV 89316
Collections: Books, manuscripts, photographs

FAMILY HISTORY LIBRARY (Salt Lake City, Utah) HOLDINGS

All microfilmed and microfiched records (unless restricted) are available to rent worldwide at branch Family History Centers and selected larger public and private libraries and societies.

Nevada, Eureka - Archives and libraries - Inventories, registers, catalogs
Inventory of the County Archives of Nevada, no. 06, Eureka County (Eureka). Prepared by the Historical Records Survey, Division of Professional and Service Projects, Work Projects Administration. Reno, Nev. : Historical Records Survey, 1939.
979.332 A3i, also on microfiche- 6100349

Nevada, Eureka - History
Hall, Shawn R. *Romancing Nevada's Past, Ghost Towns and Historical Sites of Eureka, Lander, and White Pine Counties.* Reno : University of Nevada Press, c1994.
979.3 E3h

Molinelli, Lambert. *Eureka and its Resources : a Complete History of Eureka County, Nevada, Containing the United States Mining Laws, the Mining Laws of the District, Bullion Product and Other Statistics for 1878, and a List of County Officers.*
979.332 H2e

Nevada, Eureka - Vital records
Parkin, Nona. *Eureka County Records, 1864-1983.* Salt Lake City : Filmed by the Genealogical Society of Utah, 1997
   Contents: v. 1. Birth records/notices: Eureka County records 1871-1911; Cemetery census: Eureka Cemetery with index, Palisade Cemetery with index, Safford Cemetery; Death records/obituaries: Eureka County records 1887-1911, Newspaper notices 1864-1917, Newspaper obituaries 1922-1983; Funeral home records: Mortuary records from Eureka 1883-1938; Marriage records/notices: Eureka County records 1870-1919; Newspaper "scats"; Pioneer families -- v. 2. Church records: Eureka Catholic Parish records with index, St. James records. Includes index.
Microfilm- 1598449 item 1-2   Vol. 1-2

Eureka County (Nevada). Recorder. *Marriage Records, 1870-1975.*
Microfilm- 1902340 item 10-12

Index, marriages, v. 1	27 Mar 1873-23 Jul 1913
Marriages, v. 1	22 Feb 1870-20 Jan 1873
Marr. v. A (p. 1-275)	27 Mar 1873- 8 Feb 1888

Microfilm- 1902341

Marr. v. A (p 275-end)	8 Feb 1888-25 Nov 1908
Marriages, v. B-E	30 Nov 1908-26 Jun 1975

Nevada. State Board of Health. *Birth Records for Eureka County, 1887-1972.* Salt Lake City : Filmed by the Genealogical Society of Utah, 1993.
Microfilm- 1902340 item 1-5

Index to births, v. 1	19 Apr 1887-24 May 1957
Births, v. 1	29 Apr 1887-24 May 1957
Births, v. 2	5 Jul 1911- 3 Dec 1929
Birth certificates	10 Mar 1930-31 Oct 1972
Birth notices	24 Oct 1871- 9 Jan 1907
	(abstracted from newspapers)

Nevada. State Board of Health. *Deaths Records for Eureka County, Nevada, 1887-1971.* Salt Lake City : Filmed by the Genealogical Society of Utah, 1993.
Microfilm- 1902340 item 6-9

Index of deaths	20 May 1887-18 Jun 1911
Death records	20 May 1887-29 Jul 1911
Death records	16 Jul 1911-28 Oct 1929
Death certificates	15 Jan 1930-18 Jun 1971

Nevada, Eureka, Eureka - Cemeteries
Eureka Cemetery (Eureka, Nevada).
979.3 A1 no.45
Cemetery is mostly abandoned and in care of Nevada Division of Forestry. Includes index.

Nevada, Eureka, Palisade - Cemeteries
Bonnett, Mrs. Max. *Cemetery Listing from Palisade, Eureka Co., Nevada.*
979.3 A1 no.60
Palisade is mostly a ghost town located 10 miles southwest of Carlin, Nevada.

CHAPTER EIGHT

Humboldt County

Humboldt County was one of the original counties, created at the first session of the Territorial Legislature by an act approved on 25 November 1861.

Humboldt County got its name from the Humboldt River, which enters the county in the southeastern corner, turns northwest for sixty miles, then turns southwest, to the Humboldt Sink, or lake, near the center of the southern line of the county.

CHURCHES

MC DERMITT
Assemblies of God: American Indian New Life, PO Box 455, Mc Dermitt, NV 89421 Phone: 775 532-8759
OROVADA
Independent: Community Church of Orovada, PO Box 56, Orovada, NV 89425 Phone: 775 272-3225
Latter-day Saints: Orovada Church of Latter-day Saints, Orovada, NV 89425 Phone: 272-3350
PARADISE VALLEY
Latter-day Saints: Las Vegas Thirtieth Ward, Tropicana and Burnham, Paradise Valley, NV 89426 Phone: 775 736-3550
WINNEMUCCA
Assemblies of God: Word of Light Fellowship, 1095 S. Bridge St., PO Box 962, Winnemucca, NV 89446   Phone: 775 623-3322
Baptist: Grass Valley Baptist Church, PO Box 1436, Winnemucca, NV 89446 Northeast Baptist Association, 1855 Mizpah St., Winnemucca, NV 89445
Church of Christ: Church of Christ, 155 E. 6th St., PO Box 772, Winnemucca, NV 89446 Phone: 775 632-2650
Christian Science: Church of Christ Scientist, 184 e. 4th St., Winnemucca, NV 89445
Episcopal: St. Mary Episcopalian Church, PO Box 209, Winnemucca, NV 89446 Phone: 775 623-3901
Independent Fundamentalist: Winnemucca Community Bible Church, East 4th and Reinhart, PO Box 348, Winnemucca, NV 89445 Phone: 775 623-3901

Latter-day Saints: Church of Jesus Christ Latter-day Saints, 111 W. McArthur Ave., Winnemucca, NV 89445 Phone: 775 623-4411

Lutheran: Lutheran Church Missouri Synod, 120 W. Minor St., Winnemucca, NV 89445

Zion Lutheran Church, 1350 Melarkey St., Winnemucca, MV 89445 Phone: 775 623-3796

Methodist: Battle Mountain United Methodist, 138 W. 3rd St., Winnemucca, NV 89445 Phone: 775 623-2814

Pentecostal: Full Gospel of Christ, 3275 N. Highland Dr., Winnemucca, NV 89445 Phone: 775 623-4673

Protestant: Winnemucca Christian Fellowship, 4380 Grass Valley Rd., Winnemucca, NV 89445 Phone: 775 623-5431

Roman Catholic: St. Pauls Catholic Church, E. 4th and Melarkey, PO Box 93, Winnemucca, NV 89446 Phone: 775 623-2928

Seventh Day Adventist: Seventh Day Adventist Church, 5130 E. Palisade Dr., Winnemucca, NV 89445 Phone: 775 623-2785

Southern Baptist: Grass Valley Baptist Church, 4150 E. Thomas Canyon Rd., Winnemucca, NV 89445 Phone: 775 623-5714

Winnemucca First Baptist Church, 138 W. Winnemucca Blvd, Winnemucca, NV 89445 Phone: 775 623-2085

COURTHOUSE

Humboldt County Courthouse
50 West Fifth Street, Winnemucca, NV 89445-0352
Phone: 775 623-6343
Land records: County Recorder
Naturalization records: County Clerk
Probate records: County Clerk
  Probate search service: $1.00 per year; copies $1.00 per page, no minimum; must be written request.

FUNERAL HOMES

Alberston Funeral Home
47 West First Street, Winnemucca, NV 89445
Phone: 775 623-2986

LIBRARIES

Humboldt County Library
85 E 5th St., Winnemucca, NV 89445
Phone: 775 623-6388 Fax: 775 623-6438 E-mail: jamarcin@clan.lib.nv.us
Hours: Monday, Thursday, Friday, Saturday: 9:00 a.m. to 5:00 p.m., Tuesday
& Wednesday: 9:00 a.m. to 9:00 p.m. Nevada Newspaper indexes:
  Humboldt Register, 1865-1880-currently being updated
Denio Branch Library, Denio, NV 89404; no phone
Hours: Monday & Friday: 1:00 p.m. to 5:00 p.m., Wed.: 7:00 p.m. to 9:00 p.m.
McDermitt Branch Library, McDermitt, NV 89421; Phone: 775 532-8014;
Fax: 775 532-8018
Hours: Tuesday & Thursday: 9:00 a.m. to 5:00 p.m., Wed.: 7:00 p.m. to 9:00
  p.m.

NEWSPAPERS

Newspapers	City	UNLV Library has
Chafey News	Chafey	Sept. 26, 1908 - Jan. 23, 1909 (weekly - full run)
Daily Humboldt Register	Winnemucca	January 28 - November 4, 1876
Daily Silver State	Winnemucca	April 30, 1903 - June 15, 1907
Humboldt County Bulletin	Winnemucca	December 7, 1966 - Dec. 27, 1967
Humboldt County Bulletin	Winnemucca	February 18, 1970 - May 3, 1972
Humboldt County Bulletin & Battle Mountain News	Winnemucca	January 3, 1968 - March 26, 1969
Humboldt National	Winnemucca	August 14 - October 16, 1869 (weekly - full run)
Humboldt Standard	Winnemucca	February 16 - September 28, 1903 (daily - full run)
Humboldt Star	Winnemucca	January 11, 1906 - July 20, 1925
Humboldt Star (1935)	Winnemucca	November 5, 1935 - June 30, 1949
Humboldt Star & Battle Mountain Scout	Winnemucca	January 2, 1964 - Nov. 26, 1965
Humboldt Star and the Silver State	Winnemucca	July 22, 1925 - November 4, 1935
Humboldt Sun	Winnemucca	January 19, 1972 - date
National Miner	National	Dec. 9, 1910 - Sept. 26, 1913 (weekly - full run)
Nevada Daily Bulletin	Winnemucca	July 1, 1964 - November 30, 1966

Nevada Miner	Golconda	February 15 - July 1, 1902
		(semi-monthly - full run)
Nevada Mining Record	Winnemucca	February - March 1966
Nevada News	Winnemucca	Sep. 13, 1900 - Mar. 4, 1901
News (Golconda)	Golconda	February 18, 1899 - July 14, 1900
News (Winnemucca)	Winnemucca	August 23 - September 6, 1900
Orovada Weekly Journal	Orovada	Sept. 5, 1924 - Aug. 28, 1925
		(weekly - full run)
Paradise Reporter	Paradise	May 17, 1879 - October 9, 1880
		(weekly - full run)
Paradise Sunshine	Paradise Valley	May 1906
People's Advocate Winnemucca	Winnemucca	May 17, 1898 - Apr. 28, 1899 (daily, semi weekly - full run)
Silver State (Unionville)	Unionville	March 22, 1870 - Sept. 1874 (weekly - full run)
Silver State (Winnemucca)	Winnemucca	Sep. 10, 1874 - April 29, 1903
Silver State	Winnemucca	Sep. 11, 1909 - July 11, 1925
Silver State News	Winnemucca	June 20, 1907 - Sep. 7, 1909
Territorial Enterprise (Winnemucca)	Winnemucca	April 2, 1969 - February 11, 1970
Winnemucca Argent	Winnemucca	July 23 - November 21, 1868
Winnemucca Humboldt Star & Battle Mountain Scout	Winnemucca	November 29, 1965 - Oct. 6, 1967

SOCIETIES

Northern Central Nevada Historical Society
P. O. Box 819, Winnemucca, NV 89445
Phone: 775 623-2912
Collections: Manuscripts, newspapers, photographs, oral histories

Humbolt County Genealogical Society
85 E. Fifth St., Winnemucca, NV 89445

FAMILY HISTORY LIBRARY (Salt Lake City, Utah) HOLDINGS

All microfilmed and microfiched records (unless restricted) are available to rent worldwide at branch Family History Centers and selected larger public and private libraries and societies.

Nevada, Humboldt - Newspapers
Parkin, Nona. *Humboldt County Records, 1861-1983.* Salt Lake City : Filmed by the Genealogical Society of Utah, 1997.
Birth records/notices: Newspaper notices 1868-1920; Cemetery census: Denio, Golconda, McDermitt; Paradise Valley; Unionville; Winnemucca -- v. 2. Death records/obituaries: Humboldt County records 1887-1913; Newspaper notices 1865-1918; Newspaper obituaries 1923-1983; Funeral home records: Eddy Funeral home — v. 3. Marriage records/notices: Humboldt County records 1861-1916; Newspaper notices 1874-1919; Pioneer families; Church records: Catholic Parish, Winnemucca; Winnemucca Episcopal Church.
Microfilm- 1598455 item 4-5   Vol. 1-2
Microfilm- 1598456 item 1   Vol. 3

Nevada, Humboldt - Military records - World War, 1914-1918
Banks, Raymond H. *The Banks compilation of birth data of men with links to Humboldt County Nevada, including present-day Pershing County, who were born 1873-1900 : as found in the civilian registration cards.* L.D.S. microfilm series of World War I Selective Service draft registration cards. 979.3 A1 no.52
An alphabetical listing by surname of men who completed civilian registration cards for their draft boards during 1917-1918. About 98% of men present in America and born 1873-1900 provided draft card information in 1917 or 1918. Aliens were required to register. Persons already in the military did not register.˙Includes name, date of birth, ethnic group, birth location or other information, and county or city draft board in the state where registered.

Humboldt County (Nevada). Recorder. *Birth Records, 1887-1911.* Salt Lake City : Filmed by the Genealogical Society of Utah, 1993.
Microfilm- 1888482 item 1
Birth certificates, v. A   1887-1911
Includes index at beginning of volume.

Nevada, Humboldt - Vital records
Humboldt County (Nevada). County Clerk. *Affidavits for Marriage Licenses, 1881-1950.* Salt Lake City : Filmed by the Genealogical Society of Utah, 1993.

Microfilm- 1888491 item 3	
List of licenses issued	1881-1899
Microfilm- 1888490	
Affidavits for licenses, v. 1-3	1881-1914
Affidavits for licenses, v. 4	1914-1917 (p. 1-240)
Microfilm- 1888491 item 1-2	
Affidavits for licenses, v. 4	1917 (p. 240-end)
Affidavits for licenses, v. 5	1917-1919
Microfilm- 1888491 item 4-11	
Affidavits for licenses, v. 1-8	1919-1941
Microfilm- 1888492	
Affidavits for licenses, v. 9-17	1941-1947
Affidavits for licenses, v. 18	1947 (no. 1-3546)
Microfilm- 1888493	
Affidavits for licenses, v. 18	1947
Affidavits for licenses, v. 19-27	1947-1950

Humboldt County (Nevada). Recorder. *Death Records, 1887-1911.* Salt Lake City : Filmed by the Genealogical Society of Utah, 1993.
Microfilm- 1888482 item 2   Death certificates, v. A   1887-1911
Includes index at beginning of volume.

Humboldt County (Nevada). Recorder. *Marriage Records, 1862-1951.* Salt Lake City : Filmed by the Genealogical Society of Utah, 1993.

Microfilm- 1888482 item 3-6	
Licenses and certificates, v. A-C	1862-1908
Licenses and certificates, v. D (p. 1-205)	1908-1912
Microfilm- 1888483	
Licenses and certificates, v. D (p. 205-end)	1912-1915
Licenses and certificates, v. E-H	1915-1940
Certificates, v. I (p. 1-141)	1941-1944
Microfilm- 1888484	
Certificates, v. I (p. 141-end)	1944-1946
Certificates, v. v. J-K	1946-1951
Includes index at beginning of volumes.	

Nevada, Humboldt - Voting registers
Election and Court Records of Humboldt County, Nevada, 1869-1904.
  979.3 A1 no.27
    Includes election registers, 1869-1904 and justice court records.

Nevada, Humboldt, Paradise Valley - Cemeteries
Fujii, Maggie. *Cemetery, Paradise Valley, Nevada.*
  Microfilm- 1598157 item 5
    Cemetery is owned and maintained by the local chapter of I.O.O.F. Lodge.
    ...includes German, Italian, Basque, Native Americans, Irish and a minor
    sprinkling of other races.

Nevada, Humboldt, Winnemucca - Cemeteries
Cemetery Records, Winnemucca, Humboldt, Nevada.
  979.354/W1 V3c

Parkin, Nona. *Winnemucca, Humboldt County, Nevada* [cemetery]
  979.354/W1 V3p, also on microfilm- 1033939 item 16
    Other towns in the vicinity are McDermitt, Owyhee, Battle Mountain,
    Paradise Valley, Lovelock, and the original county seat, Unionville.

Nevada, Humboldt, Winnemucca - Church records
Church of Jesus Christ of Latter-day Saints. Winnemucca Ward (Nevada).
  Annual Genealogical Report, Form E, 1941-1948. Salt Lake City : Filmed
  by the Genealogical Society of Utah, 1951.
  Microfilm- 0014927
    Microfilm of original records in the LDS Church Archives, Salt Lake City.
    Winnemucca Ward was a local unit of the Reno and Humboldt Stakes.

Nevada, Humboldt, Winnemucca - Schools
Winnada, 1929 : volume 10. Salt Lake City : Filmed by the Genealogical
  Society of Utah, 1994.
  Microfilm- 1698063 item 12
    Microfilm of yearbook published: Winnemucca, Nevada : Associated
    Student body of the Humboldt County High School, 1929. [84] p.

CHAPTER NINE

Lander County

Lander County was created by an act of the legislature on 19 December 1862, from Humboldt and Churchill counties.

The county was named in honor of General Frederick W. Lander, who was in charge of the construction, by the United States Government, of a wagon road across Nevada. He later became a Brigadier General in the Union Army during the Civil War, dying at the age of forty at Paw Paw, Virginia, 2 March 1862, from wounds received in Battle.

CHURCHES

AUSTIN
Episcopal: St. George Episcopalian Church, East Shanks St., Austin, NV 89310
Latter-day Saints: Austin Latter-day Saints Church, Austin, NV 89310 Phone: 775 964-2336
Southern Baptist: Austin Baptist Church, PO Box 183, Austin, NV 89310 Phone: 775 964-2300
Kingston Village Baptist Church, Kingston Village, Austin, NV 89310 Phone: 775 964-2444
BATTLE MOUNTAIN
Churches of Christ: Battle Mountain Church of Christ, 477 S. Reese N. 25-9, PO Box 651, Battle Mountain, NV 89820 Phone: 775 635-9097
Battle Mountain United Methodist, 152 W. 2nd St. No.B, Battle Mountain, NV 89820 Phone: 775 635-2230
Latter-day Saints: Battle Mountain Ward Latter-day Saints, 785 W. Humboldt, Battle Mountain, NV 89820 Phone: 775 635-2628
Lutheran: Christs Mission, PO Box 48, Battle Mountain, NV 89820
Penecostal: Battle Mountain Assembly God, PO Box 336, Battle Mountain, NV 89820 Phone: 775 635-2465
Presbyterian: Grace Chapel Presbyterian Church, Battle Mountain, NV 89820
Southern Baptist: First Baptist Church, Weaver Ave. & E 7th, PO Box 543, Battle Mountain, NV 89820 Phone: 775 635-2055

COURTHOUSE

Lander County Courthouse
315 South Humboldt St., Battle Mountain, NV 89820
Phone: 775 635-5738
Land records: County Clerk
    Search service: $1.00 per year; copies $1.00 each, $3.00 for certification
Naturalization records: County Clerk
    Search service: see above
Probate records: County Clerk
    Search service: see above
Vital records: County Clerk
    Search service: see above

NEWSPAPERS

Newspapers	City	Library has
Austin Sun	Austin	Sep. 2, 1933 - June 23, 1934 (weekly - full run)
Battle Mountain Bugle	Battle Mountain	May 27, 1976 - date
Battle Mountain Herald & Central Nevadan	Battle Mountain	Dec. 19, 1907 - May 18, 1911
Battle Mountain Messenger	Battle Mountain	June 18 - September 17, 1881
Battle Mountain Messenger	Battle Mountain	Apr. 26 - Dec. 26, 1884
Battle Mountain Scout	Battle Mountain	Feb. 7, 1920 - Dec. 26, 1957 (weekly - full run)
Battle Mountain Scout of Central Nevada	Battle Mountain	July 16, 1913 - January 31, 1920
Battle Mountain Weekly Messenger	Battle Mountain	Sep. 24, 1881 - April 19, 1884
Betty O'Neal Concentrator	Betty O'Nela	June 21, 1924 (weekly - 1924-1924?)
Bullion District Miner	Tenabo	July 23, 1907
Central Nevadan	Battle Mountain	January 16, 1885 - Dec. 5, 1907 (weekly - full run)
Daily Morning Democrat	Austin	August 9, 1882 - July 8, 1883 (daily - full run)
Daily Reese River Reveille	Austin	May 24, 1864 - May 25, 1869
Kimberly News	Kimberly	February 17 - December 17, 1910
Lander Press Press	Battle Mountain	July 8, 1881 - Dec. 28, 1882 (weekly - full run)

Measure for Measure	Battle Mountain	March 6 - October 9, 1875 (weekly - 1873-1875)
Nevada Progressive	Battle Mountain	Dec. 31, 1924 - October 2, 1926
Nevada Progressive	Austin	Dec. 31, 1924 - Oct. 2, 1926 (weekly - full run)
People's Advocate	Austin	Dec. 3, 1890 - January 21, 1893
Reese River Reveille	Austin	May 16, 1863 - May 21, 1864
Reese River Reveille	Austin	May 29, 1869 - Dec. 18, 1926
Reese River Reveille	Austin	January 3, 1962 - date
Reese River Reveille & Nevada Progressive	Austin	Dec. 25, 1926 - June 23, 1934
Reese River Reveille & the Austin Sun	Austin	June 30, 1934 - Dec. 31, 1949
Skookum Times	Skookum	May 23 & June 27, 1908
Valley Times	Battle Mountain	January 16 - December 31, 1981

FAMILY HISTORY LIBRARY (Salt Lake City, Utah) HOLDINGS

All microfilmed and microfiched records (unless restricted) are available to rent worldwide at branch Family History Centers and selected larger public and private libraries and societies.

Nevada, Lander - Cemeteries

Parkin, Nona. *Lander County Records, 1886-1983.* Salt Lake City : Filmed by the Genealogical Society of Utah, 1997.

V. 1. Birth records/notices: Lander County records, 1886-1915; Cemetery census: Austin Cemetery and Austin IOOF Cemetery, Battle Mountain Cemetery; Death records/obituaries: Lander County records 1887-1917, Newspaper notices 1863-1924, Newspaper obituaries, Austin 1923-1983, Newspaper obituaries, Battle Mountain 1923-1983; Marriage records/notices: Lander County records 1863-1920, Newspaper notices 1871-1920; Pioneer families -- v. 2. Church records: Austin Catholic Parish records with index, Battle Mountain Catholic Church with index. Includes index.

Microfilm- 1598450 item 1-2   Vol. 1-2

Nevada, Lander - Census

Thompson, J. S. *Lander County, Nevada 1863 Census.* Salt Lake City : Filmed by the Genealogical Society of Utah, 1995.

Microfilm- 1598348 item 15

Contents: pt. 1. Everyname index giving age (when known) and town -- pt. 2. Alphabetical listing by surname in each town.

Nevada, Lander - Military records - World War, 1914-1918

Banks, Raymond H. *The Banks Compilation of Birth Data of Men with Links to Lander County, Nevada, who Were Born 1873-1900 : as Found in the Civilian Registration Cards.* L.D.S. microfilm series of World War I Selective Service draft registration cards, for their draft boards during 1917-1918.

979.3 A1 no. 53

About 98% of men present in America and born 1873-1900 provided draft card information in 1917 or 1918. Aliens were required to register. Persons already in the military did not register. Includes name, date of birth, ethnic group, birth location or other information, and county or city draft board in the state where registered.

Nevada, Lander - Vital records

Lander County (Nevada). Recorder. *Birth and Death Records, 1887-1963.* Salt Lake City : Filmed by the Genealogical Society of Utah, 1993.

Microfilm- 1888191 item 2	Births and deaths	1887-1915
Microfilm- 1888190 item 4-8	Births	1911-1960
	Deaths	1888-1953
Microfilm- 1888191 item 1	Deaths	1953-1963

Lander County (Nevada). Recorder. *Marriage Records, 1863-1963; Indexes 1863-1993.* Salt Lake City : Filmed by the Genealogical Society of Utah, 1993.

Microfilm- 1888190 item 1-3	Index, 1863-1993	
	Marriages, v. 1-2, 1863-1963	

Nevada, Lander, Austin - History

Lewis, Oscar. *The Town That Died Laughing : the story of Austin, Nevada, Rambunctious Early-day Mining Camp, and of its Renowned Newspaper, the Reese River Reveille.* Reno, Nev. ; University of Nevada Press Lewis, c1986.

979.333 H2

CHAPTER TEN

Lincoln County

Lincoln County was created from Nye County by a legislative act approved on 26 February 1866.

The county was named in honor of Abraham Lincoln.

CHURCHES

ALAMO
Assemblies of God: Trinity Assembly of God, PO Box 592, Alamo, NV 89001
    Phone: 775 725-3317
Independent Fundamentalist: Christian Bible Church, PO Box 313, Alamo,
    NV 89001 Phone: 775 725-3327
Latter-day Saints: Alamo Church of Latter-day Saints, Alamo, NV 89001
    Phone: 775 725-3361
CALIENTE
Latter-day Saints: Latter-day Saints Church, Caliente, NV 89008
    Phone: 775 726-3668
Methodist: Community United Methodist Church, PO Box 57, Caliente, NV
    89008 Phone: 775 877-2274
United Methodist Church, PO Box 563, Caliente, NV 89008
Protestant: Caliente Christian Center, PO Box 452, Caliente, NV 89008
Roman Catholic: Holy Child Catholic Church, PO Box 247, Caliente, NV
    89008 Phone: 775 726-3669
PANACA
Protestant: Church of Jesus Christ, Panaca, NV 89042   Phone: 775 728-4426
PIOCHE
Episcopal: Christ Episcopalian Church, PO Box 351, Pioche, NV 89043
    Phone: 775 962-5835
Latter-day Saints: Church of Jesus Christ Latter-day Saints, 1 Main St.,
    Pioche, NV 89043 Phone: 775 962-5469
Protestant: Echoes of Faith, Rose Valley, Pioche, NV 89043
Southern Baptist: Beran Baptist Church, PO Box 314, Pioche, NV 89043
    Phone: 775 962-5886
Unclassified: Channel of Light Truth Centers, PO Box 186, Pioche, NV 89043

COURTHOUSE

Lincoln County Courthouse
P.O. Box 90, Pioche, NV 89043-0090
Phone: 775 962-5495 County Recorder/Auditor, P. O. Box 218; 775 962-5390
County Clerk
Land records: County Recorder/Auditor
Naturalization records: County Clerk
Probate records: County Clerk
  Probate search service: $1.00 per name, per year; costs $1.00 per page
Vital records: County Clerk

FUNERAL HOMES

Caliente

Wiscombe Funeral Home
730 Front St., Caliente, NV 89008
Phone: 775 726-3779

LIBRARIES

Lincoln County Library
P. O. Box 330, Pioche, NV 89043
Phone: 775 962-5244   Fax: 775 962-5244   E-mail: psdraper@clan.lib.nv.us
Hours: Monday, Wednesday, Friday: 12:00 noon to 4:00 p.m.
  Tuesday: 1:00 p.m. to 5:00 p.m.
Alamo Branch, P. O. Box 239, Alamo, NV 89001; Phone 775 725-3343
  Fax 775 725-3343
  E-mail: cstewart@clan.lib.nv.us
  Hours: Monday through Thursday: 11:00 a.m. to 4:00 p.m.
Caliente Branch, P. O. Box 306, Caliente, NV 89007; Phone 775 726-3104;
Fax 775 726-3104
  E-mail: crwilcox@clan.lib.nv.us
  Hours: Monday & Thursday: 1:00 p.m. to 5:00 p.m., Tuesday, Wednesday,
  Friday: 10:00 a.m. to 2:00 p.m.

NEWSPAPERS

Newspapers	City	UNLV Library has
Caliente Express	Caliente	Mar. 2, 1905 - May 31, 1906 (weekly- full run)

Caliente Herald	Caliente	March 22, 1928 - May 30, 1968 (weekly- full run)
Cliente Lode- Express	Caliente	June 30, 1906 - Dec. 26, 1908 (weekly- full run)
Caliente News	Caliente	October 21, 1920 - April 2, 1925 (weekly- full run)
Daily Journal	Pioche	April 6, 1875 - April 30, 1876
De La Mar Roaster	Delamar	March 18, 1900
De Lamar Lode	Delamar	July 26, 1898 - June 19, 1906 (varies - full run)
Ely Record (Pioche)	Pioche	September 1-15, 1872 (varies- 1870-1872)
Ferguson Lode	Delamar	Sep. 19, 1892 - Feb. 27, 1893 (weekly- full run)
Lincoln County Independent	Pioche	August 18, 1938 - Oct, 30, 1941 (weekly- full run)
Lincoln County Record	Pioche	July 6, 1900 - December 29, 1905 (weekly- full run)
Lincoln County Record	Pioche	July 2, 1925 - February 18, 1932 (weekly- full run)
Lincoln County Record	Pioche	June 6, 1968 - date
Local Messenger	Pioche	June 7, 1898 - January 5, 1901
Lode	Pioche	March 11, 1893 - July 12, 1898
Pioche Daily Record	Pioche	Sep. 27, 1872 - Dec. 31, 1876 (weekly- full run)
Pioche People's Press	Pioche	about 1944? One undated issue
Pioche Record	Pioche	December 26, 1908 - June 27, 1925
Pioche Record (1932)	Pioche	February 25, 1932 - May 30, 1968
Pioche Weekly Record	Pioche	January 6, 1877 - June 29, 1900

(Newspaper Indexes- at Nevada Museum and Historical Society *Pioche Weekly Record*, 1872-1904)

Pioche Weekly Record	Pioche	January 5, 1906 - Dec. 19, 1908
Prospector	Caliente	March 20, 1909 - Feb. 1, 1913 (weekly- full run)

FAMILY HISTORY LIBRARY (Salt Lake City, Utah) HOLDINGS

All microfilmed and microfiched records (unless restricted) are available to rent worldwide at branch Family History Centers and selected larger public and private libraries and societies.

Nevada, Lincoln - Cemeteries

Bonnett, Elaine. *Clover Valley, Nevada Cemetery.*
  979.3 A1 no.39, also on microfilm- 1750733 item 26
  Clover Valley Cemetery is about 7 1/2 miles from Panaca, Nevada

Vance, Paul. *Cemetery list of Boullionville, Caliente, and Panaca, Nevada.* Eagle Scout service project. Salt Lake City : Filmed by the Genealogical Society of Utah, 1986.
  Microfilm- 1307628 item 6
  Boullionville, or Bullionville no longer exists as a locality. It was located in Lincoln County.

Nevada, Lincoln - Church records

Church of Jesus Christ of Latter-day Saints. St. George Stake (Utah). *Annual Genealogical Report, Form E, 1907.* Salt Lake City : Filmed by the Genealogical Society of Utah, 1956.
  Saint George Stake records appear on pp. 1009-1184. Saint George Stake included the Alamo, Bunkerville, Enterprise, Gunlock, Hurricane, La Verkin, Leeds, Lund, Mesquite, Overton, Panaca, Pinto, Pine Valley, Preston, Rockville, Santa Clara, St. George East, St. George West, Springdale, Toquerville, Virgin, and Washington Wards.
  Microfilm- 0774320 item 13   Form E   1907

Nevada, Lincoln - Directories

Lincoln County (Nevada) Telephone Directory, August 1954 : including Alamo, Bristol Mine, Caliente, Caselton, Eagle Valley, Jackrabbit, Panaca, Pioche, Prince and Rose Valley.
  Microfilm- 1320969 item 12

Nevada, Lincoln - History

Koyen, Eva Hyde. *Treasures of Tempiute.* Sparks, Nev. : Western Printing & Publishing, c1967.
  979.314 H2k

Nevada, Lincoln - Military records - World War, 1914-1918

Banks, Raymond H. *The Banks Compilation of Birth Data of Men with Links to Lincoln County, Nevada, who Were Born 1873-1900 : as Found in the Civilian Registration Cards.* L. D.S. microfilm series of World War I Selective Service draft registration cards. Salt Lake City: R.H. Banks, c1996.
979.3 A1 no. 54

An alphabetical listing by surname of men who completed civilian registration cards for their draft boards during 1917-1918. About 98% of men present in America and born 1873-1900 provided draft card information in 1917 or 1918. Aliens were required to register. Persons already in the military did not register. Includes name, date of birth, ethnic group, birth location or other information, and county or city draft board in the state where registered.

Nevada, Lincoln - Vital records

Lincoln County (Nevada). County Clerk. *Marriage Licenses and Applications for License to Marry, 1871-1951.* Salt Lake City : Filmed by the Genealogical Society of Utah, 1993.

Microfilm- 1902885

Index to licenses	3 Apr 1874- 6 Mar 1993
License stubs, v. 1	11 Mar 1871-24 Mar 1873
Applications, v. 2	26 May 1873-23 Dec 1887
Application list, v. 3	1888-1898
Licenses, v. 4-6	16 Apr 1898-24 Jun 1919
Applications, v. 7-17	26 Jan 1919- 1 Jun 1936

Microfilm- 1902886

Applications, v. 18-34	6 Jun 1936- 9 Sep 1951

Nevada, Lincoln - Vital records

Parkin, Nona. *Lincoln County Records.* Salt Lake City : Filmed by the Genealogical Society of Utah, 1997.

v. 1. Birth notices: Newspaper notices 1906-1912; Cemetery census: Caliente, Logandale, Panaca, Pioche; Death records/obituaries Newspaper notices 1871-1909, Panaca 1928-1978, Pioche 1922-1974, Pioche Daily Record 1906-1926; Jurors called for duty: Lincoln County 1876 & 1893; Marriage records/notices: Lincoln County records 1872-1915, Newspaper notices 1883-1900; Newspaper "scats" — v. 2. Pioneer families; Registered voters: Buillionville 1876, Small precincts 1876 & 1890, Panaca 1890, Pioche 1876, 1886, 1888, 1890 & 1892; Tax assessment records: Lincoln County 1886, 1887, 1889, 1892; Pioche 1886, 1889-1893; Church records: Moapa Epiphany Mission 1930 (became St. Matthew's in 1931).

Microfilm- 1598462 item 2-3   Vol. 1-2

Nevada, Lincoln, Alamo - Church records
Church of Jesus Christ of Latter-day Saints. Alamo Ward (Nevada). *Record of Members 1906-1941; Annual Genealogical Report, Form E, 1907-1948.*
Salt Lake City : Filmed by the Genealogical Society of Utah, 1951.
  Microfilm of originals in the LDS Church Archives, Salt Lake City. The Form E includes records pertaining to the St. George (Utah) and Moapa (Nevada) Stakes.
  Microfilm- 0014893 item 1-2   Record of members 1906-1941
  Microfilm- 0014893 item 3   Form E   1907-1948
  Photocopies not permitted except for direct line descendants. Remove all other data from photocopy.

Nevada, Lincoln, Caliente - Church records
Church of Jesus Christ of Latter-day Saints. Caliente Ward (Nevada). *Record of Members 1930-1941; annual Genealogical Report, Form E, 1931- 1948.*
Salt Lake City : Filmed by the Genealogical Society of Utah, 1951.
  Microfilm- 0014896 item 1   Record of members 1930-1941
  Microfilm- 0014896 item 2   Form E   1931-1948
  Microfilm of original records in the LDS Church Archives, Salt Lake City.
  Photocopies not permitted except for direct line descendants. Remove all other data from photocopy.

Nevada, Lincoln, Caliente - Vital records
Marriage Records Completed by Evan H. Edwards, Justice of the Peace, Caliente, Lincoln County, Nevada : 1935-1948. [Nevada : s. n.], 1982.
Microfilm- 1292743
  Microreproduction of original records in Caliente, Lincoln County, Nevada.

Nevada, Lincoln, Panaca - Church records
Church of Jesus Christ of Latter-day Saints. Panaca Ward (Nevada). *Record of Members, 1869-1941; Annual Genealogical Report, Form E, 1907-1948.*
Salt Lake City : Filmed by the Genealogical Society of Utah, 1951.
  Microfilm of original records in the LDS Church Archives, Salt Lake City.
  The Form E includes reports from the St. George and Moapa Stakes.
  Microfilm- 0014915   Form E   1907-1948
  Microfilm- 0014914   Record of members 1869-1941
  Microfilm- 0164612 item 2   Record of members 1884

Nevada, Lincoln, Panaca - History
A Century in Meadow Valley, 1864-1964. Compiled and edited by Panaca
Centennial Book Committee ; Ruth Lee and Sylvia Wadsworth,
co-chairmen. [S.l. : s.n.], c1966 ([Salt Lake City] : Deseret News Press).
979.314/P1 H2c
Includes biographies and family histories.

Nevada, Lincoln, Pioche - Church records
Church of Jesus Christ of Latter-day Saints. Pioche Ward (Nevada). *Record of
Members, 1929-1941; Annual*
Genealogical Report, Form E, 1929- 1948. Salt Lake City : Filmed by the
Genealogical Society of Utah, 1951.
Microfilm of original records in the LDS Church Archives, Salt Lake City.
Pioche Ward, created in
1936, was formerly known as Pioche Branch.
Microfilm- 0014916 item 1-2   Record of members 1929-1941
Microfilm- 0014916 item 3   Form E   1929-1948

CHAPTER ELEVEN

Lyon County

Lyon County was one of the original counties, created by an act approved 25 November 1861. The county was named in honor of General Nathaniel Lyon, who died in the battle of Willson's Creek, near Springfield, Missouri.

CEMETERIES

Northern Nevada Veterans Memorial Cemetery
14 Veterans Way, Fernley, NV 89408
Mailing address: P. O. Box 1919, Reno, NV 89520-1919
Phone: 775 486-5920   Fax: 775 486-5923
Years of operation: 1990-present
Affiliations: State Veteran cemetery
Record: housed at Southern Nevada Veterans Memorial Cemetery
1900 Buchanan Blvd., Boulder City, NV 89005

CHURCHES

DAYTON
Southern Baptist: Calvary Baptist Church, Hwy 50 & Flowery Ave.,
   PO Box 398, Dayton, NV 89403 Phone: 775 246-0808
FERNLEY
Holiness: Free Methodist Church, PO Box 709, Fernley, NV 89408
   Phone: 775 575-4424
Independent: Faith Bible Church, 875 Freemont St., Fernley, NV 89408
   Phone: 775 575-2834
Latter-day Saints: Church of Jesus Christ of Latter-day Saints, Hwy 95
   Alternate, Fernley, NV 89408 Phone: 775 575-4474
Protestant: Living Faith Christian, PO 1215, Fernley, NV 89408
   Phone: 775 575-2105
Roman Catholic: St. Robert Bellamine Catholic Church, PO Box 473,
   Fernley, NV 89408
Southern Baptist: Fernley First Baptist Church, PO Box 617, Fernley, NV
   89408 Phone: 775 575-4565
SMITH
Methodist: Smith Valley United Methodist, 44 Rivers Rd., Smith, NV 89430

Roman Catholic: St. John's Catholic Church, 158 Grant View Dr., Smith, NV 89430 Phone: 775 465-2220
WELLINGTON
Baptist: First Baptist Church, 1441 Agate Rd., Wellington, NV 89444 Phone: 775 266-3309
Southern Baptist: Topaz First Baptist Church, 1141 Agate Rd., Wellington, NV 89444 Phone: 775 266-3476
YERINGTON
Adventist: Seventh Day Adventist Church, 71 Mason Rd., Yerington, NV 89447 Phone: 775 463-3908
Baptist: First Baptist Church, 307 Broadway St., Yerington, NV 89447 Phone 775 463-3715
Valley Baptist Church, 404 N. Oregon St., Yerington, NV 89447 Phone: 775 463-5319
Churches of Christ: Church of Christ, 14 Willhoyt Ln., Yerington, NV 89447 Phone: 775 463-4382
Episcopal: St. Alban Episcopalian Church, 12 N. West St., Yerington, NV 89447
St. Alban Episcopalian Church, PO Box 207, Yerington, NV 89447 Phone: 775 463-2182
Holiness: Church of the Nazarene, 328 N. West St., Yerington, NV 89447 Phone: 775 463-3279
Independent Fundamentalist: Trinity Evangelical Free Church, PO Box 720, Yerington, NV Phone: 775 463-2330
Latter-day Saints: Church of Jesus Christ of Latter-day Saints, 600 N. Oregon St., Yerington, NV Phone: 775 463-3600
Lutheran: Faith Lutheran Church, PO Box 861, Yerington, NV 89447 Phone: 775 463-4567
Protestant: Church at Yerington, 304 Charlotte Ave., Yerlington, NV 89447
Roman Catholic: Holy Family Catholic Church, 301 Virginia St., PO Box B. Yerlington, NV 89447 Phone: 775 463-2882

COURTHOUSE

Lyon County Courthouse
31 South Main St., Yerington, NV 89447-0816
Phone: 775 463-3341

FUNERAL HOMES

Freitas Funeral Home
14 Van Ness Street, Yerington, NV 89447
Phone: 775 463-2911

LIBRARIES

Lyon County Library
20 Nevin Way, Yerington, NV 89447
Phone: 775 463-6645   Fax: 775 463-6500
E-mail: cdfreer@clan.lib.nv.us
Hours: Monday, Wednesday, Friday: 9:00 a.m. to 6:00 p.m., Tuesday &
Thursday: 9:00 a.m. to 9:00 p.m., Saturday: 9:00 a.m. to 6:00 p.m.
Dayton Valley Branch Library, P.O. Box 1729, 321 "Old" Dayton Valley
Road, Dayton, NV 89403
Phone: 775 246-6212
Hours: Monday & Tuesday: 11:00 a.m. to 6:30 p.m., Wednesday: 11:00 a.m. to
7:00 p.m., Sunday: 12:00 noon to 5:00
Fernley Branch Library, P.O. Box 647, Lyon County Complex, 575 Silver
Lace Blvd, Fernley, NV 89408 Phone: 775 575-3366;
E-mail: plzdunic@clan.lib.nv.us
Hours: Monday, Wednesday, Friday: 10:00 a.m. to 6:00 p.m., Tuesday: 10:00
a.m. to 9:00 p.m., Saturday: 11:00 a.m. to 4:00 p.m.
Ida Compston Branch Library, P.O. Box 156, 2001 Hwy 2008, Wellington,
NV 89444
Phone: 775 465-2369
Hours: Wednesday & Thursday: 10:00 a.m. to 6:00 p.m., Friday: 10:00 a.m. to
4:30 p.m.
Silver Springs Branch Library, 3905 Hwy. 50 West, Silver Springs, NV
89429; Phone: 775 577-5015
E-mail: cmmack@clan.lib.nv.us
Hours: Wednesday: 2:00 p.m. to 7:00 p.m., Thursday & Friday: 10:00 a.m. to
7:00 p.m., Saturday: 11:00 a.m. to 4:00

NEWSPAPERS

Newspapers	City	UNLV Library has
Esmeralda Sun	Pine Grove	May 18, 1872
Fernley Enterprise	Fernley	December 6, 1919 & Feb. 7, 1920
Independent	Sutro	April 21, 1879 - Nov. 29, 1880
Lyon County Monitor	Yerington	June 8, 1900 - March 7, 1902 (weekly - full run)
Lyon County Times	Silver City	July 4, 1874 - December 11, 1880 (varies - full run)
Lyon County Times	Dayton	Dec. 18, 1880 - July 27, 1901 (weekly - full run)

Lyon County Times	Yerington	August 10, 1901 - Sep. 14, 1907 (weekly - full run)
Lyon County Wasp	Yerington	Sep. 3, 1912 - Feb. 27, 1913 (weekly - full run)
Mason Valley News	Mason	Mar. 19, 1909 - Nov. 28, 1914 (weekly - full run)
Mason Valley News	Yerington	December 5, 1914 - date
Mason Valley Tidings	Greenfield	March 25, 1893 - March 29, 1894
Mason Valley Tidings	Yerington	April 5 - November 29, 1894
News Reporter	Dayton	March 4, 1886 - June 30, 1887
Pick and Shovel	Pine Grove	about July 1872, one undated issue
Pine Grove and Rockland Star	Rockland	one undated issue
Pine Grove Burlesque	Pine Grove	May 4, 1872
Pine Grove Chronicle	Pine Grove	June 15, 1872
Pine Grove Observer	Pine Grove	one undated issue
Silver City Reporter	Silver City	October 5 - Dec. 5, 1876 (twice weekly - full run)
Sutro Independent	Sutro	Sep. 25, 1875 - Mar. 1, 1879 (weekly - 1875-1880)
Yerington Rustler	Yerington	Feb. 28, 1895 - May 25, 1900 (weekly - full run)
Yerington Times	Yerington	Sep. 21, 1907 - Dec. 23, 1931 (weekly - 1907-1932)

FAMILY HISTORY LIBRARY (Salt Lake City, Utah) HOLDINGS

All microfilmed and microfiched records (unless restricted) are available to rent worldwide at branch Family History Centers and selected larger public and private libraries and societies.

Nevada, Lyon - Military records
Draft and Enlistment Lists Published in the Yerington Times : Lyon County, 1917-1918.
979.3 A1 no. 3, also on microfilm- 0962211 item 2

Nevada, Lyon - Military records - World War, 1914-1918
Banks, Raymond H. *The Banks Compilation of Birth Data of Men with Links to Lyon County, Nevada, Who Were Born 1873-1900 : as Found in the Civilian Registration Cards.* L.D.S. microfilm series of World War I Selective Service draft registration cards. Salt Lake City : R.H. Banks, c1996.
979.3 A1 no. 55
   An alphabetical listing by surname of men who completed civilian

registration cards for their draft boards during 1917-1918. About 98% of men present in America and born 1873-1900 provided draft card information in 1917 or 1918. Aliens were required to register. Persons already in the military did not register. Includes name, date of birth, ethnic group, birth location or other information, and county or city draft board in the state where registered.

Nevada, Lyon - Newspapers
Parkin, Nona. *Lyon County Records*. Salt Lake City : Filmed by the Genealogical Society of Utah, 1996.
V. 1. Birth records/notices: Newspaper notices 1911-1918; Cemetery census: Dayton Cemetery with index, Forest Grove and Fort Churchill, Hillcrest, McLeod and Missouri Flat, Silver City, Small cemeteries, Yerington, St. Joseph's Catholic (near Yerington) -- v. 2. Death records/obituaries: Newspaper notices 1863-1914, Newspaper notices Hillcrest 1971-1973 and McLeod 1890-1912, Newspaper obituaries Dayton and surrounding area 1912-1919, Newspaper obituaries 1922-1983, Newspaper obituaries Silver City and Silver Springs 1930-1983 -- v. 3. Divorces; Funeral home records: Freitas funeral records with index; Marriage records/notices: Lyon County records 1862-1919, Newspaper notices 1871-1919; Pioneer families; Church records. Includes some indexing.
Microfilm- 1598460 item 5   Vol. 1
Microfilm- 1598461 item 1-2 Vol. 2-3

Nevada, Lyon - Vital records
Parkin, Nona. *Miscellaneous Records from Lyon County, Nevada*. Salt Lake City : Filmed by the Genealogical Society of Utah, 1971.
Microfilm- 0869278 item 5
Dayton Cemetery (Nevada) -- Silver City Cemetery (Nevada) -- Draft and enlistment lists, 1917-1918 (Lyon County, Nevada) -- Voting registration, 1918 (Lyon County, Nevada) -- Births, marriages and deaths, 1910-1919 taken from the Yerington Times newspaper.

Parkin, Nona. *Death Records, March, 1909-March, 1919 : From the Yerington Times and Births, Marriages, divorces and Deaths from Yerington Times and Lyon County*.
979.358 V2p

Lyon County (Nevada). Recorder. *Birth and Death Records, 1887-1968*. Salt Lake City : Filmed by the Genealogical Society of Utah, 1993.
Includes index and indexes at beginning of volumes.
Microfilm- 1902307

Index to v. A, births and deaths,	1887-1911
Births, and deaths, v. A	1887-1956
Births, v. 1 B	3 July 1911-11 Mar 1917
Birth certificates	1908-1911
Births, v. 2 B-3 B	13 Apr 1911-11 Aug 1952
Death certificates	1906-1911
Microfilm- 1902308 item 1-3	
Deaths, v. 1 D-3 D	20 Jul 1911-26 Mar 1968

Lyon County (Nevada). County Clerk. *Marriage Records, 1861-1960.* Salt
Lake City : Filmed by the Genealogical Society of Utah, 1993.
Includes index and indexes at beginning of volumes.

Microfilm- 1902308 item 4-5	
Index, certificates, v. A	1862-1887
Certificates, v. A	1862-1887
Microfilm- 1902309 item 11-13	
Certificates, v. B-C	17 Jan 1888-19 Sep 1905
Certificate index, v. D	4 Jan 1922-20 Apr 1954
Microfilm- 1902310	
Certificates, v. D	15 Dec 1921-23 Sep 1960
Microfilm- 1902308 item 6-10	
Affidavit of application for marriage license	
Vol. 1-5	20 Mar 1869-29 Apr 1909
Microfilm- 1902309 item 1-3	
Vol. 6-8	31 Mar 1909- 3 Jan 1922
Fiche- 6334617	
Vol. 9 (2 fiches)	29 May 1922-16 Jun 1925
Microfilm- 1902309 item 4-10	
Vol. 10-16	26 Aug 1926-23 Apr 1952

Nevada, Lyon - Voting registers
Parkin, Nona. *Official List of Primary Voting Registration in Lyon County,
Nevada : Taken From the Yerington Times, Yerington, Nevada, 1918.*
979.3 A1 no.5, also on microfilm- 0962209 item 15

Nevada, Lyon, Fort Churchill - Cemeteries
Larsen, Annie D. *Cemetery inscriptions, Old Fort Churchill, Nevada.* Salt Lake
City : Filmed by the Genealogical Society of Utah, 1974.
Microfilm- 0962289 item 8

Nevada, Lyon, Fort Churchill - History

Paterson, Verna S. *Fort Churchill Once Active Center of Life in Nevada but Now is All Desolation.* Salt Lake City : Filmed by the Genealogical Society of Utah, 1990.

Microfilm- 1320996 item 23

Nevada, Lyon, Dayton - Cemeteries

Parkin, Nona. *Miscellaneous Records From Lyon County, Nevada.* Salt Lake City : Filmed by the Genealogical Society of Utah, 1971.

Microfilm- 0869278 item 5

    Dayton Cemetery (Nevada) -- Silver City Cemetery (Nevada) -- Draft and enlistment lists, 1917-1918 (Lyon County, Nevada) --Voting registration, 1918 (Lyon County, Nevada) -- Births, marriages and deaths, 1910-1919 taken from the Yerington Times newspaper.

CHAPTER TWELVE

Mineral County

Mineral County was formed on 10 February 1911 out of the northern portion of Esmeralda County.

It was named for the minerals found in the county.

CHURCHES

MINA
Baptist: Mina Baptist Church, PO Box 276, Mina, NV 89422
  Phone: 775 573-2523
SCHURZ
Methodist: Schurz United Methodist Church, General Delivery, churz, NV
  89427 Phone: 775 463-2174
Southern Baptist: Walker River Baptist Church, PO Box 250, Schurz, NV
  89427 Phone: 775 773-2588
HAWTHORNE
Adventist: Jehovah's Witnesses, PO Box 1512, Hawthorne, NV 89415
  Phone: 775 945-5200
Assemblies of God: First Assembly of God, Fourth and J Streets,
  PO Box 1507. Hawthorne, NV 89415 Phone: 775 945-2775
Baptist: Bethel Baptist Church, PO Box 57, Hawthorne, NV 89415
  Phone: 775 945-3772
First Regular Baptist Church, 8th & C Sts., Hawthorne, NV 89415
  Phone: 775 945-3556
Greater St. Paul Missionary Baptist, PO Box 151, Hawthorne, NV 89415
  Phone: 775 945-3781
Churches of Christ: Church of Christ, PO Box 565, Hawthorne, NV 89415
  Phone: 775 945-5174
Episcopal: St. Philip Desert Episcopalian, PO Box 117, Hawthorne, NV 89415
  Phone: 775 945-2510
Holiness: Church of the Nazarene, PO Box 837, Hawthorne, NV 89415
  Phone: 945-5511
Latter-day Saints: Church of Jesus Christ of Latter-day Saints, 207 A St.,
  Hawthorne, NV 89415 Phone: 775 945-2847

Lutheran: Bethany Lutheran Church, PO Box 1207, Hawthorne, NV 89415
Phone: 775 945-2332
Pentecostal: Trinity Temple Church of God, 110 W. 10[th,] Hawthorne, NV
89415 Phone: 775 945-5875
Presbyterian: Community Presbyterian Church, PO Box 1096, Hawthorne,
NV 89415 Phone: 775 945-3545
Roman Catholic: Our lady of Perpetual Help Church, 8th & A St., Hawthorne,
NV 89415 Phone: 775 945-2020
Seventh Day Adventist: Hawthorne Seventh Day Adventist Church,
PO Box 1666, Hawthorne, NV 89415 Phone: 775 945-2055
Southern Baptist: Walker Lake Baptist Church, 330 Golden Willow Dr.,
Hawthorne, NV 89415   Phone: 775 945-2424
Unclassified: Post Chapel Hawthorne Army Ammunition, Hawthorne, NV
89415

COURTHOUSE

Mineral County Courthouse
P.O. Box 1450, Hawthorne, NV 89415-1450
Phone: 775 945-2446
Land records: $1.00 per page, County Clerk
Naturalization records: to 23 August 1957
Probate records: County Clerk
   Probate search service: $1.00 per name, per year; copies $1.00 per page
Vital records: Marriages

FUNERAL HOMES

Hawthorne Funeral Home
10th & G Streets, Hawthorne, NV 89451
Phone: 775 945-2047

LIBRARIES

Mineral County Public Library
First & A Street, P.O. Box 1390, Hawthorne, NV 89415
Phone: 775 945-2778   Fax: 775 945-0703   E-mail: adellamo@clan.lib.nv.us
Founded: 1955
Hours: Monday through Thursday: 10:00 a.m. to 9:00 p.m., Friday: 10:00 a.m.
   to 6:00 p.m., Saturday: 12:00 noon to 3:30 p.m.
Summer Hours: Monday: 10:00 a.m. to 9:00 p.m., Tuesday through Friday:
   10:00 a.m. to 6:00 p.m., Saturday: 12:00 to 3:30
Special Collections: State of Nevada History Collection

Mina-Luning Community, P.O. Box 143, Mina, NV 89422;
Phone: 775 573-2505
Hours: Monday & Wednesday: 1:00 p.m. to 5:00 p.m., Tuesday & Thursday:
4:00 p.m. to 8:00 p.m., Friday: 1:00 p.m. to 4:00 p.m.

NEWSPAPERS

Newspapers	City	UNLV Library has
Agal Dicutta Yaduan	Schurz	Sep. 8, 1975 - Jun. 24, 1977 (bimonthly - full run)
Aurora Borealis	Aurora	December 23, 1905 (weekly - 1905-1906?)
Aurora Daily Times	Aurora	November 27 - Dec. 12, 1863
Bovard Booster	Bovard	April 28, 1908
Cholordie Belt	Candelaria	Dec. 10, 1890 - Dec. 24, 1892 (weekly - full run)
Dutch Creek News	Dutch Creek	February 1 - May 1, 1907
Esmeralda Daily Union	Aurora	March 23 - November 12, 1864 (daily - full run)
Esmeralda Herald	Hawthorne	August 18, 1883 - April 19, 1884 (weekly - full run)
Esmeralda News	Hawthorne	January 1, 1887 - May 18, 1889 (weekly - full run)
Esmeralda Star	Aurora	May 17 & September 20, 1862; December 30, 1863
Esmeralda Union	Aurora	Nov. 14, 1864 - Mar. 15, 1865 (varies- 1864-1868)
Granite Times	Granite	April 17 & May 1, 1908
Hawthorne - Lucky Boy News	Hawthorne	April 25, 1909
Hawthorne- Lucky Boy News	Hawthorne	May 12 - October 12, 1909 (weekly - full run)
Hawthorne News	Hawthorne	Jan. 14, 1931 - June 14, 1935 (weekly - 1928-1935)
Inter-Tribal Council of Nevada Newsletter	Schurz	March - May 1964
Luckyboy Mining Record	Luckyboy	June 10 - September 17, 1909
Mineral County Democrat	Hawthorne	January 12 - 26, 1961
Mineral County Forum	Hawthorne	February 9 - September 6, 1961 (weekly - full run)
Mineral County Independent	Hawthorne	March 1, 1933 - July 10, 1935 (weekly - full run)

Mineral County Independent &		
Hawthorne News	Hawthorne	July 24, 1935 - May 6, 1987
Mineral County Independent		
News	Hawthorne	May 13, 1987 - date
Oasis	Hawthorne	September 8, 1881
Rawhide Daily Press	Rawhide	February 1 - 20, 1908
Rawhide News	Rawhide	March 7 & August 1, 1908
Rawhide Press- Times	Rawhide	Feb. 28, 1908 - Jan. 20, 1911 (varies - full run)
Rawhide Rustler	Rawhide	January 16, 1908 - April 17, 1909
Times of Mineral County	Hawthorne	September 14, 1978 - December 29, 1981
Walker Lake Bulletin	Hawthorne	Mar. 14, 1883 - Oct. 25, 1924 (weekly - 1883-1926)
Western Nevada Miner	Mina	Sept. 19, 1908 - Oct. 27, 1924
Western Nevada Miner &		
Mineral County News	Mina	November 2, 1928 - Dec. 12, 1930

FAMILY HISTORY LIBRARY (Salt Lake City, Utah) HOLDINGS

All microfilmed and microfiched records (unless restricted) are available to rent worldwide at branch Family History Centers and selected larger public and private libraries and societies.

Nevada, Mineral - Cemeteries

Parkin, Nona. *Mineral County Records*. Salt Lake City : Filmed by the Genealogical Society of Utah, 1997.
> v. 1. Birth records/notices: Newspaper notices 1876-1909; Cemetery census: Aurora, Candelaria and Hawthorne; City directories: Rawhide-Fallon 1908-1909; Death records/obituaries: Newspaper notices 1882-1916; Newspaper obituaries: Mineral County Independent News 1933-1963 with index; Newspaper obituaries miscellaneous 1890-1962; Newspaper obituaries, Rawhide and Schurz 1922-1973; Newspaper obituaries 1922-1983 -- v. 2. Marriage records/notices: Mineral County records 1911-1944; Pioneer families; Church records: St. Phillip's Episcopal Church.
> Microfilm- 1598449 item 5-6   Vol. 1-2

Nevada, Mineral - Military records - World War, 1914-1918

Banks, Raymond H. *The Banks Compilation of Birth Data of Men with Links to Mineral County, Nevada, who Were Born 1873-1900 : as Found in the Civilian Registration Cards*. L.D.S. microfilm series of World War I Selective Service draft registration cards. Salt Lake City : R.H. Banks,

c1996.
979.3 A1 no.56
An alphabetical listing by surname of men who completed civilian registration cards for their draft boards during 1917-1918. About 98% of men present in America and born 1873-1900 provided draft card information in 1917 or 1918. Aliens were required to register. Persons already in the military did not register. Includes name, date of birth, ethnic group, birth place or other information, and county or city draft board in the state where registered.

Nevada, Mineral - Vital records

Mineral County (Nevada). County Clerk. *Marriage License Applications, 1911-1952.* Salt Lake City : Filmed by the Genealogical Society of Utah, 1993.
Includes indexes at beginning of volumes.
Microfilm- 1902325
    License with app. v.1   10 Jun 1911-26 Jun 1919
    Applications, v. 2-6   16 Aug 1919-12 Jun 1948
Microfilm- 1902326
    Applications, v. 7   16 Jun 1948- 8 Nov 1952

Mineral County (Nevada). Recorder. *Marriage Records, 1911-1958.* Salt Lake City : Filmed by the Genealogical Society of Utah, 1993.
Includes indexes at beginning of volumes.
Microfilm- 1902324   Vol. 1-2   11 Jun 1911- 7 Aug 1958

Nevada, Mineral - Vital records - Indexes

Anderson, Mary. *Index to Mineral County, Nevada, Marriage Records.*
979.351 V25a

Nevada, Mineral, Hawthorne - Cemeteries

Cemetery and Death Records, Hawthorne, Mineral County, Nevada.
979.351/H1 V3h, also on microfilm- 0874352 item 3

Nevada, Mineral, Hawthorne - Church records

Church of Jesus Christ of Latter-day Saints. Hawthorne Ward (Nevada).
Annual Genealogical Report, Form E, 1941-1948. Salt Lake City : Filmed by the Genealogical Society of Utah, 1951.
Microfilm of original records in the LDS Church Archives, Salt Lake City.
Microfilm- 0014903   Form E   1941-1948

CHAPTER THIRTEEN

Nye County

Nye County was organized 16 February 1864 from Esmeralda County.

Nye County is named in honor of Governor J. W. Nye.

CHURCHES

AMARGOSA VALLEY
Churches of Christ: Amargosa Valley Church of Christ, RR Box 546-C, Amargosa Valley, NV 89020 Phone: 775 372-5432
Protestant: Church of Amargosa, St Rte 15 Nox 495R, Amargosa, NV 89020
BEATTY
Baptist: Community Church, PO Box 429, Beatty, NV 89003
Phone: 775 553-2481
Episcopal: Good Shepard Episcopalian Church, PO Box 338, Beatty, NV 89003
Latter-day Saints: Church of Jesus Christ Latter-day Saints, General Delivery, Beatty, NV 89003 Phone: 775 553-2051
Protestant: Beatty Community Church, General Delivery, Beatty, NV 89003
Phone: 775 553-2088
GABBS
Latter-day Saints: Gabbs Church of Latter-day Saints, General Delivery, Gabbs, NV 89409 Phone: 775 285-2653
Pentecostal: Gabbs Assembly of God, PO Box 85, Gabbs, NV 89409
Phone: 775 285-2653
Roman Catholic: St. Michaels Catholic Church, PO Box 146, Gabbs, NV 89409 Phone: 775 972-7462
PAHRUMP
Assemblies of God: Trinity Assembly of God, PO Box 1374, Pahrump, NV 89041 Phone: 775 727-4514
Churches of Christ: Amargosa Valley Church of Christ, PO Box 1087, Pahrump, NV 89041
Church of Christ, PO Box 374, Pahrump, NV 89041
Church of Christ, Hwy 52 & Lola Ln., PO Box 74, Pahrump, NV 89041
Pahrump Church of Christ, Boling Av., Pahrump, NV 89041
Phone: 775 727-5007

Latter-day Saints: Church of Jesus Christ of Latter-day Saints, Wilson Ave., Pahrump, NV 89041

Pentecostal: Church of Pentecostal, PO Box 606, Pahrump, NV 89041 Phone: 775 727-6681

Roman Catholic: Our Lady of the Valley, PO Box 1506, Pahrump, NV 89041 Phone: 775 727-6096

Southern Baptist: First Southern Baptist Church, PO Box 399, Pahrump, NV 89041 Phone: 775 727-6038

ROUND MOUNTAIN

Assemblies of God: Trinity Assembly of God, PO Box 85, Round Mountain, NV 89045 Phone: 775 727-4514

Protestant: Smoky Valley Community Church, PO Box 29, Round Mountain, NV 89045 Phone: 775 377-9903

Southern Baptist: Smokey Valley Baptist Church, PO Box 225, Round Mountain, NV 89045 Phone: 775 377-9903

TONOPAH

Adventist: Jehovah's Witnesses Hall, 584 Central, Tonopah, NV 89049 Phone: 775 482-6846

Assemblies of God: First Assembly of God, PO Box 174, Tonopah, NV 89049 Phone: 775 482-6686

Baptist: Tonopah First Baptist Church, PO Box 461, Tonopah, NV 89049 Phone: 775 482-3558

Churches of Christ: Church of Christ, Tonopah, NV 89049

Episcopal: St. Mark Episcopalian Church, PO Box 447, Tonopah, NV 89049

Lutheran: Faith Lutheran Church, PO Box 1163, Tonopah, NV 89049 Phone: 775 463-4870

Presbyterian: Tonopah Presbyterian Church, PO Box 787, Tonopah, NV 89049 Phone: 775 482-3660

Protestant: Calvary Fellowship, 459 Mizpah Cir., Tonopah, NV 89049 Phone: 775 482-9485

Roman Catholic: St. Patricks Catholic Church, PO Box 325, Tonopah, NV 89049 Phone: 775 482-6746

COURTHOUSE

Nye County Courthouse
P.O.Box 1031, Tonopah, NV 89049
Phone: 775 482-8127
Land records: Recorder's Office, P.O. Box 1111, Tonopah, NV 89049
Naturalization records: Records of Naturalization 1865-1929, County Clerk
Letter of Naturalization 1939-1949
Probate records: 1864 to present, County Clerk
Probate search service: $1.00 per year; copies, $1.00 per page

Vital records: Recorders Office
Marriages: 1864 to present; $7.00 per copy
Births: 1887-1911; $4.00 per copy
Deaths: 1887-1911; $4.00 per copy

FUNERAL HOMES

Tonopah Mortuary Service
200 Bryan, Tonopah, NV 89049
Phone: 775 482-5200

LIBRARIES - SOCIETIES

Amarogosa Valley

Amarogosa Valley Community Library
HCR 69, Box 401T, Amarogosa Valley, NV 89020-9701
Phone: 775 372-5340   Fax: 775 372-1188   E-mail: mrdelee@clan.lib.nv.us
Founded: 1977
Hours: Monday: 9:00 a.m. to 8:00 p.m., Tuesday to Friday: 9:00 a.m. to 6:00
p.m., Sunday: 9:00 a.m. to 8:00 p.m.

Beatty

Beatty Community Library
Fourth & Ward, P.O. Box 129, Beatty, NV 89003
Phone: 775 553-2257   Fax: 775 553-2257   E-mail: llgad@clan.lib.nv.us
Founded 1966
Hours: Monday through Friday: 9:00 a.m. to 5:00 p.m., Saturday (except
summer): 11:00 a.m. to 1:00 p.m.
Subject interests: Local history
Special collections: Lincoln & Civil War, Nevada

Gabbs

Gabbs City Library
P.O. Box 206, Gabbs, NV 89409
Phone: 775 285-2686   E-mail: mjlumsde@clan.lib.nv.us
Hours: Monday: 9:00 a.m. to 12:00 noon, Tuesday through Thursday: 9:00
   a.m. to 3:00 p.m., Tuesday: 7:00 p.m. to 9:00 p.m.
Summer Hours: Tuesday: 9:00 a.m. to 12:00 noon & 7:00 p.m. to 9:00 p.m.,
   Wednesday: 2:00 p.m. to 5:00 p.m.

Manhattan

Manhattan Library
P.O. Box 95, Manhattan, NV 89022
Phone: 775 487-2326   E-mail: llhansen@clan.lib.nv.us
Hours: Monday, Tuesday & Thursday: 10:30 a.m. to 4:30 p.m.

Pahrump

Pahrump Community Library
2101 E Calvada Blvd., P.O. Box 578, Pahrump, NV 89041
Phone: 775 727-5930   Fax: 775 727-6209   E-mail: imlewis@clan.lib.nv.us
Hours: Tuesday & Friday: 9:00 a.m. to 5:00 p.m., Wednesday & Thursday:
   9:00 a.m. to 7:00 p.m., Saturday: 11:00 a.m. to 5:00

Round Mountain

Round Mountain Public Library
P.O. Box 1265, Round Mountain, NV 89045
Phone: 775 377-2215   Fax: 775 377-2699   E-mail: dcanfiel@clan.lib.nv.us
Hours: Monday & Friday: 8:00 a.m. to 5:00 p.m., Tuesday through Thursday:
   8:00 a.m. to 8:00 p.m., Saturday: 10:00 a.m. to 4:00 p.m.

Tonopah

Central Nevada Museum
Central Nevada Historical Society
P.O. Box 326, Logan Field Rd., Tonopah, NV 89049
Phone: 775 482-9676
Collections: Books, manuscripts, maps, newspapers, photographs, oral histories
Central Nevada Museum was found in 1981 by the Central Nevada Historical
   Society. The museum is dedicated to the preservation and display of the
   history of central Nevada which includes Nye and Esmeralda counties and
   nearby areas. This includes towns such as: Belmont, Bullfrog, Gilbert,
   Goldfield, Gold Point, Ione, Manhattan, Rawhide, Round Mountain,
   Rhyolite, Tonopah, Tybo, and Weepah.
Research Service: Fees- Postage, copies $.25 per page, if lengthy research,
   charge time. No charge if information not located
Cemetery records:
   Goldfield Cemetery: Information from both county and tombstone records.
   Mostly from tombstones.
   Tonopah Cemetery: Information from county records.
County Records: Partially indexed

Nye County deed indexes
Directories: Goldfield City Directories 1907/1908-indexed in card file, 1940 to
  date
Histories: Local histories- indexed in card file
Map file
Mining company records: Partially indexed
Newspapers: Newspaper clipping index (articles relating to the area)
  Goldfield News, partially indexed
  Tonopah Times Bonanza, partially indexed: Years- 1930 to present
Oral Histories, indexed in card catalog and computer
Photographs: indexed, statewide
Vertical files: Various business records

Tonopah

Tonapah Library District
P.O. Box 449, Tonapah, NV 89049
Phone: 775 482-3374   Fax: 775 482-5143   E-mail: dmhartso@clan.lib.nv.us
Hours: Monday through Friday: 10:00 a.m. to 1:00 p.m. & 2:00 p.m. to 4:00
  p.m., 1st & 3rd Saturday: 10:00 a.m. to 2:00 p.m.

NEWSPAPERS

Newspapers	City	UNLV Library has
Advertiser	Ione	September 17 - October 29, 1864 (weekly - full run)
Beatty Amargosa Times	Beatty	July 23, 1982 - July 15, 1983
Beatty Bullfrog Miner	Beatty	April 8, 1905 - October 24, 1908 (weekly - full run)
Belmont Courier	Belmont	February 14, 1874 - Mar. 2, 1901 (weekly - full run)
Bullfrog Miner	Bullfrog	June 9, 1905 - March 23, 1906
Bullfrog Miner	Rhyolite	March 30, 1906 - Sep. 25, 1909
Carrara Miner	Carrara	July 11, 1929
Carrara Obelisk	Carrara	Feb. 7, 1914 - Sep. 9, 1916 (weekly - 1913-1916)
Death Valley Gateway Gazette	Beatty	July 23, 1983 - date
Death Valley Prospector	Rhyolite	November - December 1907
Gabbs Gab	Gabbs	June 14, 1943 - August 25, 1944
Gabbs Valley Enterprise	Gabbs	Sep. 26, 1974 - April 6, 1976
Gold Center News	Gold Center	Sep. 29, 1906 - Jan. 12, 1907 (weekly - full run)

Grantsville Bonanza	Grantsville	May 7 & July 30, 1881 (daily - 1880-1884?)
Knocker	Manhattan	about September 1911, one issue
Manhattan Magnet	Manhattan	May 25, 1917 - Sep. 9, 1922 (weekly - full run)
Manhattan Mail	Manhattan	May 16, 1906 - June 24, 1911 (weekly - full run)
Manhattan News	Manhattan	April 7, 1906 - July 7, 1907 (weekly - full run)
Manhattan Post	Manhattan	Oct. 15, 1910 - May 30, 1914 (weekly - full run)
Manhattan Times	Manhattan	July 13 - October 7, 1907 (weekly - full run)
Monarch Tribune	Monarch	August 25, 1906
Mountain Champion	Belmont	June 3, 1868 - April 24, 1869 (weekly - full run)
Nevada Democratic Record	Tonopah	April 1962 - October 1970
Nevada Mining Record	Tonopah	May 15, 1926 - Nov. 16, 1929
Nevada Mining Record & Reporter	Tonopah	Nov. 23, 1929 - May 14, 1932
Nevada West & Pahrump Valley Times	Pahrump	March 1971 - November 26, 1976
Nevada West, Pahrump Valley Times	Pahrump	January - February 1971
Nugget	Round Mountain	October 2 - 23, 1910
Nye County News	Ione	July 1 - October 28, 1865; July 28 & August 11, 1866
Pahrump Tribune	Pahrump	1979 - December 1983
Pahrump Valley Times	Pahrump	December 3, 1976 - July 31, 1981
Pahrump Valley Times	Pahrump	September 5, 1986 - date
Pahrump Valley Times - Star	Pahrump	August 7, 1981 - August 29, 1986
Pioneer Topics	Pioneer	February 24 - July 24, 1909
Quartz Mountain Miner	Tonopah	June 16, 1926
Rhyolite Daily Bulletin	Rhyolite	Sep. 23, 1907 - June 8, 1909
Rhyolite Herald	Rhyolite	May 5, 1905 - June 22, 1912
Round Mountain Nugget	Round Mountain	June 2, 1906 - May 21, 1910
Silver Bend Reporter	Belmont	May 25, 1867 - July 29, 1868
Silver Bow Standard	Silver Bow	January 6, 1906
Tonopah Bonanza	Tonopah	June 15, 1901 - Dec. 25, 1909
Tonopah Daily Bonanza	Tonopah	October 24, 1906 - Nov. 15, 1929
Tonopah Daily Sun	Tonopah	January 10, 1905 - Jan.1, 1909
Tonopah Daily Sun Saturday		

Mining Edition	Tonopah	January 27, 1906 - Feb. 9, 1907
Tonopah Daily Times	Tonopah	December 2, 1916 - Nov. 17, 1929
Tonopah Daily Times &		
Bonanza	Tonopah	Nov. 18, 1929 - Mar. 26, 1943
Tonopah Miner	Tonopah	June 26 - November 5, 1921
Tonopah Mining Reporter	Tonopah	Aug. 27, 1921 - Nov. 16, 1929
		(weekly - full run)
Tonopah Nevadan	Tonopah	October 8 - Dec. 31, 1912
		(weekly - full run)
Tonopah Sun	Tonopah	May 11 - July 20, 1904
Tonopah Sun (1909)	Tonopah	January 2, 1909 - July 16, 1910
Tonopah Sun Saturday Mining		
Edition	Tonopah	March 2, 1907 - May 7, 1910
Tonopah Times Bonanza	Tonopah	April 2, 1943 - June 24, 1949
Tonopah Times Bonanza &	Tonopah	January 4, 1963 - date
Goldfield News		
Transvaal Miner	Beatty	April 14, 1906
Tybo Sun	Tybo	September 15 - Nov. 24, 1877
Tybo Weekly Sun	Tybo	December 1, 1877 - Sep. 13, 1879
Weekly Silver Bend Reporter	Belmont	March 30 - May 11, 1867

FAMILY HISTORY LIBRARY (Salt Lake City, Utah) HOLDINGS

All microfilmed and microfiched records (unless restricted) are available to rent worldwide at branch Family History Centers and selected larger public and private libraries and societies.

Nevada, Nye - Archives and libraries - Inventories, registers, catalogs
Inventory of the County Archives of Nevada, no. 12, Nye County (Tonopah).
Prepared by the Nevada Historical Records Survey Project, Division of Professional and Service Projects, Work Projects Administration. Reno, Nev. Historical Records Survey, 1940.
979.334 A3i, also on microfilm- 1320792 item 7

Nevada, Nye - Cemeteries
Parkin, Nona. *Nye County Records*. Salt Lake City : Filmed by the Genealogical Society of Utah, 1997.
Census: Belmont, Ione, Laurel Hill Cemetery, Hamilton, Rhyolite; Small cemeteries; Death records/ obituaries: Newspaper notices 1866-1919, Newspaper obituaries 1922-1983; Jurors called for duty -- v. 2.
Newspaper abstracts; Pioneer families; Registered voters: Belmont Precinct 1884 & 1888, Ione Precinct 1896, Tybo Precinct 1884 & 1896; Tax assessment records Nye County, 1886, 1887, 1888, 1893, 1895 &

1896; Church records: Tonopah Catholic Parish.
Microfilm- 1598448 item 3-4 Vol. 1-2

Paterson, Verna S. *Desert Hill Cemetery, Beatty, Nye County, Nevada and other Cemeteries.* Salt Lake City : Filmed by the Genealogical Society of Utah, 1990.
Microfilm- 1320996 item 26
Cemetery records are alphabetized by county or town. Contains inscriptions from Desert Hill Cemetery (Beatty), Manhattan and   Rhyolite Cemeteries, Reese River (an Indian cemetery), Tybo in Nye County; Lewis (Lander County), and Fish Lake Valley (Esmeralda County), Orena (Pershing County), Galena (Washoe County), Schellbourne and Teasure Hill (White Pine County), Wonder City (Churchill County) Nelson (Clark County), Marietta and Rawhide (Mineral County), Nevada.

Nevada, Nye - Directories
Nevada Territory Directories.
Microfilm- 1377106

1862	First directory of Nevada Territory, by Commercial Steam Presses, Valentine & Co.
1863	Second directory of Nevada Territory, by J. Wells Kelly; published by Valentine & Co.
1864/65	Mercantile guide and directory for Virginia City, Gold Hill, Silver City and American City... by Agnew & Deffenbach, Book and Job Printers
1864/65	San Francisco business directory and mercantile guide... by B. F. Stilwell & Co.
1865/66	None published
1866	Harrington's directory of the city of Austin... by Myron Angel; published by J. D. Fairchild & Co.
1878/68	None published
1868/69	The Nevada directory... by William Gillis
1869	Not available
1870/71	None published

Microfilm- 1377107

1871/72	Storey, Ormsby, Washoe and Lyon Counties directory... by County Directory Publishing Company
1871/73	The Pacific Coast business directory by Henry G. Langley
1872	Wells, Fargo & Co.'s express directory
1872	McKennys' gazetteer and directory of the Central Pacific Railroad and its branches ... by Directory Publishing Company

Microfilm- 1377108

1873/74	The Virginia and Truckee railroad directory... by John F. Ehlhorn; published by H. S. Crocker & Co.

1873/74 The Virginia and Truckee railroad   directory... by John F.
         Ehlhorn; published by H. S. Crocker & Co.
1874/75 None published
1875   A general business and mining directory of Storey, Lyon,
         Ormsby, and Washoe Counties, Nevada... by John D. Bethel &
         Co.
1876/77 None published
1877   Business directory of San Francisco and principal towns of
         California and Nevada ... by L. M. McKenney
1878   Business directory of the Pacific States and Territories... by L.
         M. McKenney
Microfilm- 1377109
1878/79 Bishop's directory of Virginia City, Gold Hill, Silver City,
         Carson City and Reno... by B. C. Vandall
1879/82 Not available
1880/81 Pacific Coast directory... by L. M. McKenney & Co.
1881/82 None published

Nevada, Nye - History - Newspapers
Basso, David. *Nye County*. Sparks, Nev. : Dave's Print. & Pub., c1972.
979.3 A1 no. 20

Nevada, Nye - Land and property
Nye (Nevada). County Recorder. *Chronicle List of Papers on File, 1866-1907*.
Salt Lake City : Filmed by the Genealogical Society of Utah, 1992.
   Arranged alphabetically by name of participant or recipient. Includes lis
   pendens, executions, sheriff's sales, attachments, bonds, oaths, judgments,
   appointments, sales, etc.
Microfilm- 1863897 item 5   Index, v. 1 1866-1907

Nye (Nevada). County Recorder. *Deeds, 1864-1902; Index 1864-1905*. Salt
Lake City : Filmed by the Genealogical Society of Utah, 1992.
Microfilm- 1863898 item 4-6   Index, v. 1-3 A-J (part)   1864-1905
Microfilm- 1863899   Index, v. 3 J (part) - Z   1902-1905
                               Deeds, v. A-C (p. 1-359)   1864-1867
Microfilm- 1863900   Vol. C (p. 359-end) - E   1865-1867
Microfilm- 1863901   Deeds, v. F-H (p. 1-553)   1867-1875
Microfilm- 1863902   Deeds, v. H (p. 553-end) - K (p.1-44)
                               1875-1881
Microfilm- 1863903   Deeds, v. K (p. 440-end) - N (p.1-73)
                               1881-1894
Microfilm- 1863904 item 1-2Deeds, v. N (p. 73-end) - O   1894-1902

Nye (Nevada). County Recorder. *Mining Records and Other Miscellaneous Land Records, 1864-1904.* Salt Lake City : Filmed by the Genealogical Society of Utah, 1992.

Includes mining locations, names, notices and land records such as indentures, agreements, water rights, liens, bonds, incorporations, bill of sales, and judgments.

Microfilm- 1869550 item 2-6

Index to locators	1864-1903
Index to name of claim	1864-1903
Mining notices, v. A	1864-1904
Mining locations, v. A-B	1864-1890
Mining locations, v. C (p. 1-179)	1891-1892

Microfilm- 1869551 item 1-2

Mining locations, v. C (p. 179-end)	1892-1895
Mining locations, v. D	1895-1901

Microfilm- 1863904 item 3-4

Misc. records, v. A	1864-1882
Misc. records, v. B (p. 1-68)	1876-1884

Microfilm- 1869549 item 1-3

Misc. records, v. B (p. 68-end)	1877-1884
Misc. records, v. C-D	1884-1902

Nye (Nevada). County Recorder. *Powers of Attorney and Mortgages, 1864-1905; Index 1864-1915.* Salt Lake City : Filmed by the Genealogical Society of Utah, 1992.

Microfilm- 1863898 item 1	Index to powers of attorney	1864-1915
Microfilm- 1869551 item 3	Index to mortgages	1864-1908
Microfilm- 1863898 item 2-3	Powers of attorney & mortgages, v. A 1864-1868	
	Powers of attorney, v. B	1868-1905
Microfilm- 1869551 item 4	Chattel mortgages, v. A	1886-1904

Nye (Nevada). County Recorder. *Trust Deeds, 1864-1877.* Salt Lake City : Filmed by the Genealogical Society of Utah, 1992.

Microfilm- 1869549 item 4	Vol. A (p. 1-403)	1864-1870
Microfilm- 1869550 item 1	Vol. A (p. 403-end)	1870-1877

Nevada, Nye - Military records

Nye (Nevada). County Recorder. *Army and Navy Discharge Papers, v. 1, 1919-1953.* Salt Lake City : Filmed by the Genealogical Society of Utah, 1992.

Microfilm- 1869551 item 5

Nevada, Nye - Military records - World War, 1914-1918
Banks, Raymond H. *The Banks Compilation of Birth Data of Men with Links to Nye County, Nevada, Who Were Born 1873-1900 : as Found in the Civilian Registration Cards.* L.D.S. microfilm series of World War I Selective Service draft registration cards. Salt Lake City : R.H. Banks, c1996.
979.3 A1 no.57
An alphabetical listing by surname of men who completed civilian registration cards for their draft boards during 1917-1918. About 98% of men present in America and born 1873-1900 provided draft card information in 1917 or 1918. Aliens were required to register. Persons already in the military did not register. Includes name, date of birth, ethnic group, birth place or other information, and county or city draft board in the state where registered.

Nevada, Nye - Vital records
Nye (Nevada). County Recorder. *Births and Deaths, 1887-1911.* Salt Lake City : Filmed by the Genealogical Society of Utah, 1992.
Includes index at beginning of volumes.
Microfilm- 1863589 item 1-3   Births and deaths, v. A-C   1887-1911
Microfilm- 1863589 item 7   Misc. birth certificates, v. G-H 1879-1911

Nye (Nevada). County Recorder. *Marriages, 1887-1957.* Salt Lake City : Filmed by the Genealogical Society of Utah, 1992.
Microfilm- 1869548 item 2-3
    Index, applications and licenses   1868-1951
Microfilm- 1869548 item 1
    Index, applications and licenses A-E   1870-1962
Microfilm- 1863589 item 5-6
    Index to marriages, v. B   1916-1947
    Index to marriages, v. C (A-R)   1948-1972
Microfilm- 1863897 item 1
    Index to marriages, v. C (S-Z)   1948-1972
Microfilm- 1863589 item 4
    Marriage certificates, v. A   1864-1915
Microfilm- 1863897 item 2-4
    Marriage certificates, v. B-D   1915-1957
Microfilm- 1869548 item 4-5
    Marriage licenses, no. 1-199   1885-1904

Nevada, Nye, Amargosa Valley - History
McCracken, Robert D. *A History of Amargosa Valley, Nevada : the Modern Pioneers.*
    979.334/A1 H2m, also on microfilm- 2055147 item 6
    The Amargosa Valley, about ninety miles northwest of Las Vegas in Nye County, Nevada.

Nevada, Nye, Beatty - History
McCracken, Robert D. *A History of Beatty, Nevada : Frontier Oasis.* Tonopah, Nev. : Nye County Press, c1992.
    979.344/B1 H2m, also on microfilm- 2055147 item 9

Nevada, Nye, Gabbs - History
Danner, Ruth Fenstermaker. *Gabbs Valley, Nevada : its History and Legend.* Gabbs, Nevada : R. Danner, c1992.
    979.334/G1 H2d

Nevada, Nye, Pahrump - History
McCracken, Robert D. *A History of Pahrump, Nevada : a Valley Waiting to Become a City.* Tonopah, Nev. : Nye County Press, 1992, c1990.
    979.334/P1 H2m, also on microfilm- 2055147 item 7

Nevada, Nye, Tonopah - History
Paher, Stanley W. *Tonopah, Silver Camp of Nevada.* Las Vegas, Nev. : Nevada Publications, c1978.
    979.3 A1 no.44

McCracken, Robert D. *A History of Tonopah, Nevada : the Greatest, the Richest, and the Best Mining Camp in the World.* Tonopah, Nev. : Nye County Press, 1992, c1990.
    979.334/T1 H2m, also on microfilm- 2055147 item 8

CHAPTER FOURTEEN

Ormsby County

Carson City

Ormsby County was an original county, organized 25 November 1861. It was consolidated with Carson City in 1969 to form the consolidated municipality.

Ormsby County was named after Major William M. Ormsby, who was one of the pioneers and prominent citizens of the county. He died at the battle of Pyramid Lake, where the force under his command was defeated by the Indians.

CEMETERY

Walton's Carson Gardens
1281 N. Roop St., Carson City, NV 89706
Phone: 775 882-4965

CHURCHES

CARSON CITY
Assemblies of God: Capital Assembly of God, PO Box 2890, Carson City, NV 89702 Phone: 775 883-3355
Baptist: Stewart Community Baptist Church, 5340 Snyder Ave., Carson City, NV 89701 Phone: 775 882-0622
Churches of Christ: Airport Road Church of Christ, 3209 Airport Rd., Carson City, NV 89706 Phone: 775 882-5046
Carson City Church of Christ, 2049 California St., Carson City, NV 89701 Phone: 775 882-3390
Christian Science: First Church of Christ Scientist, 213 N. Minnesota St., Carson City, NV 89703 Phone: 775 882-3600
Episcopal: St. Peter's Episcopalian Church, 305 N. Minnesota St., Carson City, NV 89703 Phone: 775 882-1534
Evangelical Lutheran: St. Paul's Lutheran Church, 1201 N. Saliman Rd., Carson City, NV 89701 Phone: 775 882-3020
Holiness: Church of the Nazarene, PO Box 1851, Carson City, NV 89702 Phone: 775 882-4959

Good Shepherd Wesleyan Church, 1505 Railroad Dr., Carson City, NV 89701
Phone: 775 885-8361

Independent Fundamentalist: Calvary Bible Church, 449 W. King St.,
Carson City, NV 89703 Phone: 775 882-7500

Latter-day Saints: Carson City First Ward, 1331 McKay Dr., Carson City, NV
89701 Phone: 775 882-5335

Carson City Group Church of Latter-day Saints, 503 E. Telegraph St.,
Carson City, NV 89701

Lutheran: Bethlehem Lutheran Church, 1837 N. Mountain St., Carson City,
NV 89703 Phone: 775 882-5252

The Lutheran Missouri Synod, 505 Pat Ln., Carson City, NV 89701
Phone: 775 882-0901

Metaphysical: United Church of Religious Science, 675 Fairview Dr.Ste 241,
Carson City, NV 89701 Phone: 775 882-0901

Methodist: First United Methodist Church, 412 W. Musser St., Carson City,
NV 89703 Phone: 775 882-1436

Pentecostal: Carson Valley Community Church, PO Box 2376, Carson City,
NV 89775 Phone: 775 882-1626

Christian People Church, PO Box 2322, Carson City, NV 89702
Phone: 775 885-0444

Vineyard Christian Fellowship, 1601 Fairview Dr., Carson City, NV 89701
Phone: 775 883-8078

Word of Life Fellowship, Corner of Roop and Fairview, Carson City, NV
89701 Phone: 775 883-8239

Pentecostal Church of God: Carson City Church of God, 3101 S. Carson City,
NV 89701 Phone: 775 883-1683

The Lighthouse Church of God, PO Box 2492, Carson City, NV 89702
Phone: 775 885-0880

Presbyterian: First Presbyterian Church, 110 N. Nevada St., Carson City, NV
89703 Phone: 882-1032

Protestant: Carson Interfaith Center, 2039 Bunch Way, Carson City, NV
89706

Christ Body Life Ministry, 1132 Fremont St., Carson City, NV 89701

Fountainhead Church, PO Box 2775, Carson City, NV 89702

Lakeview Community Church, 3835 Pershing Ln., Carson City, NV 89704
Phone: 775 883-7926

Ranchos Community Church, 3375 Alpine View Ct., Carson City, NV 89705
Phone: 775 265-2501

Roman Catholic: Corpus Christi Catholic Church, 5335 Snyder Ave.,
Carson City, NV 89701 Phone: 775 882-1967

St. Teresa of Avia Catholic Church, 108 M. Minnesota St., Carson City, NV
89703 Phone: 775 882-2130

Seventh Day Adventist: Seventh Day Adventist Church, 3 Wild Sage Ct.,
    Carson City, NV 89704 Phone: 775 882-3541
Southern Baptist: Capitol City Baptist Church, PO Box 642, Carson City, NV
    89702 Phone: 775 882-1946
First Baptist Church, 1750 N. Mountain St., Carson City, NV 89703
    Phone: 775 882-1851
Unclassified: Baha'i Faith, 616 E. John St. Apt. 6, Carson City, NV 89706
    Phone: 775 882-0515

COURTHOUSE

Carson City Courthouse
198 North Carson Street, Carson City, NV 89701
Phone: 775 887-2260
Land records: Recorder's Office, above address
Naturalization records: Court Clerk's Office or Recorder's Office, above address
Probate records: Contact Clerk
Probate search service: $1.00 per year;
    Copies: $1.00 per page, no minimum
Vital records: State Office

FUNERAL HOME

FitzHenry's Funeral Home & Crematory
833 N. Edmonds Dr., Carson City, NV 89701
Phone: 775 882-2644

LIBRARIES

Carson City Library
900 N Roop St., Carson City, NV 89701
Phone: 775 887-2244 Fax: 775 887-2273 E-mail: ejdailey@clan.lib.nv.us
Founded 1966
Hours: Monday, Friday & Saturday: 10:00 a.m. to 6:00 p.m., Tuesday,
    Wednesday, Thursday: 10:00 a.m. to 9:00 p.m.
Special Collections: Nevada

Carson Family History Center
Mail: 4845 E 5th St, Carson City, NV 89701
Phone: 775 884-2064

178 Nevada Guide to Genealogical Records

Nevada State Library & Archives
100 Stewart St., Carson City, NV 89710
Phone: 775 687-8313 Fax: 775 687-8330 (ILL, Reference)
Internet: http://www.clan.lib.nv.us
Hours: 8 a.m. to 5 p.m. Monday through Friday, except holidays
Founded 1859

NEWSPAPERS

Nevada Appeal
P.O. Box 2288, Carson City, NV 89702
Phone: 775 882-2111 ext. 211 Fax: 775 882-2111 ext. 249
Northern Nevada Newspapers, back issues
Internet: http://www/tahoe.com/backissues.html

Newspapers	City	UNLV Library has
Carson Boys	Carson City	September 16, 1885 - May 12, 1886
Carson Chronicle	Carson City	February 2 - December 28, 1967
Carson Chronicle	Carson City	Dec. 18, 1969 - Dec. 30, 1969; January 1973 - January 25, 1984
Carson City Chronicle	Carson City	August 9, 1935 - June 27, 1952
Carson City Daily Appeal	Carson City	July 10, 1907 - April 30, 1930 (daily - full run)
Carson City Daily Appeal	Carson City	Dec. 31, 1936 - Dec. 31, 1946
Carson City Daily Appeal & *Carson City News*	Carson City	May 1, 1930 - December 30, 1936
Carson City Enlightener	Carson City	August 5 - September 4, 1914
Carson City Nevada Appeal	Carson City	January 2, 1947 - Oct. 20, 1948
Carson City Nevada Appeal	Carson City	December 7, 1956 - Aug. 30, 1968
Carson City News	Carson City	August 25, 1902 - May 1, 1930
Carson City News (1961)	Carson City	January 5 - April 27, 1961
Carson Daily Appeal	Carson City	May 16, 1865 - October 9, 1870
Carson Daily Appeal (1873)	Carson City	March 11, 1873 - Feb. 28, 1877
Carson Daily Independent	Carson City	September 1, October 8, Dec. 5 & 20, 1863; June 5, 1864
Carson Daily Index	Carson City	September 29, 1885 - July 3, 1887 (daily - full run)
Carson Daily Morning News	Carson City	March 11 - October 25, 1892
Carson Daily Times	Carson City	June 14, 1880 - June 11, 1881
Carson Evening Gazette	Carson City	July 21 & 23, 1914
Carson Free Lance	Carson City	March 2, 1885 - Nov. 29, 1886 (weekly - full run)

Carson Morning Chronicle	Carson City	October 1 & November 19, 1964; January 14, 1965
Carson Morning News	Carson City	October 26, 1892 - Oct. 31, 1895
Carson Press	Carson City	January 1, 1892 - Dec. 30, 1893
Carson Review	Carson City	Nov. 25, 1970 - Nov. 9, 1973
Carson Times	Carson City	April 9 - June 1, 1880
Carson Times (1977)	Carson City	August 10, 1977 - March 26, 1980
Carson Valley Chronicle	Carson City	January 2 - December 11, 1969
Carson Weekly	Carson City	February 29, 1892 - Dec. 2, 1895
Carson Weekly (1897)	Carson City	February 1, 1897 - Jan. 2, 1899
Carson Weekly (1906)	Carson City	February 26, 1906 - Nov. 7, 1918
Celebration Gazetteer	Carson City	July 3 - 6, 1892?
Daily Appeal	Carson City	May 3, 1906 - July 8, 1907
Daily Bee	Carson City	July 14 - November 18, 1882
Daily Evening Herald	Carson City	August 20 - September 9, 1875 (daily - full run)
Daily Index	Carson City	Dec. 25, 1880 - Sep. 27, 1885
Daily Morning Post	Carson City	March 16 & April 15, 1865
Daily Nevada Tribune	Carson City	August 9, 1875 - April 5, 1896 (daily - full run)
Daily Silver Age	Carson City	August 26 & October 20, 1861
Daily State Register	Carson City	Dec. 29, 1870 - Nov. 30, 1872 (daily - full run)
Desert News	Carson City	June 5 - October 1973
Flash	Carson City	October 10, 1969 - April 10, 1970
Indian Advance	Carson City	September 1, 1899 - Sep. 1, 1903 (daily - full run)
Inter-Tribal Council of Nevada Newsletter	Carson City	June 1964 - April 1965
Monday Weekly	Carson City	April 27, 1903 - Feb. 19, 1906
Morning Appeal	Carson City	May 1, 1877 - May 2, 1906 (daily - full run)
Native Nevadan	Carson City	May 1965 - January 13, 1966
Nevadan American	Carson City	April 4, 1914
Nevada Appeal	Carson City	October 21, 1948 - June 30, 1949
Nevada Appeal (1968)	Carson City	September 1, 1968 - date
Nevada Appeal, Chronicle Edition	Carson City	February 1, 1984 - date
Nevada Capitol News	Carson City	December 1950
Nevada Index- Union	Carson City	July 6, 1887 - July 3, 1888 (daily - full run)
Nevada Patriot	Carson City	July 11 - August 3, 1876 (weekly - full run)

Nevada State Journal	Carson City	May 15 - 23, 1866
Nevada State Recorder	Carson City	January 17, 1984 - June 18, 1986
Nevada Statesman	Carson City	January 26 - April 22, 1966
Nevada Tribune	Carson City	Sep. 17, 1873 - August 7, 1875 (varies - full run)
Nevada Union	Carson City	August 4, 1886 - July 5, 1887 (daily - full run)
Nevada State Veteran	Carson City	March - December 1949
Nevadan Times	Carson City	October 9, 1931 - July 26, 1935
New Daily Appeal	Carson City	Sep. 9, 1872 - March 9, 1873 (daily - full run)
New Indian	Carson City	January & Nov. 1903; July 1904
News	Carson City	June 21, 1891 - March 10, 1892
News (1895)	Carson City	Nov. 2, 1895 - Aug.t 23, 1902
Ormsby County Ledger	Carson City	about 1900, one undated issue
Parish Rubic	Carson City	February 1898; March & April 1901; June 1904
Silver Age	Carson City	July 13 & 20, & August 20, 1861
Tahoe Chronicle	Carson City	October 5, 1967 - Nov. 25, 1968
Weekly	Carson City	August 17, 1891 - Feb. 22, 1892
Weekly (1895)	Carson City	December 9, 1895 - Jan. 25, 1897
Weekly (1900)	Carson City	January 28, 1900 - April 20, 1903
White Ribbon	Carson City	July 6 - 9; 12- 14, 17, 19,21, 1894

FAMILY HISTORY LIBRARY (Salt Lake City, Utah) HOLDINGS

All microfilmed and microfiched records (unless restricted) are available to rent worldwide at branch Family History Centers and selected larger public and private libraries and societies.

Nevada, Carson City (Independent City) - Cemeteries

Daughters of the American Colonists. Reno Chapter. *Cemetery Inscriptions from Lone Mountain Cemetery, Veteran's Military Cemetery and St. Theresa's Cemetery, Carson City, Nevada.* Salt Lake City : Filmed by the Genealogical Society of Utah, 1959.
Microfilm- 0176647

Parkin, Nona. *Nevada Cemetery Inscriptions.* Salt Lake City : Filmed by the Genealogical Society of Utah, 1971.
Microfilm- 0869278 item 4
Microfilm of original records in the D.A.R. Library in Washington, D.C.
Contents: Carson City, Ormsby County cemetery inscriptions -- Genoa (Douglas County) cemetery inscriptions -- Mottsville (Douglas County)

cemetery inscriptions -- Aurora Cemetery (Mineral County) inscriptions.

Paterson, Verna S. *Cemetery inscriptions, Carson City, Ormsby County, Nevada : Lone Mountain Cemetery (Protestant), Veteran's Military Cemetery, St. Theresa's Cemetery (Catholic).* Salt Lake City : Filmed by the Genealogical Society of Utah, 1959.
Microfilm- 0899791

Nevada, Carson City (Independent City) - Church records
Daughters of the American Colonists (Nevada). *Nevada Records of Marriages, Wills, and Miscellaneous Data.* Salt Lake City : Filmed by the Genealogical Society of Utah, 1959.
Microfilm- 0176646
Includes marriage records 1890-1896, First Presbyterian Church, Carson City, Nevada; abstracts of Wills 1906-1926, Fallon, Nevada; report of Stanton Post, no. 29, located at Carson City, County of Ormsby, Department of California, G.A.R. for third quarter of 1870; tax list of Lyon County, Nevada, for the year 1897. Includes a partial index.

Church of Jesus Christ of Latter-day Saints. Carson City Branch (Nevada). *Record of Members, 1940-1941;Annual Genealogical Report, Form E, 1941- 1942.* Salt Lake City ; Salt Lake City : Filmed by the LDS Church Historian's Office : Filmed by the Genealogical Society of Utah, 1966, 1951.
Carson City Branch, organized in Feb. 1941, was dissolved in July 1943.Includes index.
Microfilm- 0889387 item 3   Record of members   1940-1941
Microfilm- 0014898   Form E   1941-1942
Photocopies not permitted except for direct line descendants. Remove all other data from photocopy.

Nevada, Carson City (Independent City) - Directories
R. L. Polk and Company. *Carson City (Washoe County, Nevada) Directory, 1964.*
979.357 E4p
Library has: 1964, 1968.

Nevada, Carson City (Independent City) - History
Scott, Edward B. *The Saga of Lake Tahoe : a Complete Documentary of Lake Tahoe's Development Over the Last One Hundred Years.*
979.438 H2s

Nevada, Carson City (Independent City) - History - Newspapers
Basso, David. *Carson City.* Reno, Nev. : s.n., c1971.
979.3 Al no. 19

Nevada, Carson City (Independent City) - Land and property
Ormsby County (Nevada). Recorder. *Miscellaneous Mortgages, Powers, Plats and Contracts, 1855-1897.* Salt Lake City : Filmed by the Genealogical Society of Utah, 1993.
> Ormsby County was consolidated into Carson City in 1969. Includes indexes at beginning of volumes. Includes a few scattered marriages.
> Microfilm- 1901696 item 3-7
> Index, v. E; Vol. E, 1855-1861
> Index, v. 3, 7, 13; Vol. 3, 7, 1862-1869
> Microfilm- 1901697 item 1-3
> Vol. 13, 1869-1879; Index, v. 20, Vol. 20, 1879-1897

Nevada, Carson City (Independent City) - Military records - World War, 1914-1918
Banks, Raymond H. *The Banks Compilation of Birth Data of Men with Links to Ormsby County, (now Carson City) Nevada, Who Were Born 1873-1900 : as Found in the Civilian Registration Cards.* L.D.S. microfilm series of World War I Selective Service draft registration cards.
979.3 Al no. 58
> About 98% of men present in America and born 1873-1900 provided draft card information in 1917 or 1918. Aliens were required to register. Persons already in the military did not register.

Nevada, Carson City (Independent City) - Newspapers
Parkin, Nona. *Orsmby County Records.* Salt Lake City : Filmed by the Genealogical Society of Utah, 1997.
> Contents: v. 1. Birth records/notices: Newspaper notices 1866 and 1920; Cemetery census: Carson City (all cemeteries) with index, Carson City Catholic, Carson City Masonic Cemetery with index, Empire Cemetery with index -- v. 2. Death records/ obituaries: Newspaper notices 1863-1908, Newspaper obituaries 1906-1981, Newspaper obituaries 1922-1983; Funeral home records, Kitzmeyer and Elges, Ross Burke burials in Carson City and vicinity -- v. 3. Marriage records/ notices: Ormsby County records; Pioneer records; Union membership rolls; Church records: St. Terese Catholic Church, St. Peter's Episcopal Church. Includes some indexing.
> Microfilm- 1598450 item 3-4   Vol. 1-2
> Microfilm- 1598451 item 1   Vol. 3

Nevada, Carson City (Independent City) - Societies
International Order of Good Templers (Carson City, Nevada). *I.O.G.T.*
(Independent Order of Good Templers) Carson City, Nevada Attendance
Book, 1879.
  979.3 A1 no.1
  Record of a temperance group in Carson City.

Nevada, Carson City (Independent City) - Vital records
Carson City (Independent City (Nevada)). Recorder. *Births, Burials and*
Marriages, 1887-1902. Salt Lake City : Filmed by the Genealogical Society
of Utah, 1993.
  Microfilm- 1901695 item 5-9

Birth certificates, v. 2	1903-1911
Birth duplicate certificates	1911-1949
Birth certificates	1949-1951
Death certificates, v. 1 (p.1-227)	1895-1909

  Microfilm- 1901696 item 1-2

Death certificates, v. 1 (p.227-end)	1909-1911
Death certificates	1949-1953

Carson City (Independent City (Nevada)). Recorder. *Marriage Records,*
1899-1951. Salt Lake City : Filmed by the Genealogical Society of Utah,
1993.
  Includes indexes at beginning of volumes.
  Microfilm- 1901697 item 4-5

Certificates, v. 2-3	28 Sep 1899-14 Jun 1919

  Microfilm- 1901698

Certificates, v. 4-7	17 Jun 1919-27 Apr 1934

  Microfilm- 1901699

Certificates, v. 8-10	27 Apr 1934-16 Jun 1937
Certificates, v. 11	16 Jun 1937-15 Sep 1937 (p. 1-223)

  Microfilm- 1901700

Certificates, v. 11	15 Sep 1937-31 May 1938 (p. 223-end)
Certificates, v. 12-13	31 May 1938-1 Nov 1939
Certificates, v. 14	1 Nov 1939-30 Dec 1939 (p. 1-181)

  Microfilm- 1901701

Certificates, v. 14	30 Dec 1940-17 Jun 1940(p. 181-end)
Certificates, v. 15-16	17 Jun 1940-14 Jan 1941
Certificates, v. 17	14 Jan 1941-17 Feb 1941 (p. 1-107)

  Microfilm- 1901702

Certificates, v. 17	1 Mar 1941-30 Jun 1941 (p. 107-end)
Certificates, v. 18-19	30 Jun 1941-2 Jan 1942

  Microfilm- 1901703

Certificates, v. 20-22	2 Jan 1942-30 Sep 1943
Microfilm- 1901704	
Certificates, v. 23-25	30 Oct 1943-4 Sep 1946
Microfilm- 1901705	
Certificates, v. 26-27	4 Sep 1946-9 Sep 1947
Certificates, v. 28	9 Sep 1947-5 Mar 1948 (p. 1-485)
Microfilm- 1901706	
Certificates, v. 28	27 Jan 1948-14 Apr 1948 (p. 422-end)
Certificates, v. 29-30	14 Apr 1948-14 Jun 1949
Certificates, v. 31	14 Jun 1949-24 Aug 1949 (p. 1-231)
Microfilm- 1901707	
Certificates, v. 31	24 Aug 1949-3 Dec 1949 (p. 231-end)
Certificates, v. 32-33	3 Dec 1949-24 Nov 1950
Certificates, v. 34	24 Nov 1950-26 Feb 1951 (p. 1-185)
Microfilm- 1901708	
Certificates, v. 34	24 Feb 1951-25 Jun 1951
Licenses	1898-1919

Ormsby County, Nevada Births, 1886, Marriages 1880, 1899. Salt Lake City : Filmed by the Genealogical Society of Utah, 1990.
Microfilm- 1320996 item 24

Ormsby County (Nevada). Recorder. *Births, Burials and Marriages, 1887-1902.* Salt Lake City : Filmed by the Genealogical Society of Utah, 1993.
Orsmby County was consolidated into Carson City in 1969. Includes index.
Microfilm- 1901695 item 1-4

Index, births, v. H	1887-1902
Index, burials, v. H	1889-1894
Index, marriage certificates, v. H	1887-1899
Births, v. H	1887-1902
Burials, v. H	1887-1894
Marriage certificates, v. H	1887-1899

CHAPTER FIFTEEN

Pershing County

Pershing County was organized in 1919 from Humboldt County.

CHURCHES

LOVELOCK

Adventist: Jehovah's Witnesses, 1650 Franklin Ave., Lovelock, NV 89419
Phone: 775 273-7445

Assemblies of God: Lovelock First Assembly of God, PO Box 758, Lovelock, NV 89419 Phone: 775 273-2453

Churches of Christ: Church of Christ, 1180 Elmhurst St., PO Box 795, Lovelock, NV 89419

Episcopal: St. Francis Episcopalian Chapel, PO Box 1043, Lovelock, NV 89419

St. Francis Episcopalian Church, PO Box 295, Lovelock, NV 89419

Latter-day Saints: Church of Jesus Christ Latter-day Saints 14th, Lovelock, NV 89419 Phone 775 273-2714

Lovelock Ward Church of Latter-day Saints, 220 Maple Drive., Lovelock, NV 89419 Phone: 775 273-7214

Lutheran: Redeemer Lutheran Church, PO Box 837, Lovelock, NV 89419 Phone: 775 273-7152

Methodist: Grace United Methodist Church, PO Box 334, Lovelock, NV 89419

Roman Catholic: St. John the Baptist Church, PO Box 177, Lovelock, NV 89419 Phone: 775 273-2189

Southern Baptist: First Baptist Church, PO Box 433, Lovelock, NV 89419 Phone: 775 273-7589

COURTHOUSE

Pershing County Courthouse
P.O. Box 820, Lovelock, NV 894-0820
Phone: 775 273-2408 Recorder/Auditor, Box 736; 775 273-2208 Clerk
Land records: from 1919, County Recorder
Naturalization records: 1919 to May 1961, County Clerk
Probate records: from 1919, County Clerk
    Probate search service, $1.00 per page, no minimum
Vital records: from 1919

FUNERAL HOMES

Belanger Funeral Home
655 11th Street, Lovelock, NV 89419
Phone: 775 273-2117

LIBRARY

Pershing County Library
P.O. Box 781, 1125 Central, Lovelock, NV 89419
Phone: 775 273-2216 Fax: 775 273-7058 E-mail: meolejni@clan.lib.nv.us
Founded: 1930
Hours: Monday & Tuesday: 9:00 a.m. to 5:00 p.m., Wednesday: 9:00 a.m. to
    5:00 p.m. & 7:00 p.m. yo 9:00 p.m. Thursday & Friday: 10:00 a.m. to 5:00
    p.m., Saturday: 9:00 a.m. to 3:00 p.m.

NEWSPAPERS

Newspapers	City	UNLV Library has
Argus (Lovelock)	Lovelock	Jan. 5, 1901 - Jan. 27, 1905 (weekly 1900-1905)
Humboldt Register	Unionville	May 2, 1863 - May 29, 1869; Nov. 13, 1869 - Dec. 1, 1876
Lovelock Review	Lovelock	Aug. 21, 1908 - Dec. 30, 1910 (weekly 1908-1911)
Lovelock Review Miner	Lovelock	May 24, 1929 - March 11, 1987
Lovelock Review Miner &		
Lovelock Tribune	Lovelock	March 19, 1897 - date
Lovelock	Lovelock	May 21, 1898 - February 1, 1912
Lovelock Tribune	Lovelock	January 15 - March 12, 1987
Lovelocks Courier	Lovelock	1 issue, about 1900

Mining Topics	Unionville	Dec. 6, 1921 - July 13, 1922 (varies 1921-1925)
Nevada Legionnaire	Locklock	August 7, 1934 - Sep. 1950 (monthly 1932-1950)
Nevada New Era	Lovelock	October 21, 1893 - June 2, 1894 (weekly full-run)
Northern Nevada Weekly Mine Review	Lovelock	August 11 - December 29, 1915
Review - Miner	Lovelock	October 24, 1913 - May 17, 1929
Rochester Journal	Rochester	Feb. 2, 20, & 27, 1913; March 6 & May 1, 1913 (weekly Jan- May 1913)
Rochester Miner	Rochester	January 22, 1913 - Jan. 7, 1914 (weekly full-run)
Seven Troughs & Lovelock Review-Miner	Lovelock	January 6, 1911 - Oct. 17, 1913
Seven Troughs District News	Mazuma	Sep. 19, 1908 - Jan. 16, 1909 (weekly full-run)
Seven Troughs Miner	Vernon	September 7, 1907 - Oct. 1, 1910
Vernon Miner	Vernon	March 1, 1907
Vernon Review	Vernon	June 29 - October 12, 1907

FAMILY HISTORY LIBRARY (Salt Lake City, Utah) HOLDINGS

All microfilmed and microfiched records (unless restricted) are available to rent worldwide at branch Family History Centers and selected larger public and private libraries and societies.

Nevada, Pershing - Cemeteries

Kemmerle, Fred W. *Cemeteries of Pershing County, Nevada, 1989.* [S.l.] : Kemmerle, 1989.

    979.3 A1 no.30

        Includes Unionville Cemetery, Unionville; Indian Cemetery, Big Meadow Cemetery, and Lone Mountain Cemetery, Lovelock; and Solitary Grave, Dun Glen.

Nevada, Pershing - History

Shamberger, Hugh A. *The Story of Seven Thoughts, Pershing County, Nevada : a Little About the Seven Thoughts Mining District, its People, its Towns, its Mines, its Quest for Water; and its Promoters, All of Which Made an Interesting Chapter in the Mining History of Nevada.* Carson City, Nev. : [s.n.], 1972.

    979.3 A1 no.16

Nevada, Pershing - Vital records
Parkin, Nona. *Pershing County Records, 1922-1975.* Salt Lake City : Filmed
by the Genealogical Society of Utah, 1997.
    v. 1. Cemetery census: Big Meadow, Lone Mountain, small cemeteries;
Death records/obituaries: Newspaper obituaries, 1922-1975 -- v. 2.
Marriage records/ notices, Pioneer families, Church records: Lovelock.
Includes newspaper clippings.
    Microfilm- 1598449 item 3-4   Vol. 1-2

Pershing County (Nevada). Recorder. *Affidavits of Application for Marriage
License, 1919-1951.* Salt Lake City : Filmed by the Genealogical Society of
Utah, 1993.
    Microfilm- 1888665 Vol. 1-22 (no. 1-1903)   1919-1950
    Microfilm- 1888666 Vol. 22-24 (no. 1903-2050) 1949-1951

Pershing County (Nevada). Recorder. *Marriage Records, 1919-1959.* Salt
Lake City : Filmed by the Genealogical Society of Utah, 1993.
    Includes indexes at beginning of volumes.
    Microfilm- 1888664   Marriage licenses, v. 1-3   1919-1959

Nevada, Pershing, Lovelock - Church records
Church of Jesus Christ of Latter-day Saints. Lovelock Branch (Nevada).
Record of Members, 1932-1933. Salt Lake City : Filmed by the Genealogical
Society of Utah, 1954.
    Microfilm of original records in the LDS Church Archives, Salt Lake City.
    Microfilm- 0001955 item 4   Record of members 1932-1933

CHAPTER SIXTEEN

Storey County

Storey County was one of the original counties, formed by an act approved on 25 November 1861.

It was named after Captain Edward Faris Storey, a frontiersman, who after the death of Major Ormsby at the battle of Pyramid Lake, raised a force of riflemen. On 2 June 1860 they attacked the fortified camp of Piutes and defeated them.

CHURCHES

VIRGINIA CITY
Presbyterian: First Presbyterian Church, PO Box 87, Virginia City, NV 89440
   Phone: 775 847-0298
Roman Catholic: St. Mary in the Mountain Catholic Church, PO Box 328,
   Virginia City, NV 89440 Phone: 775 847-0797

COURTHOUSE

Storey County Courthouse
P.O. Box 493, Virginia City, NV 89440
Phone: 775 847-0967
Land records: from 1859 to present, County Recorder
Probate records: County Clerk
   Probate search service: $1.00 per page; copies $1.00 per page
Vital records: County Recorder
   Births: 1887-1949
   Deaths: 1887-1949
   Marriage: all marriages to present (indexes start 1862)

LIBRARIES

Storey County Library
P.O. Box 14, Virginia City, NV
Phone: 775 847-0956 Fax: 775 847-0996 E-mail: lwbouldi@clan.lib.nv.us
Hours: Tuesday & Wednesday: 2:00 p.m. to 8:00 p.m., Thursday: 2:00 p.m. to
5:00 p.m., Saturday: 10:00 a.m. to 2:00 p.m.
Summer Hours: Tuesday & Wednesday: Noon to 8:00 p.m., Thursday: Noon to
5:00 p.m., Saturday: 10:00 a.m. to 2:00 p.m.

NEWSPAPERS

Newspapers	City	UNLV Library has
Campaign Notes	Virginia City	October 8 - November 6, 1900
Daily Independent	Virginia City	October 31, 1874 & Jan. 5, 1875 (daily full-run)
Daily Old Piute	Virginia City	May 17 & June 18, 1864 August 25 & 27, 1864
Daily Safeguard	Virginia City	October 5, 1868 - Feb. 1, 1869 (daily full-run)
Daily Stage	Virginia City	October 9, 1878 - Nov. 5, 1880
Daily Territorial Enterprise	Virginia City	Nov. 17, 1861 - May 8, 1863; April 9, 1865 - January 15, 1893; Dec. 3, 1893 - May 30, 1916 (varies 1860-1916)
Daily Trespass	Virginia City	February 6, 1867 - Oct. 3, 1868
Evening Report	Virginia City	Feb. 2, 1887 - Dec. 31, 1903 (daily 1887-1904)
Footlight	Virginia City	February 16, 1874; Nov. 8, 1875 - January 25, 1887 (varies 1872-1887)
Gold Hill Daily News	Gold Hill	October 12, 1863 - April 8, 1882 (daily full-run)
Gold Hill News	Gold Hill	June 3, 1974 - October 31, 1978
Lariat	Virginia City	August 1877
Monday Budget	Virginia City	December 24, 1917 - Nov. 4, 1918
Monday Budget (1927)	Virginia City	August 29, 1927 - Dec. 23, 1929
Occasional	Virginia City	August 19, 1886
People's Tribune	Gold Hill	January - June 1870
Ramsey Recorder	Ramsey	August 5, 1906 - Nov. 8, 1908 (weekly full-run)

Republican Principles	Virginia City	about 1888, two issues not dated
Sun Mountain Sentinel	Virginia City	January 1, 1964 - February 1965
Territorial Enterprise	Virginia City	March 13 - June 12, 1946
Territorial Enterprise & Virginia		
City News	Virginia City	May 2, 1952 - March 28, 1969
		(weekly 1952-1970)
Territorial Enterprise & Virginia		
City News (1985)	Virginia City	January 11, 1985 - Dec.24, 1986
Virginia City Legend	Virginia City	November 23, 1970; August 5,
		1971 -December 28, 1973
Virginia City News	Virginia City	March 13, 1936 - June 30, 1951
Virginia City Times	Virginia City	1958, 1959 & 1961
Virginia City Times Bonanza	Virginia City	August 8 - December 27, 1969
Virginia City Union	Virginia City	January 21, 1863 - Feb. 5, 1867
Virginia Evening Bulletin	Virginia City	July 6, 1863 - May 16, 1864
		(daily full-run)
Virginia Evening Chronicle	Virginia City	April 8, 1872 - August 6, 1927
Washoe Stock Circular	Virginia City	May 25, 1864

SOCIETIES

Storey County Historical Society
P. O. Box 846, Virginia City, NV 89440

FAMILY HISTORY LIBRARY (Salt Lake City, Utah) HOLDINGS

All microfilmed and microfiched records (unless restricted) are available to rent worldwide at branch Family History Centers and selected larger public and private libraries and societies.

Nevada, Storey - Cemeteries

Parkin, Nona. *Storey County Records*. Salt Lake City : Filmed by the Genealogical Society of Utah, 1997.

v. 1. Birth records/notices: Storey County records 1869-1912; Cemetery census: American Flat and Gold Hill with index, City of Gold Hill Cemetery record, Virginia City Cemetery with index -- v. 2. Death records/notices: Newspaper notices 1862-1912, Storey County death records 1887-1991 with index, Storey County records from 1875, Virginia City death records 1879-1890, Newspaper obituaries, Storey County 1922-1983, Storey County Coroner's records 1879-1887 -- v. 3. Funeral home records: Register of funerals, Virginia City 1879-1914, Old mortuary records 1891-1918, Virginia City mortuary records 1879-1883 with index; City directories: American City, Gold Hill and Silver City

1864-1865 -- v. 4. Marriage records/notices: Storey County marriage records 1862-1929 with index, Newspaper notices 1875-1912 -- v. 5. Newspaper "scats", Pioneer families, Union membership rolls -- v. 6. Church records: Gold Hill Catholic Church, St. Paul's Episcopal Parish, Virginia City -- v. 7. Church records: Virginia City Catholic Church, St. Paul Episcopal Church. Includes some indexing.

Microfilm- 1598459 item 3-5   Vol. 1-3
Microfilm- 1598460 item 1-4   Vol. 4-7

Nevada, Storey - History

Parkin, Nona. *Various years -- Taken From "Scats" at the Nevada Historical Society Library, Reno, Nevada, 1863-1881.*

979.3 A1 no.11, also on microfilm- 0962643 item 10

Typescript. Various people, firms and organizations listed in articles and ads of the Gold Hill Evening News.

Nevada, Storey - Military records - World War, 1914-1918

Banks, Raymond H. *The Banks Compilation of Birth Data of Men with Links to Storey County, Nevada, Who Were Born 1873-1900 : as Found in the Civilian Registration Cards.* L.D.S. microfilm series of World War I Selective Service draft registration cards. Salt Lake City : R.H. Banks, c1996.

979.3 A1 no.59

About 98% of men present in America and born 1873-1900 provided draft card information in 1917 or 1918. Aliens were required to register. Persons already in the military did not register. Includes name, date of birth, ethnic group, birth location or other information, and county or city draft board in the state where registered.

Nevada, Storey - Names, Geographical - History

Ansari, Mary B. *Comstock Place Names : the Names of Storey County, Nevada.* Reno, Nev. : Camp Nevada, c1986.

979.356 E2a

Nevada, Storey - Vital records

Brodek, R. T. *Coroner's Record of Deaths, Storey County, Nevada, 1879-1887.* Salt Lake City : Filmed by the Genealogical Society of Utah, 1993.

Includes name, nativity, gender, age, time and place of death, and cause of death.

Microfilm- 1889228 item 1

Coroner's records   6 Jan 1879-30 May 1887

Parkin, Nona. *Affadavits of Birth 1869-1914 : Filed in the Office of the County Recorder of Storey County, Nevada.*
979.3 A1 no.7, also on microfilm- 0962208 item 3

Parkin, Nona. *Coroner's Records, 1879-1887 : Deaths, April 1887-1911, Storey County, Nevada.*
979.356 V23 , also on microfilm- 0874350 item 4

Storey County (Nevada). County Clerk. *Marriage License Applications and Affidavits, 1874-1950.* Salt Lake City : Filmed by the Genealogical Society of Utah, 1993.
Microfilm- 1901583
  Index, v. 1-2   1875-1940
  Applications, v. 1-10   23 Dec 1874- 4 May 1912
Microfilm- 1901584
  Applications, v. 11-19   2 Dec 1919-1 Feb 1941
  no. 1-200, no. 201-600   (filmed in reverse order)
  no. 1000-601(filmed in reverse order), no. 1416-1001(filmed in reverse order), no. 1842-1666 (filmed in reverse order)
Microfilm- 1901585
  Applications,   1 Feb 1941-12 Dec 1947
  no. 1666-1417 (filmed in reverse order), no. 2292-1843 (filmed in reverse order), no. 2672-2293 (filmed in reverse order), no. 3242-2673 (filmed in reverse order), no. 3605-3243 (filmed in reverse order), no. 4169-3906 (filmed in reverse order)
Microfilm- 1901586
  Applications,   12 Dec 1947-30 Dec 1950
  no. 3906-3606 (filmed in reverse order), no. 4659-4170 (filmed in reverse order)

Storey County (Nevada). County Recorder. *Recorded Birth and Death Certificates, 1887-1949.* Salt Lake City : Filmed by the Genealogical Society of Utah, 1993.

Microfilm- 1889226 item 7	Index, v. A-B	1887-1911
Microfilm- 1889227 item 4	Index, deaths	1890-1896
Microfilm- 1889226 item 8		
Births, v. A	10 Nov 1887- 6 Mar 1905	
Deaths , v. A	6 Mar 1887-27 Dec 1888	
Microfilm- 1889227 item 1-3		
Deaths, v. A	28 Dec 1888-27 Dec 1890	
Births, v. B	1 Jul 1911	
Births, v. E	5 Dec 1926-12 May 1947	
Microfilm- 1889227 item 5-10		

Deaths, v. B-F	5 Oct 1890- 7 Jun 1943
Deaths,	4 Aug 1943-24 Aug 1949

Storey County (Nevada). County Recorder. *Recorded Marriage Certificates, 1862-1952.* Salt Lake City : Filmed by the Genealogical Society of Utah, 1993.
Microfilm- 1889225

Index, groom & bride	24 Feb 1862-Oct 1902
Certificates, v. A-F (v. F p. 1-153)	24 Feb 1862-19 Jul 1939

Microfilm- 1889226 item 1-6

Certificates, v. F-K (v. F p. 153-end)	19 Jul 1939- 9 Aug 1952

Nevada, Storey, Gold Hill - Church records
Daughters of the American Colonists. Delight Camp Cowles Chapter (Reno,Nevada). *St. John's Episcopal Church (Gold Hill, Nevada) Records, 1862-1886.* Salt Lake City : Filmed by the Genealogical Society of Utah, 1959.
Microfilm- 0176648
Includes history, baptisms, marriages, and burials. Includes index.

Nevada, Storey, Virginia City - Cemeteries
Parkin, Nona. *Cemetery Records Virginia City, Storey County, Nevada.*
979.356 V3p, also on microfilm- 0874352 item 4
Contains the city cemetery and the old Jewish burial grounds of Virginia City, Nev.

Nevada, Storey, Virginia City - Church records
Daughters of the American Colonists (Nevada). *Church Register of St. Paul's Episcopal Church, Virginia City, Nevada 1862-1868.* Salt Lake City : Filmed by the Genealogical Society of Utah, 1959.
Microfilm- 0176650

Nevada, Storey, Virginia City - History
McMillen, Erma. *Index to Eliot Lord's "The Drama of Virginia City."* Salt Lake City : Filmed by the Genealogical Society of Utah, 1987.
Microfilm- 1421750 item 3
This is a surname index for Eliot Lord's *The Drama of Virginia City.*

Zauner, Phyllis. *Virginia City: A Mini-History.* Tahoe Paradise, Ca. : Zanel Publications, c1979.
979.356/V1 H2z

Nevada, Storey, Virginia City - Vital records
Gold Hill Cemetery Record Book, 1863-1884. Salt Lake City : Filmed by the
  Genealogical Society of Utah, 1993.
  Microfilm- 1889228 item 2

CHAPTER SEVENTEEN

Washoe County

Washoe County was an original county approved by an act on 25 November 1861. Until then it had been part of Carson County, Utah.

The county takes it name from the aboriginal tribe who inhabited the strip of country from along the base of the Sierra Mountains, from the head of the Carson River to the Truckee River.

CEMETERIES

Masonic Memorial Gardens
437 Stoker Avenue, Reno, NV 89503
Phone: 775 329-2635
Years of operation: 1893-present
Affiliations: Fraternal and non-sectarian
Records: Housed on-site; searches by office personnel only

Mountain View Cemetery
P. O. Box 5118, Reno, NV 89503
Phone: 775 329-9231 Fax: 775 329-9225
Years of operation: 1871-present
Affiliations: Non-sectarian
Records: Located at 435 Stoker Avenue, Reno, NV 89503
Written searches accepted at mailing address

Our Mother of Sorrows
2700 N. Virginia, Reno, NV 89507
Phone: 775 323-0133 Fax: 775 323-1229
Years of operation: 1933-present
Affiliations: Catholic
Records: housed on-site

Sierra Memorial Gardens
Highway 395, Reno, NV 89503
Phone: 775 323-1835   Fax: 775 322-8866
Years of operation: 1980-present
Affiliations: non-sectarian
Records: located at 142 Bell Street, Reno, NV 89503

Incline Village

Tahoe Memorial Columbarium
341 Village Blvd., Incline Village, NV 89451
Phone: 775 831-1612

Verdi

Verdi Cemetery
P.O. Box 221, Verdi, NV 89439-0021
Phone: 775 345-0202
Years of operation: 1864-present
Affiliations: non-sectarian
Records: searches by appointment at 150 Bridge Street, Verdi, NV 89439

CHURCHES

BLACK SPRINGS
Baptist: First Baptist Church, Coreta Way, Black Springs, NV 89506
    Phone: 775 972-9370
CRYSTAL BAY
Pentecostal: United Foursquare Church, 918 Northwood, Crystal Bay, NV
    89402
INCLINE VILLAGE
Episcopal: St. Patrick Episcopalian Church, PO Box 3158, Incline Village, NV
    89450 Phone: 775 831-1418
    St. Patrick's Episcopalian Church, 591 Village Blvd., Incline Village, NV
    89451 Phone: 775 831-0213
Metaphysical: Lakeside Christian Essene, PO Box 4468, Incline Village, NV
    89450
Presbyterian: Incline Village Presbyterian, McCourry Blvd & Mt., PO Box F.
    Incline Village, NV 89450 Phone: 775 831-3726
Protestant: Church of the Lake, 250 Village Blvd., Incline Village, NV 89451
    Phone: 775 831-5030
Roman Catholic: St. Francis of Assisi, PO Box 4226, Incline Village, NV
    890490 Phone: 775 831-0490

NIXON
Assemblies of God: Pyramid Lake Assembly, PO Box 222, Nixon, NV 89424
Phone: 775 574-0121
Episcopal: St. Mary the Virgin Episcopalian Church, Nixon, NV 89424
Phone: 775 574-0198
RENO
Adventist: Jehovah's Witnesses Hall, 601 Spokane St., Reno, NV 89512
Phone: 775 329-6842
Nevada Utah Conference Seventh Day Adventist, PO Box 10730, Reno, NV
89510
African Methodist: Bethel African Methodist Episcopal Church, 220 Bell St.,
Reno, NV 89503 Phone: 775 322-1043
Assemblies of God: Assembly of God, 11000 Lemmon Valley Dr., Reno, NV
89506 Phone: 775 972-1088
First Assembly of God Church, 425 Gentry Way, Reno, NV 89502
Phone: 775 825-4448
Little Portion Assembly, 355 Denslowe Dr., Reno, NV 89512
Phone: 775 329-1959
Truckee Meadows Christian Center, 524 Bell St., Reno, NV 89503
Phone: 775 323-7827
Baptist: Calvary Regular Baptist Church, 1881 Harvard Way, Reno, NV 89502
Phone: 775 322-0393
Community Baptist Church, 1001 Wheeler Ave., Reno, NV 89502
Phone: 775 323-3556
Faith Baptist Church, PO Box 10943, Reno, NV 89510 Phone: 775 826-9019
Fellowship Baptist Church, 4050 Casa Blanca Rd., Reno, NV 89502
Phone: 775 786-0406
First Baptist Church, 1330 Foster Dr., Reno, NV 89509 Phone: 775 323-7141
First Baptist of Black Springs, 100 Coretta Way, Reno, NV 89506
Phone: 775 322-8730
Greater New Hope Baptist, 1810 Helena Ave., Reno, NV 89512
Phone: 775 329-6260
Nevada Area Baptist Convention, 406 California Ave., Reno, NV 89509
Phone: 775 322-0895
Northgate Community Baptist Church, 1300 Stardust, PO Box 70605, Reno,
NV 89570 Phone: 775 786-6933
Pilgrim Rest Baptist Church, 1395 Montello St., Reno, NV 89512
Phone: 775 329-4779
Buddist: Eikoyi Institute of America, 548 California Ave., Reno, NV 89509
Mountain Seminar Center, PO Box 1328, Reno, NV 89504
Pansophic Institute, Box 2422, Reno, NV 89505
Silver Mountain Sangha, 3060 Sagitarius, Reno, NV 89504
Phone: 775 786-1484

Churches of Christ: Church of Christ, 2850 Wrondel Way, Reno, NV 89502
Phone: 775 825-0191

First Christian Church of Reno, 820 Plumas St., Reno, NV 89509
Phone: 775 322-8642

First Church of Christ, 501 Riverside Dr., Reno, NV 89503
Phone: 775 322-5142

Virginia Street Church of Christ, 1505 N. Virginia St., Reno, NV 89503
Phone: 775 972-0419

Wedekind Road Church of Christ, 1555 Wedekind Rd., Reno, NV 89512
Phone: 775 322-5635

Christian Science: First Church of Christ Scientist, 485 E. Plumb Ln., 89502

Congregational: Reno First Congregational Church, 627 Sunnyside Dr., Reno, NV 89503 Phone: 775 747-1414

Sierra Meadows United Church of Christ, 1000 Zolezzi Ln., Reno, NV 89511
Phone: 775 853-1013

Episcopal: Holy Spiritual Episcopalian Church, 3140 W. Plumb Ln., Reno, NV 89509

St. Paul's Episcopalian Church, 2390 W. 7th St., Reno, NV 89503
Phone: 775 747-4949

St. Stephen Episcopalian Church, 2400 W. 7th St., Reno, NV 89503
Phone; 775 747-4900

Trinity Episcopalian Church, Rainbow & Island Ave., PO Box 2246, Reno, NV 89505 Phone: 775 329-4279

Evangelical Lutheran: Faith Evangelical Lutheran Church, 2075 W. 7th St., Reno, NV 89503 Phone: 775 747-3246

Good Shepherd Lutheran Church, 501 California Ave., Reno, NV 89509
Phone: 775 329-0696

Holy Cross Lutheran Church, 4895 S. McCarran Blvd, PO Box 71137, Reno, NV 89570 Phone: 775 827-4822

Holiness: Calvary Church of the Nazarene, 8820 Paloma Way, Reno, NV 89506 Phone: 775 972-7401

Community Alliance Church, PO Box 9745, Reno, NV 89507
Phone: 775 331-8511

First Church of God, 1201 Yori Ave., Reno, NV 89502 Phone: 775 322-0684

First Church of the Nazarene, 7400 Del Monte Lane, Reno, NV 89511
Phone: 775 853-2018

Reno-Sparks Gospel Mission, 145 W. 3rd St., Reno, NV 89501
Phone: 775 323-0386

Salvation Army, 180 W. 5th St., Reno, NV 89503 Phone: 775 322-6927

Salvation Army, 835 E. 2nd St., Reno, NV 89502 Phone: 775 689-2240

Independent Fundamentalist: Faith Bible Church, 244 Courtney Ln, Reno, NV 89523 Phone: 775 747-6366

First Evangelical Free Church, 3195 Everett Dr., Reno, NV 89503
Phone: 775 747-1217

Grace Community Church, PO Box 10943, Reno, NV 89510
Phone: 775 348-9777

Mount Rose Evangelical Free Church, 9725 S. Virginia St., Reno, NV 89511
Phone: 775 852-7383

Jewish: Temple Emanu-El, 1031 Manzanita Ln., Reno, NV 89509
Phone: 775 825-5600

Temple Sinal, 3405 Gulling Rd., Reno, NV 89505 Phone: 775 747-5508

Latter-day Saints: Church of Jesus Christ Latter-day Saints,
1309 Buena Vista Ave., Reno, NV 89503 Phone: 775 786-8542

Church of Jesus Christ Latter-day Saints, 95 W. 11th St., Reno, NV 89503
Phone: 775 322-0493

Las Vegas First Ward, 501 9th St., Reno, NV 89503 Phone: 775 387-9275

Mount Rose Fourth Ward Church of Latter-day Saints, 4751 Neil Rd., Reno,
NV 89502 Phone: 775 826-0555

Mount Rose Second Ward Church of Latter-day Saints, 1095 Golconda Dr.,
Reno, NV 89509 Phone: 775 825-8794

Reno Church of Latter-day Saints, 1375 Coleman Dr., Reno, NV 89503
Phone: 775 747-9988

Reno Second Ward Church of Latter-day Saints, 2505 Kings Row, Reno, NV
89503 Phone: 775 747-6612

University Ward Church of Latter-day Saints, 1309 Buena Vista Ave., Reno,
NV 89503 Phone: 775 323-1838

Valley Second Ward of Latter-day Saints, 8080 Lemmon Dr., Reno, NV 89506
Phone: 775 972-0776

Washoe Valley Latter-day Saints Ward, 440 McCellan Dr., Reno, NV 89511
Phone: 775 849-1170

Lutheran: Shepherd of the Mountains Lutheran, 955 W. Peckham Ln., Reno,
NV 89509 Phone: 775 827-4242

Lutheran- Missouri Synod: St. Luke's Lutheran Church, 3835 Lakeside Dr.,
Reno, NV 89509 Phone: 775 825-0588

Metaphysical: Church of the Cosmos, 701 Marsh Ave., Reno, NV 89509

Faith in God Spiritual Church, 11925 Jean Way, Reno, NV 89506
Phone: 775 972-3337

First Church Religious Science, 4685 Lakeside Dr., Reno, NV 89509
Phone: 775 826-0566

Reno Unity Center, 847 N. Center St., Reno, NV 89501 Phone: 775 322-2024

Spiritual Regeneration Move, 1 E. 1st St., Reno, NV 89501

Unity Church of Reno, 2207 Kings Row, Reno, NV 89503 Phone: 747-2207

Methodist: First United Methodist Church, W. 1st and West St., Reno, NV
89501 Phone: 775 322-4564

St. Paul's United Methodist Church, 1660 Grandview Ave., Reno, NV 89503
Phone: 775 747-1431

South Reno United Methodist Church, 4342 Loreta Lane, Reno, NV 89502
Phone: 775 851-1181

Muslin: Alarkam Mosque, 1095 N. Virginia St. No. 3, Reno, NV 89503
Phone: 775 786-2522

North Nevada Muslin Commun, PO Box 9117, Reno, NV 89507

Orthodox: Greek Orthodox Church, 4795 Lakeside Dr., Reno, NV 89509
Phone: 775 825-5365

St. James Orthodox Church, 1170 Codel Way, Reno, NV 89503
Phone: 775 786-5545

Pentecostal: Believers Fellowship, 120 Hubbard Way, Reno, NV 89502
Phone: 775 827-0333

Glory Temple, 16255 S. Virginia St., Reno, NV 89511 Phone: 775 849-1002

Lighthouse Full Gospel Ministry, 2500 Dickerson Rd., Apt.192, Reno, NV 89503

Reno Christian Fellowship, 1700 Zolezzi Lane, Reno, NV 89511
Phone: 775 853-4234

Pentecostal Church of God: Church of God, PO Box 7841, Reno, NV 89510
Phone: 775 826-3460

Faith Deliverance Church of God, 710 Autumn Hills Dr., Reno, NV 89511

Trinity Temple Church of God, 2580 Cannan St., Reno, NV 89512

United Church of God, PO Box 5241, Reno, NV 89513

Presbyterian: Temple Sinai Reformed Presbyterian, 3405 Gulling Rd., Reno, NV 89503 Phone: 775 747-5508

Presbyterian (U.S.A.): Covenant Presbyterian Church, 3690 Grant Dr., Reno, NV 89509 Phone: 775 827-4110

Protestant: All Faiths Spiritual Center, PO Box 7101, Reno, NV 89510

Center of Light and Fellowship, 7675 Hughes Dr., Reno, NV 89506

Church in the Valley, 635 S. Arlington Ave., Reno, NV 89509
Phone: 775 329-5660

Church of the Covenant, 62 Court St., Reno, NV 89501

Church of the Second Advent, 16010 S. Virginia St., Reno, NV 895111
Phone: 775 853-6660

Fellowship of Believers, PO Box 50205, Reno, NV 89513

Friends Reno Meeting, PO Box 20636, Reno, NV 89515 Phone: 775 329-9400

Little Church of the Sierras, 130 W. 1ˢᵗ St., Reno, NV 89501
Phone: 775 322-3474

Sierra Community Church, 124 W. Taylor St., Reno, NV 89509

University Family Fellowship, PO Box 50545, Reno, NV 89513
Phone: 775 786-8884

Victory Chapel, 6200 Meadowood Mall Cir., Reno, NV 89502
Phone: 775 825-1393

Roman Catholic: Church of St. Albert the Great, 1259 Saint Alberts St., Reno, NV 89503 Phone: 775 747-0722

Little Flower Catholic Church, 1280 Casazza Dr., Reno, NV 89502 Phone: 775 323-2931

Our Lady of the Snows, 1138 Wright St., Reno, NV 89509 Phone: 775 323-6894

Our lady of Wisdom Catholic Church, 1001 N. Virginia St., Reno, NV 89503 Phone: 775 329-7462

St. Michael's Catholic Church, 14075 Mount Vida St., Reno, NV 89506 Phone: 775 972-7462

St. Theresa Infant Jesus Church, 875 E. Plumb Lane, Reno, NV 89502 Phone: 775 322-2255

St. Thomas Aquinas Cathedral, 310 W. 2nd St., Reno, NV 89503 Phone: 775 329-2571

Seventh day Adventist: Seventh Day Adventist Church, 1200 S. Arlington Ave., Reno, NV 89509 Phone: 775 322-9642

Sparks Seventh Day Adventist Church, Rock and McCaren, Reno, NV 89502 Phone: 775 827-5613

Southern Baptist: Fellowship Baptist Church, 130 Hydraulic St., PO Box 60283, Reno, NV 89506 Phone: 775 972-1555

First Southern Baptist Church, 2301 Kings Row, Reno, NV 89503 Phone: 775 747-3073

Granite Hills Baptist Church, 4950 Texas Ave., Reno, NV 90506 Phone: 775 972-0887

Reno Second Baptist Church, 1265 Montello St., Reno, NV 89512 Phone: 775 786-1017

Steamboat Baptist Church, 1480 Geiger Grade Rd., Reno, NV 89511 Phone: 775 851-8891

Unclassified: Baha'i Faith, 503 Modoc St., Reno, NV 89509 Phone: 775 322-2813

Eckankar Satsung Society, 1450 E. 2nd St., Reno, NV 89502

Metro Community Church of the Sierras, PO Box 21192, Reno, NV 89515 Phone: 775 829-8602

Metropolitan Community Church, 120 Thoma St., Reno, NV 89501 Phone: 775 348-7377

Unification Church, 1410 E. 9th St., Reno, NV 89512 Phone: 775 786-1858

Unitarian Universalist Fellowship, 780 Del Monte Lane, Reno, NV 89511 Phone: 775 851-7100

SPARKS

Adventist: Jehovah's Witness, 5555 Lupin Dr., Sparks, NV 89433
Phone: 775 673-4777
Jehovah's Witnesses Hall, 3400 Spanish Springs Rd., Sparks, NV 89436
Phone: 775 331-5153
Assemblies of God: New Life Christian Assembly, 1327 Pyramid Way,
Sparks, NV 89431 Phone: 775 358-2232
Baptist: Emmanuel First Baptist Church, 1100 12th St., Sparks, NV 89431
Phone: 775 358-7259
Lighthouse Baptist Church, 2751 Wabash Cir., Sparks, NV 89434
Mount Hope Baptist Church, PO Box 5056, Sparks, NV 89432
Phone: 775 972-8479
New Jerusalem Baptist Church, 1315 Prater Way, Sparks, NV 89431
Phone: 775 331-0330
Second Baptist Church, 983 Lepori Way, Sparks, NV 89431
Christian Church of Christ: Church of Christ, 475 E. Queen Way, Sparks,
NV 89431 Phone: 775 358-0479
Church of Christ Truckee Meadows, 605 Spice Island Dr., Sparks, NV 89431
Phone: 775 331-4313
First Christian Church, 445 Queen Way, Sparks, NV 89431
Phone: 775 358-0507
Episcopal: St. Paul's Episcopalian Church, 12th and Oddie Blvd., Sparks, NV
89431 Phone: 775 358-4474
Evangelical Lutheran: Lord of Mercy Lutheran Church, 3400 Pyramid Way,
Sparks, NV 89431 Phone: 775 358-7863
Holiness: Community First Church of God, 198 Richards Way, Sparks, NV
89431 Phone: 775 358-7215
First Church of the Nazarene, 2200 El Rancho Dr., Sparks, NV 89431
Shepherd of the Valley Nazarene Church, 205 W. Gepford Pky., Sparks, NV
89433 Phone: 775 673-2700
Independent: First Evangelical Free Church, 1913 Rosemary Dr., Sparks, NV
89434
Latter-day Saints: Sparks Second Ward of Latter-day Saints, 1114 Prater
Way, Sparks, NV 89431 Phone: 775 358-6785
Valley First Ward of Latter-day Saints, 2955 Rock Blvd., Sparks, NV 89431
Phone: 775 359-6713
Lutheran: Our Savior Lutheran Church, 1900 1st St., Sparks, NV 89431
Phone: 775 358-0743
Metaphysical: Living Church Religious Science, PO Box 567, Sparks, NV
89432 Phone: 775 356-7053
Methodist: Sparks United Methodist Church, 1231 Pyramid Way, Sparks, NV
89431 Phone: 775 358-0925

Pentecostal: Calvary Chapel, 3095 Round Mountain Rd., Sparks, NV 89434
Phone: 775 356-7902
Christian Faith Fellowship, 230 Coney Island Dr., Sparks, NV 89431
Phone: 775 358-1986
The Cornerstone Church, PO Box 2223, Sparks, NV 89432
Phone: 775 329-1916
First United Pentecostal Church: 615 Queen Way, Sparks, NV 89431
Phone: 775 358-5116
Sparks Foursquare Church, 2308 Coney Island Dr., Sparks, NV 89431
Phone: 775 331-3147
Pentecostal Church of God: Holy Temple Church of God, 2760 Probasco Way,
Sparks, NV 89431 Phone: 775 355-8600
Sparks Church of God, 1400 Russell Way, Sparks, NV 89431
Sparks Church of God, 416 Pyramid Way, Sparks, NV 89431
Presbyterian: Reno Presbyterian Church, 148 Richards Way, Sparks, NV
89431 Phone: 775 358-4544
Westminister Presbyterian Church, 2655 N. Rock Blvd. #P, PO Box 1983,
Sparks, NV 89432 Phone: 775 358-2100
Protestant: Agape Faith Ministries, PO Box 20418, Sparks, NV 89433
Phone: 775 673-5695
Fresh Wind Christian Fellowship, 1129 Brooktree Dr. Apt. 2, Sparks, NV
89434
International Constitutional Church, 1015 Spanish Springs Rd., Sparks, NV
89434
Living Word Ministries, 5390 Madeiros Dr., Sparks, NV 89433
New Hope Covenant Church, 1864 Deming Way, Sparks, NV 89431
Phone: 775 358-0281
Search Within Fellowship, 6300 Blackwood Rd., Sparks, NV 89433
University Family Fellowship, 2105 Capurro Way No. C., Sparks, NV 89431
Phone: 775 359-2222
Roman Catholic: Catholic Church, 225 E. 5th Ave., Sparks, NV 89433
Phone: 775 673-3313
Holy Cross Catholic Church, 3175 Goldy Way, Sparks, NV 89434
Phone: 775 358-2544
Immaculate Conception Catholic Church, 590 Pyramid Way, Sparks, NV
Phone: 775 358-5977
St. Peter Canisius Church, 225 E. 5th Ave., Sparks, NV 89433
Southern Baptist Convention: First Baptist Church, 525 E. 4th Ave., Sparks,
NV 89433 Phone: 775 673-1118
Temple Baptist Church, 1125 Stanford Way, Sparks, NV 89431
Phone: 775 358-2138
Unclassified: Church of Inner Reality, 1303 Probasco Way, Sparks, NV 89431

WADSWORTH
Episcopal: St. Michael of All Angels Church, Wadsworth, NV 89442

COURTHOUSE

Washoe County Courthouse
P.O. Box 11130, Reno, NV 89520-0027
Phone: 775 328-3661, County Recorder; 775 328-3260, County Clerk;
775 328-2400, County Health Department;
775 328-3110, Court Clerk
Land records: 1862 to present, County Recorder; research area available for public use
Copy costs: $1.00 per page, plus $3.00 for certification
Naturalization records: County Clerk, $1.00 per page, $4.00 for each certificate
Probate records: County Clerk, copy costs $1.00 per page
Vital records: County Health Department
Births: mid-1900s to present, $11.00 per copy
Deaths: mid-1900s to present, $8.00 per copy
Marriages: $7.00 per copy; no personal checks-money order or cashier's check only

FUNERAL HOMES

Reno

Northern Nevada Memorial Cremation & Burial Society
616 South Wells Avenue, Reno, NV
Phone: 775 322-2772, Fax: 775 322-5814

O'Brien-Rogers-Crosby Funeral Home
600 West Second, Reno, NV 89503
Phone: 775 323-6191

Ross, Burke & Knobel Mortuary
2155 Kietzke Lane, Reno, NV 89502
Phone: 775 323-4154

Walton's Sierra Chapel
875 West 2nd Street, Reno, NV 89503
Phone: 775 323-7189

Sparks

Ross, Burke & Knobel Mortuary
1538 "C" Street, Sparks, NV 89431
Phone: 775 359-0440

Waltons Sparks Funeral Home
1745 Sullivan Lane, Sparks, NV 89431
Phone: 775 359-2210

LIBRARIES

Reno Family History Center
4751 Neil Rd, Mail: 2931 Randolph Court, Reno, NV 89502
Phone: 775 826-1130

University of Nevada, Reno
Noble H. Getchell Library, Reno, NV 89557-0044
Phone: 775 784-6533   Fax: 775 784-1751   Internet:
http://www.library.unr.edu
Founded: 1886

Washoe County Library
301 S Center Street, P.O. Box 2151, Reno, NV 89505
Phone: 775 785-4190   Fax: 775 785-4609   Internet:
http://www.washoe.lib.nv.us
Reference e-mail: reference@washoe.lib.nv.us   Periodicals e-mail:
periodicals@washoe.lib.nv.us
Founded: 1902
Billinghurst Branch Library, 6685 Chesterfield Lane, Reno, NV 89503;
Phone: 775 746-5858
Fax: 775 746-5859
Hours: Tuesday & Wednesday: 2:00 p.m. to 8:00 p.m., Thursday & Friday:
   2:00 p.m. to 6:00 p.m., Saturday: 10:00 a.m. to 2:00 p.m.
Galena, 3600 Butch Cassidy Way, 89511; Phone: 775 851-5639;
Fax: 775 851-5636
Hours: Tuesday & Wednesday: 2:00 p.m. to 8:00 p.m., Thursday & Friday:
   2:00 p.m. to 6:00 p.m., Saturday: 10:00 a.m. to 2:00 p.m.
Gerlach Branch, 555 E Sunset Blvd, Gerlach, NV 89412;
Phone: 775 557-2447; Fax: 775 557-2450
Hours: Monday through Friday: 8:30 a.m. tp 3:00 p.m., Tuesday: 5:30 to 7:30
p.m.

Incline Branch Library, 846 Tahoe Blvd, Incline Villae, NV 89451;
Phone: 775 832-4130
Fax: 775 832-4145; E-mail: incline@washoe.lib.nv.us
Hours: Monday to Friday: 11:00 a.m. to 6:00 p.m., Sat.: 11:00 a.m. to 3:00
p.m.
Mendive Branch Library, 1900 Whitewood Drive, Sparks, NV 89434;
Phone: 775 353-5989
Fax: 775 353-5988
Hours: Tuesday & Wednesday: 2:00 p.m. to 8:00 p.m., Thursday & Friday:
2:00 p.m. to 6:00 p.m., Saturday: 10:00 a.m. to 2:00 p.m.
Peavine Branch Library, 1075 N Hills Blvd #340, Reno,NV 89506;
Phone: 775 972-0281
Fax: 775 972-6810; E-mail: peavine@washoe.lib.nv.us
Hours: Monday through Wednesday: 10:00 a.m. to 8:00 p.m., Thursday: 10:00
a.m. to 5:00 p.m., Friday & Saturday: 10:00 a.m. to 1:00 p.m.
Reno Branch Library, P.O. Box 2151, 301 S Center, Reno, NV 89505;
Phone: 775 785-4190
Fax: 775 785-4609
E-mail: reference@washoe.lib.nv.us
E-mail: periodicals@washoe.lib.nv.us
Hours: Monday through Wednesday: 10:00 a.m. to 8:00 p.m., Thursday &
Friday: 10:00 a.m. to 6:00 p.m., Sat.: 10:00 a.m. to 5:00 p.m., Sunday: Noon
to 5:00 p.m.

Sierra View Branch Library, 4001 S Virginia St, Reno,NV 89502
Phone: 775 827-3232
Fax: 775 827-8792; E-mail: sierraview@washoe.lib.nv.us
Hours: Monday through Thursday: 10:00 a.m. to 8:00 p.m., Friday & Saturday:
10:00 a.m. to 6:00 p.m., Saturday: Noon to 5:00 p.m.
Sparks Branch Library, 1125 12th St, Sparks, NV 89431;
Phone: 775 352-3200; Fax: 775 352-3207
E-mail: sparks@washoe.lib.nv.us
Hours: Monday through Wednesday: 10:00 a.m. to 8:00 p.m., Thursday &
Friday: 10:00 a.m. to 6:00 p.m., Saturday: 10:00 a.m. to 5:00 p.m.
Traner-Duncan Branch Library, 1700 Carville Dive, Reno, NV 89512;
Phone: 775 333-5134
Fax: 775 333-5076
Hours: Tuesday through Friday: 2:00 p.m. to 6:00 p.m., Saturday: 10:00 a.m. to
2:00 p.m.
Verdi Branch Library, 250 Bridge St, Verdi, NV 89439;
Phone: 775 345-8104; Fax: 775 345-7277
Hours: Tuesday through Friday: 2:00 p.m. to 6:00 p.m., Saturday: 10:00 a.m. to
2:00 p.m.

NEWSPAPERS

Gazette Journal
P.O. Box 22000, Reno, NV 89520
Phone: 775 788-6200, 800 848-5048   Fax: 775 788-6438

Newspapers	City	UNLV Library has
Ahora	Reno	July 23, 1987 - date
Air Age News	Reno	March 14, 1867 - March 12, 1968
Air Age News	Sparks	March 26, 1968
Bolletino del Nevada	Reno	June 19, 1915 - May 26, 1944 (weekly full-run)
Boots and Chutes	Reno	February 5, 1954 - April 15, 1955
CAPReno	Reno	April 1948 - June 1949
Citizen	Reno	Dec. 15, 1965 - Aug. 30, 1966
Cyclone Occasional	Reno	May 23, 1891
Daily Evening Crescent	Reno	February 12 - June 16, 1875
Daily Lantern	Reno	December 10, 1907 - Nov. 1, 1912
Daily Morning Star	Reno	October 21, 1884
Daily Nevada Democrat	Reno	June 30 - August 26. 1875
Daily Nevada State Journal	Reno	April 2, 1874 - Sep. 24, 1907
Daily Nevada Tribune	Reno	April 22 - July 15, 1896
Daily Nevadan Democrat	Reno	June 30 - August 26, 1875
Daily Nevada State Journal	Reno	April 2, 1874 - Sep. 24, 1907
Daily Nevada Tribune	Reno	April 22 - July 15, 1896
Daily Sparks Tribune	Sparks	June 27, 1988 - date
Eastern Slope	Washoe City	March 31, 1866 - June 20, 1868
Evening Telegram	Reno	April 9 & 23, June 24 & 25, 1903
Fighting Mechanic	Reno	August 10, September 7 & 14, & November 2, 1918
Flyer	Reno	January 9, 1943 - Nov. 2, 1945
Forum	Sparks	August 2, 1909 - April 27, 1910
Free Lance	Reno	Clippings: November 13, 1889 & Dec 1889
Gerlach Express	Gerlach	June 19, 1914
Harriman Herald	Harriman	February 13 - March 26, 1904
Hearth and Home	Reno	July 29 - October 28, 1966
High Sierra Times	Incline Village	Nov. 26, 1976 - Sep. 13, 1978
Home and the Range	Reno	February - July 1968
Intermountain Liberal	Reno	February 1 - September 1, 1925
Italian - French Colony	Reno	Nov.r 14, 1908 - Feb. 20, 1909
Jumbo Miner	Jumbo	April 4 - July 25, 1908

Lake Tahoe's North Shore Villager	Crystal Bay	January 4 & 10, 1963
Lantern	Reno	Dec. 25, 1919 - April 8, 1928
Magnet	Sparks	February 9, 1910
Mining Digest	Reno	December 1, 1908
Mining Press	Reno	August 31, 1938 - July 1949
Native Nevadan (Reno)	Reno	February 18, 1966 - date
Nevadan Bugle	Reno	June 29, August 3 & 10, 1912
Nevadan Churchman	Reno	December 1908 - Dec. 1912 (monthly full-run)
Nevadan Citizen (Reno)	Reno	June & December 1897
Nevada Democrat	Reno	October 10, 1914 - Sep. 3, 1915 (weekly full-run)
Nevada Federal Journal	Sparks	September 1964
Nevada Federationist	Reno	April 25, 1917 - June 5, 1919
Nevada Federationist and Home Industry Advocate	Reno	Sep. 24, 1915 - April 18, 1917
Nevada Forum	Sparks	January 8, 1905 - July 30, 1909
Nevada Home Builder	Reno	October 19, 1917 - Oct. 10, 1919
Nevada Independent	Reno	August 13 - October 15, 1938 (weekly full-run)
Nevada Independent & Reno Reporter	Reno	March 9 - June 29, 1950
Nevada Labor Record	Reno	March 4, 1932 - Sep. 22, 1933 (weekly full-run)
Nevada Legionnaire	Sparks	October 1950 - February 1958 (monthly full-run)
Nevada Liberal	Reno	August 1, 1924 - January 1, 1925
Nevadan Liberal (1926)	Reno	June 1 - October 27, 1926
Nevada Methodist	Sparks	September 1907
Nevada Miner	Reno	September 15, 1902
Nevada Mines & Farms	Reno	Dec. 26, 1911 - Dec. 31, 1912
Nevada Mining Investor	Reno	October 15, 1906 - June 15, 1907
Nevada Mining News (Reno)	Reno	July 27, 1907 - May 27, 1909 (weekly full-run)
Nevada Mining Press	Reno	Sep. 9, 1921 - May 22, 1931 (varies 1918-1931)
Nevada Observer	Reno	January 2, 1904 - March 9, 1908
Nevada Observer (1917)	Reno	Dec. 12, 1917 - May 15, 1918
Nevada Rancher	Sparks	May, 1971 - date
Nevada Register	Reno	January 4, 1963 - August 30, 1973
Nevada Rockroller	Reno	June 27 - September 16, 1914

(weekly full-run)

Nevada Searchlight	Reno	September 14, 1922
Nevada Socialist	Reno	September - October 26, 1914
Nevada Socialist (1916)	Reno	July 1 - November 1, 1916
Nevada Sportsman	Sparks	March 23, 1956 - Sep. 20, 1957
Nevada State Builder	Reno	May 7, 1927 clipping
Nevada State Builder	Reno	April 24, 1931 - January 29, 1932
Nevada State Journal	Reno	Nov. 23, 1870 - July 31, 1875
Nevada State Journal	Reno	Sep. 25, 1907 - Sep. 30, 1983
Nevada State Labor News	Reno	September 1941 - Nov. 10, 1949
Nevada State Public Observer	Sparks	December 1964
Nevada Tribune (Reno)	Reno	December 15, 1945
Nevada Veterans Journal	Reno	April 1963 - October 1970
Nevada Voice	Reno	March 1926 - April 1927
Nevadan	Reno	October 17 - 31, 1916
Nevadan	Reno	January 1979 - October 1981
Nevadan Times	Wadsworth	December 16, 1927
News From the Base	Reno	Apr 7, Sep 1, Oct 19 & Nov 2, 1945
North Lake Tahoe Bonanza	Incline Village	September 2, 1981 - date
North Tahoe World	Crystal Bay	May 1, 1969 - April 17, 1970
Plaindealer	Reno	March 28, 1881 - Oct. 28, 1899
Recreations Whirlwind	Reno	December 1, 1938
Reno Annual Advertiser	Reno	December 25, 1878
Reno Bazaar	Reno	December 1882
Reno Courier	Reno	about 1905, one issue
Sparks Headlight	Sparks	January 21, 1905
Sparks Reno Tribune	Sparks	June 19, 1985 - October 29, 1986
Sparks Tribune	Sparks	Sep. 1, 1910 - March 5, 1980
Sparks Tribune (1983)	Sparks	October 5, 1983 - June 12, 1985
Sparks Tribune (1986)	Sparks	October 30, 1986 - June 23, 1988
Star	Reno	February 11, 1904
Student Record	Reno	October 19, 1893 - May 25, 1910
Theatre Herald	Reno	October 4, 1921 - March 25, 1922
This Week in Reno	Reno	October 2 - 9, 1931
Tribune	Sparks	March 12, 1980 - Sep. 28, 1983
University of Nevada, Reno		
Sagebrush	Reno	August 29, 1910 - August 4, 1967
Valley Green Sheet	Sparks	November 8 - December 20, 1972
Valley Outlook	Sun Valley	Dec. 18, 1972 - July 12, 1973
Valley Press	Gerlach	Dec. 15, 1961 - February 23, 1962
Vigilant Reporter	Reno	August 22 - October 4, 1957
Voice of the People	Reno	October 10, 1910 - June 22, 1911

Wadsworth Dispatch	Wadsworth	Sep. 21, 1892 - July 22, 1899 (semi-weekly full run)
Wadsworth Semi-Weekly Dispatch	Wadsworth	July 28, 1899 - Dec. 23, 1904 (semi-weekly full run)
Washoe County Citizen	Reno	October 24, 1960 - June 22, 1961 (weekly full-run)
Washoe Times	Washoe City	Jan 10, 24 & 31; Sep 19 & Nov 7,1863
Washoe Weekly Star	Washoe City	August 27 & December 31, 1864
Washoe Weekly Times	Washoe City	January 28 - November 4, 1865 (weekly full-run)
Weekly Nevada State Journal	Reno	August 7, 1875 - Dec. 26, 1891
Western Miner	Reno	May 31, 1915 - June 30, 1916; April 30 - June 16, 1919; March 15 - May 10, 1927
Western Wildlife	Reno	June 1977

SOCIETIES

Nevada Historical Society, Museum-Research Library
1650 N Virginia Street, Reno, NV 89503
Phone: 775 688-1191   Fax: 775 688-2917
Founded: 1904
Special collections: Nevada History collection, photographs
Nevada newspaper indexes:
  Eastern Slope, 1865-1868
  Nevada State Journal, 1870-1876; 1880-1884 (currently being updated)
  Reno Crescent, July 1868-March 1874
  Territorial Enterprise, 1859-1881 (currently being updated)
  Washoe Times, 1862-1863
  Washoe Weekly Star, 1864-1865, *Washoe Weekly Times*, 1865-1868

FAMILY HISTORY LIBRARY (Salt Lake City, Utah) HOLDINGS

All microfilmed and microfiched records (unless restricted) are available to rent worldwide at branch Family History Centers and selected larger public and private libraries and societies.

Nevada, Washoe - Archives and libraries - Inventories, registers, catalogs
Inventory of the County Archives of Nevada, no. 16, Washoe County (Reno). Prepared by the Historical Records Survey, Division of Women's and Professional Projects, Works Progress Administration. Reno, Nev. Historical Records Survey, 1938.
979.355 A3i, also on microfiche- 6100372

Nevada, Washoe - Biography
Bixler, W.K. *A Dozen Sierra Success Stories, Twelve Individualists of Our Time : Eva Adams, Norman Biltz, Paul Claiborne, Clel Georgetta, Harvey Gross, Raymond Knisley, Wayne Poulsen, George Probasco, Archie D. Stevenot, Lester D. Summerfield, Harvey West, Jim A.E. Wilson.* Tahoe Valley, Calif. : s.n., 1964.
979.4 D3bw

Nevada, Washoe - Cemeteries
Cemetery Records of Nevada.
979.35 V3c, also on microfilm- 1421873 item 11
Record contains tombstone inscriptions from the following cemeteries: Catholic, Protestant, Masonic, Knights of Pythias and Hebrew (all in Virginia City), Protestant and Catholic (Gold Hill), Silver City and Dayton (Lyon County) and Washoe City (Washoe County).

Nevada, Washoe - Census - 1862
1862 Census of Washoe County, Territory of Nevada. [S.l. : s.n.], 1983.
Microfilm- 1705177

Nevada, Washoe - Dwellings
Mapes, Gloria Millicent. *Bowers Mansion.* [S.l. : s.n.], 1952.
979.3 A1 no.26
Eilley Orrum Bowers built this mansion, which is located between Reno and Carson City, Nevada in 1862.

Nevada, Washoe - Genealogy - Periodicals
The Nevada Desert. -- Vol. 6, no. 5 Reno, Nev. : Nevada State Genealogical
   Society, 1987.
   979.355 D25n
   Monthly. Continues: Nevada State Genealogical Society newsletter.
   Description based on:Vol.6, no.5

Nevada, Washoe - History
Parkin, Nona. *Excerpts From Memories of George E. Peckham, Printed by
   Nevada Historical Society Papers, 1917-1920.*
   979.3 A1 no.4, also on microfilm- 0962211 item 3
   Brief record of people and events in Galena, Reno, etc.

Hummel, N. A. *General History and Resources of Washoe County, Nevada.*
   Reno, Nev. : Evening Gazette Job Print., 1888.
   979.3 A1 no.18, also on microfilm- 0908706 item 4.

Nevada, Washoe - History - Newspapers
Basso, David. *Washoe County.* Reno, Nev. : s.n., c1971.
   979.3 A1 no.21

Nevada, Washoe - Military records - World War, 1914-1918
Banks, Raymond H. *The Banks Compilation of Birth Data of Men with Links
   to Washoe County, Nevada, Who Were Born 1873-1900 : as Found in the
   Civilian Registration Cards.* L.D.S. microfilm series of World War I
   Selective Service draft registration cards. Salt Lake City : R.H. Banks,
   c1996.
   979.355 M28b
   An alphabetical listing by surname of men who completed civilian
   registration cards for their draft boards during 1917-1919. About 98% of
   men present in America and born 1873-1900 provided draft card
   information in 1917 or 1918. Aliens were required to register. Persons
   already in the military did not register. Includes name, date of birth, ethnic
   group, birth place or other information, and county or city draft board in
   the state where registered.

Nevada, Washoe - Naturalization and citizenship
Nevada. District Court (Washoe County). *Naturalization Records, 1861-1908.*
   Salt Lake City : Genealogical Society of Utah, 1975.
   Microreproduction of ms. at the Federal Record Center at San Bruno,
   Calif. Includes partial index.
   Microfilm- 0977771
   Declarations of intention, v. 1-2   1861-1888

Decl. of intention	1875-1880
Decl. of intention, v. OO (p.1-131)	1880-1906
Microfilm- 0977772	
Decl. of intention, v. OO (p.131-end)	1880-1906
Decl. of intention, v. O	1906-1908
Final papers, v. 1-3	1877-1906

Nevada, Washoe - Vital records

Parkin, Nona. *Washoe County Records*. Salt Lake City : Filmed by the
Genealogical Society of Utah, 1997.
    Contents: v. 1. Birth records/notices: Washoe County records 1878-1910;
Newspaper notices 1866-1879; Cemetery census: Hebrew Cemetery
(Reno) Hillside Cemetery (Reno), Holy Cross Cemetery (Sparks),
Masonic Memorial Garden (Reno), Native American Cemeteries
(Nixon and Wadsworth), Verdi Cemetery (Verdi), Wadsworth
Cemetery (Wadsworth), Washoe City Cemetery, Small cemeteries:
Bowers, Glendale (Steele Ranch), Holcomb or Huffaker Cemetery,
Logomarsino Canyon, Olinghouse, Wheeler and Winters Ranch -- v. 2.
Cemetery census: Mountain View Cemetery (Reno); Index to an earlier
census with an explanation -- v. 3. Cemetery census: Mountain View
Cemetery, Reno, supplemental census; Mountain View Cemetery,
Episcopal & Catholic areas; Mountain View Cemetery, new section,
veterans's section and mausoleum; Mountain View Cemetery,
regulation section arranged alphabetically; Mountain View Cemetery,
Native American section, Chinese section and County section -- v. 4.
Cemetery census: Mater Delorosa Cemetery, Reno (Our Mother of
Sorrows) -- v. 5. Death records/obituaries: Washoe County death
records, 1896-1912; Newspaper death notices, 1864-1915; Death
records by community: Gerlach, Gold Hill, Washoe and Nixon; Sparks
N.S.H., Verdi, Wadsworth, Newspaper obituaries by cemetery; Hebrew
Cemetery (Reno); Hillside Cemetery (Reno) -- v. 6. Records/
obituaries: Newspaper notices IOOF Cemetery, 1904-1925; Newspaper
obituaries by Cemetery F&AM -- v. 7. Death records/ obituaries: by
cemetery, Knights of Pythias, Reno; Newspaper obituaries with index,
1926-1982 and newspaper notices, 1905-1922; St. Thomas Catholic
Cemetery, Reno -- v. 8. Death records/obituaries: by cemetery, Our
Mother of Sorrows (Mater Delorosa) 1924-1975 -- v. 9. Death
records/obituaries: Newspaper obituaries, Reno area, 1922-1983;
Newspaper obituaries, Reno Evening Gazette with index, 1942-1944 --
v. 10. Funeral home records: Mortuary death records of Reno,
1891-1939; Native American death records, Ross-Burke 1909-1913;
Limited mortuary records, 1896-1912 -- v. 11. Funeral home records:
O'Brien-Rogers Mortuary records (Reno), 1891-1939; Native American

burials from O'Brien-Rogers, 1930-1937 -- v. 12. Marriage records/ notices: Washoe County marriage licenses, 1903-1906, Washoe County marriage licenses, April 1907-December 1907; Washoe County records, 1903-1905; Newspaper notices, 1869-1920; Newspaper "scats" -- v. 13. Pioneer families: Families in Washoe County before 1864; Early day pioneer families with index -- v. 14. Church records: Reno Catholic Parish, 1890-1921; Episcopal Church, Reno, 1869-1950; Sparks Catholic Parish, 1889-1933; Church of the Immaculate Conception, Sparks, 1904-1917.

Microfilm- 1598451 item 2-5   Vol. 1-4
Microfilm- 1598452   Vol. 5-9
Microfilm- 1598453 item 1-5   Vol. 10-14

Nevada, Washoe - Voting registers

Lists of Registered Voters in Nevada, Various Precincts, Year 1882.
    979.3 A1 no.6, also on microfilm- 0962208 item 4
      These lists were taken from the "Reno Evening Gazette" and "Nevada State Journal" of Reno. The places involved are: Wadsworth, Verdi precinct, Franktown districts Buffalo Springs precinct, Brown's precinct, Glendale Precinct.

Nevada, Washoe, Reno - Cemeteries

Nevada Death and Funeral Records in the Possession of the Ross-Burke Funeral Home, Reno, Nevada. Salt Lake City : Filmed by the Genealogical Society of Utah, 1954.

Microfilm- 0014921   Funeral records   1900-1953
Microfilm- 0014922   Funeral records   1870-1906
Microfilm- 0014923   Funeral records   1869-1938

Parkin, Nona. *Burial Records, Knights of Pythias Cemetery, Amity Lodge no. 8, Reno, Nevada : With Data Added From Old Newspapers and Mortuary Records.*
    979.355/R1 V3k, also on microfilm- 0874347 item 3.

Parkin, Nona. *Newspaper obituaries from Mountain View Cemetery, Reno with indexes by alphabet, 1924-1975.* Salt Lake City : Filmed by the Genealogical Society of Utah, 1997.
      Obituaries are arranged alphabetically by surname and also chronologically with the earliest date at the back of the designated letter.
      v. 1. A-B -- v. 2. C-D -- 3. v. 3. E-G -- v. 4. H-J -- v. 5. K-O --l v. 6. P-R -- v. 7. S-U -- v. 8. V-Z. Includes index of kin mentioned in obituaries.
Microfilm- 1598456 item 3-5   Vol. A-G
Microfilm- 1598457 item 1-5   Vol. H-Z

Byars, Steven. *Hebrew Cemetery, Reno Nevada, Yizkor Book.* Salt Lake City :
Filmed by the Genealogical Society of Utah, 1995.
    Microfilm- 1598281 item 1
        Hebrew Cemetery is located near the University of Nevada, Reno,
        Nevada. Includes alphabetical list of names.

Nevada, Washoe, Reno - Church records
Church and Cemetery Records of Washoe County, Nevada. Salt Lake City :
Filmed by the Genealogical Society of Utah, 1971.
    Microfilm- 0869278 item 6
        Microfilm of original records in the D.A.R. Library in Washington, D.C.
        Library also has a film copy of the records of Trinity Episcopal Church,
        1873-1882 (SEE film number: 176649). Contents Trinity Episcopal
        Church (Reno, Nevada), 1873-1882 -- History of early Washoe County
        cemeteries -- Hillside Cemetery (Reno, Nevada) -- St. Thomas Cemetery
        (Reno, Nevada) -- Crystal Peak Cemetery (Verdi, Nevada).

Nevada, Washoe, Reno - Directories
R. L. Polk and Company. *Reno, Sparks, Washoe County, and Carson City
Directory : Contains Buyer's Guide and a Complete Classified Business
Directory. -- 1915.*
    979.35 E4pr, also on microfilm, 1915, 1425609 item 6
        Library has: 1915 (photocopy), 1917, 1923, 1970, 1973, 1981.

Nevada, Washoe, Reno - History
Rowley, William D. *Reno, Hub of the Washoe County : an Illustrated History.*
Woodland Hills, Calif. : University of Nevada Reno, c1984 (Windsor
Publications).
    979.355 H2r

Nevada, Washoe, Reno - Newspapers
Reno Evening Gazette (Reno, Nevada). *Marriages and Decrees, 1967-1970.*
Salt Lake City : Filmed by the Genealogical Society of Utah, 1989.
    Microfilm- 1597626 item 10   Vol. 2   1967-1970
    Microfilm- 1597626 item 9   Index to 1967-1970, by Ruth Berentsen

Slagle, Eleanor. *Eleanor Slagle Index Card Collection.* Salt Lake City : Filmed by the Genealogical Society of Utah, 1994.

Microfilm- 1307683

Extracted information taken from the Reno Evening Gazette mainly from 1876-1892, with a few after 1900 and some from the Nevada Appeal. Material extracted includes births, deaths, marriages, probate notices, registered voters and some information from accidents, crimes, illnesses, moves and other individual activities.

Nevada, Washoe, Reno - Obituaries
Trissel, Cynthia Lynn Sugden. *Obituary and Will Records, Misc. Towns, Counties, and States, 1887-1986.* Newhall, Calif. : C.L. Trissel, [1986?].

973 A1 no.282, also on microfilm- 1697416 item 10

Includes index. Contains a few wills and a few obituaries from the following newspapers: Reno Gazette--Journal, Reno, Nevada ; The Mooreland Leader, Mooreland, Oklahoma ; The Ames Newspaper, Ames, Kansas ; Times--Republican Newspaper, Marshalltown, Iowa.

Nevada, Washoe, Reno - Vital records
Parkin, Nona. *Mortuary Death Records, O'Brien Rogers Funeral Home, Reno, Washoe County, Nevada, 911-1939.*

979.355/R1 V38p, also on microfilm- 0874347 item 2

Parkin, Nona. *Reno Evening Gazette Births, Marriages and Deaths, 1878-1882 and Reno Gazette and Stockman Marriages and Deaths, 1888.*

979.3 A1 no.10, also on microfilm- 0962208 item 6

Nevada, Washoe, Sparks - Church records
Church of Jesus Christ of Latter-day Saints. Sparks Branch (Nevada). *Record of Members, 1910-1941;Annual Genealogical Report, Form E, 1941- 1948.* Salt Lake City : Filmed by the Genealogical Society of Utah, 1951-1954.

Microfilm of original records in the LDS Church Archives, Salt Lake City.

Microfilm- 0001955 item 5-7   Record of members   1910-1941
Microfilm- 0014925   Form E   1941-1948

Nevada, Washoe, Sparks - Vital records
Parkin, Nona. *Nevada State Hospital Death Records, 1882-1962.*

979.355/S1 V2p, also on microfilm- 0874352 item 5

CHAPTER EIGHTEEN

White Pine County

White Pine County was created from Lander County by an act of the legislature on 1 April 1869.

CEMETERIES

City of Ely Cemetery
P.O. Box 299, Ely, NV 89301
Phone: 775 289-4602
Years of operation: 1868?-present
Affiliations: non-sectarian cemetery
Records: housed on-site; searches by personnel only

CHURCHES

ELY
Assemblies of God: Assembly of God, 700 Ave. M, PO Box 869, Ely, NV 89301 Phone: 775 289-2697
Baptist: Ely First Baptist Church, 936 Pioche Hwy, Ely, NV 89301 Phone: 775 289-8221
Episcopal: St. Bartholomew Episcopalian Church, PO Box 387, Ely, NV 89301
Latter-day Saints: Church of Jesus Christ of Latter-day Saints, 900 Ave. E., Ely, NV 89301 Phone: 775 289-2241
Lutheran: Immanuel Lutheran Church, PO Box 375, Ely, NV 89301 Phone: 775 289-6353
Methodist: McGill United Methodist Church, PO Box 848, Ely, NV 89301 Phone: 775 289-8345
Orthodox: St. Alexios, Greek Orthodox Church, PO Box 1203, Ely, NV 89301
Roman Catholic: Sacred Hearth Catholic Church, PO Box 26, Ely, NV 89301

LUND
Latter-day Saints: Church of Jesus Christ Latter-day Saints, Main St., Lund, NV 89317 Phone: 775 238-5207

MC GILL
Orthodox: St. Barbara Greek Orthodox Church, PO Box 1352, Mc Gill, NV
89318 Phone: 775 235-7341

COURTHOUSE

White Pine County Courthouse
P.O. Box 68, Ely, NV 89301
Phone: 775 289-3016 County Assessor; 775 289-2341 County Clerk; 775 289-
4567 County Recorder
Land records: County Assessor
Naturalization records: from 1900, County Clerk, Box 659
Probate records: 1900 to present, County Clerk
    Probate search service: $1.00 per year, copy costs $1.00 per page
Vital records: County Recorder

FUNERAL HOMES

Wilson-Bates Mortuary
450 Mill Street, Ely, NV 289-2651

LIBRARIES - SOCIETIES

White Pine County Library
950 Campton, Ely, NV 89301
Phone: 775 289-3737   Fax: 775 289-1555   E-mail: avnye@ckab.lib.nv.us
Founded: 1961
Hours: Monday-Thursday: 10:00 a.m. to 6:00 p.m., Friday: 10:00 a.m. to 5:00
    p.m., Saturday: 10:00 a.m. to 2:00 p.m.
Special Collections: Nevada materials; local history (White Pine County
    Historial Society), photographs, oral history
Newspaper Indexes:
    Copper Ore, 1910
    Daily Inland Empire, 1867-1870
    Eureka Daily Sentinel, 1873-1874
    Eureka Sentinel, 1870-1871
    Kimberly News, 1910
    Reese River Reveille, 1863-1868
    Ward Miner, 1876-1877
    White Pine Evening Telegram, 1869
    White Pine News, 1869-1906

White Pine Historical Society
McGill Highway, Ely, NV 89310
Collections: Books, manuscripts, maps, newspapers, photographs, oral histories

NEWSPAPERS

The Ely Daily News
P.O. Box 1139, Ely, NV 89301
Phone: 775 289-4491   Fax: 775 289-4566

Newspapers	City	UNLV Library has
Cherry Creek Miner	Cherry Creek	April 15, 1903
Copper Ore	McGill	February 11, 1909 - June 11, 1914
Ely Daily Daily Mining Expositor	Ely	June 28, 1907 - January 31, 1915
Ely Daily Times	Ely	April 19, 1920 - date (daily full-run)
Ely Mining Expositor	Ely	October 11, 1906 - May 9, 1907
Ely Mining Record	Ely	Aug. 4, 1906 - Dec. 26, 1908 (weekly full-run)
Ely Record (Ely)	Ely	January 1, 1909 - August 15, 1981
Ely Weekly Mining Expositor	Ely	May 16, 1907 - Dec. 26, 1912 (weekly 1906-1912)
Inland Empire	Hamilton	March 27, 1869 - Nov. 9, 1870 (daily full-run)
Mining Record	Ely	March 4, 1905 - July 28, 1906 (weekly full-run)
Ward Reflex	Ward	April 9, 1877 - May 17, 1884 (varies full-run)
White Pine Daily News	Hamilton	February 7, 1870 - Nov. 16, 1872
White Pine Evening Telegram	Shermantown	June 2 - August 18, 1869
White Pine News	Cherry Creek	January 1, 1881 - August 15, 1885
White Pine News	East Ely	October 24, 1920 - Dec. 31, 1923
White Pine News	Ely	Sep. 15, 1888 - Dec. 25, 1906
White Pine News	Ely	October 31, 1907 - June 30, 1910
White Pine News	Hamilton	January 15 - February 5, 1870
White Pine News	Hamilton	Nov. 23, 1872 - Dec. 16, 1880
White Pine News	Taylor	August 22, 1885 - Sep. 8, 1888
White Pine News	Treasure City	December 26, 1868 - Jan. 8, 1870
White Pine News Daily Edition	Ely	Dec. 26, 1906 - Oct. 30, 1907
White Pine News Weekly Mining Review	Ely	January 12, 1907 - Oct. 17, 1920

White Pine Reflex	Taylor	June 21, 1884 - August 12, 1885
		(weekly full-run)
White Pine Suffragist	Ely	October 31, 1914

FAMILY HISTORY LIBRARY (Salt Lake City, Utah) HOLDINGS

All microfilmed and microfiched records (unless restricted) are available to rent worldwide at branch Family History Centers and selected larger public and private libraries and societies.

Nevada, White Pine - Cemeteries
Ely Nevada Stake Genealogical Library. *Cemetery Inscription for the Communities, Ranches, and Ghost Towns of the Area in the Ely Nevada Stake.* Salt Lake City : Filmed by the Genealogical Society of Utah, 1979.
Microfilm- 1206354 item 1
> Hot Creek, Preston, and Lund Cemetery records. Contains records of the cemeteries in all of White Pine County except Ely, part of Nye County, Nevada and...Western Millard County, Utah.

Parkin, Nona. *White Pine County Records.* Salt Lake City : Filmed by the Genealogical Society of Utah, 1997.
> V. 1. Birth records/notices: Newspaper notices 1890, White Pine County records 1881-1920; Cemetery census: Cherry Creek Ely Cemetery, Hamilton Cemetery, Lund Cemetery, Small cemeteries: Osceola, Parton Schellbourne, Treasure Hill and Ward; Death records/obituaries: White Pine County records 1887-1911, Newspaper notices 1869-1911, Newspaper obituaries 1889-1890, Newspaper obituaries, Ely 1926-1983, Newspaper obituaries: Cherry Valley, Lund and Preston 1933-1979 -- v. 2. Divorces 1890; Marriage records/ notices: White Pine County records 1884-1915; Pioneer families; Tax assessment records: Delinquent tax list 1890; Church records: St. Luke's Protestant Episcopal Church, Hamilton, Nevada, St. Bartholomew Ely, Nevada. Includes some indexing.
Microfilm- 1598461 item 3-4   Vol. 1-2

Nevada, White Pine - History
Patera, Alan H. *Rush to White Pine.* [S.l.] : The Depot, c1988.
979.3 A1 no.42
> Western mining interest was focused on the White Pine as the district swelled to a population of 16,000 and then declined as other mining strikes were made. Bibliography: p. 68. Includes index.

Read, Effie Oxborrow. *White Pine Lang Syne : a True History of White Pine County, Nevada.* Denver : Big Mountain Press, 1965.
979.315 H2r

Robison, George Swallow. *White Pine County [Nevada] Pioneers.* Salt Lake City : Filmed by the Genealogical Society of Utah, 1979.
Microfilm- 1036429 item 7
Historical sketch of the Robison and Swallow families, Mormons, who settled in White Pine County, Nevada.

Nevada, White Pine - Military records - World War, 1914-1918

Banks, Raymond H. *The Banks Compilation of Birth Data of Men With Links to White Pine County, Nevada, Who Were Born 1873-1900 : as Found in the Civilian Registration Cards.* L.D.S. microfilm series of World War I Selective Service draft registration cards. Salt Lake City : R.H. Banks, c1996.
979.315 M28b
An alphabetical listing by surname of men who completed civilian registration cards for their draft boards during 1917-1918. About 98% of men present in America and born 1873-1900 provided draft card information in 1917 or 1918. Aliens were required to register. Persons already in the military did not register. Includes name, date of birth, ethnic group, birth location or other information, and county or city draft board in the state where registered.

Nevada, White Pine - Vital records

Parkin, Nona. *White Pine News, Ely, Nevada, 1890 : an Extract of Births, Divorces, Marriages, Deaths and Delinquent Tax List From the White Pine News in 1890.*
979.3 A1 no.8

Nevada. State Board of Health. *Death Records for White Pine County, 1887-1952.* Salt Lake City : Filmed by the Genealogical Society of Utah, 1993.
Includes indexes at beginning of volumes.
Microfilm- 1902446 item 5
Deaths, v. Old 1 53   27 Oct 1887-26 Apr 1911
Microfilm- 1902447
Deaths, v. 1-4   3 Jul 1911-23 Jul 1939
Deaths, v. 5 (p. 1-313)   4 Aug 1939- 1 Nov 1944
Microfilm- 1902448 item 1-3
Deaths, v. 5 (313-end)   1 Nov 1944-22 Nov 1948
Deaths, v. 6-7   1 Dec 1948-26 Dec 1952

White Pine County (Nevada). County Clerk. *Marriage License Stubs,*
1885-1950. Salt Lake City : Filmed by the Genealogical Society of Utah,
1993.
Microfilm- 1902543
 Vol. 1-20   25 Feb 1885-29 Oct 1928
Microfilm- 1902544
 Vol. 21-52   10 Nov 1928-16 Mar 1943
Microfilm- 1902545 item 1-28
 Vol. 53-80   27 Mar 1943- 8 Aug 1947
Microfilm- 1902546 item 1
 Vol. 81   9 Aug 1947- 1 Oct 1947
Microfilm- 1902545 item 29
 Vol. 82   4 Oct 1947- 3 Jan 1948
Microfilm- 1902546 item 2-16
 Vol. 83-97   3 Jan 1948-31 Dec 1950

White Pine County (Nevada). Recorder. *Birth Records, 1887-1951.* Salt Lake
City : Filmed by the Genealogical Society of Utah, 1993.
 Includes indexes at beginning of volumes.
Microfilm- 1902444
 Births, old 1 52   13 Aug 1887-30 May 1911
 Births, v. 1-4   5 Jun 1911-31 Mar 1928
 Births, v. 5, index   12 Apr 1928-30 Nov 1932
Microfilm- 1902445
 Births, v. 5   12 Apr 1928-30 Nov 1932
 Births, 6-7   16 Dec 1932-28 Mar 1942
 Births, v. 8 (p. 1-285)   3 Apr 1942-14 Feb 1944
Microfilm- 1902446 item 1-4
 Births, (285-end)   14 Feb 1944- 7 Aug 1945
 Births, v. 9-11   8 Aug 1945- 1 Nov 1951

White Pine County (Nevada). Recorder. *Marriage Records, 1884-1953.* Salt
Lake City : Filmed by the Genealogical Society of Utah, 1993.
 Includes indexes at beginning of volumes.
Microfilm- 1902448 item 4-7
 Marriages, v. Old 1 51   31 Dec 1884- 9 Jul 1913
 Marriages, v. 2   9 Jul 1913- 6 Jun 1917
 Marriages, v. 80   6 Jun 1917- 2 Nov 1936
 Marr. v. 124 (p.1-307)   7 Nov 1936-16 Oct 1941
Microfilm- 1902449
 Marr. v. 124 (307-end)   16 Oct 1941-19 Jul 1944
 Marriages, v. 139-150   22 Jul 1944-27 Feb 1953

Nevada, White Pine, Baker - Church records

Church of Jesus Christ of Latter-day Saints. Garrison Branch (Utah). *Record of Members, 1925-1941; Annual Genealogical Report, Form E, 1925- 1948.* Salt Lake City : Filmed by the Genealogical Society of Utah, 1951.
Microfilm of original records in the LDS Church Archives, Salt Lake City. Garrison Branch, created in 1941, was formerly known as the Snake Valley Branch. Snake Valley Branch was headquartered in Baker, Nevada. Includes partial index. Photocopies not permitted except for direct line descendants. Remove all other data from photocopy.

| Microfilm- 0025972 item 1 | Record of members | 1925-1941 |
| Microfilm- 0025972 item 2 | Form E | 1925-1948 |

Nevada, White Pine, Cherry Creek - Voting registers

Cherry Creek (Nevada). Registrar. *Voter Registration List and Poll List for the 1904 General Election.* Salt Lake City : Filmed by the Genealogical Society of Utah, 1988.
Microfilm- 1421885 item 4
Registration list and poll list of voters in the 1904 general election.

Nevada, White Pine, Ely - Cemeteries

Cemetery Records, Ely, White Pine County, Nevada. Salt Lake City : Filmed by the Genealogical Society of Utah, 1956.
Microfilm- 0002112 item 5

Nevada, White Pine, Ely - Church records

Church of Jesus Christ of Latter-day Saints. Ely Ward (Nevada). *Record of Members, 1926-1941; Annual Genealogical Report, Form E, 1927- 1948.* Salt Lake City : Filmed by the Genealogical Society of Utah, 1951.
Microfilm of original records in the LDS Church Archives, Salt Lake City. Photocopies not permitted except for direct line descendants. Remove all other data from photocopy.

| Microfilm- 0014899 item 1-3 | Record of members | 1926-1919, 1926-1941 |
| Microfilm- 0014899 item 4 | Form E, 1927-1948 | |

Nevada, White Pine, Ely - Directories

R. L. Polk and Company. *Ely (White Pine County, Nevada) City Directory : Including East Ely, McGill, Ruth, and White Pine County, Contains Buyers' Guide and a Complete Classified Business Directory. -- 1964.*
979.315 E4p

Nevada, White Pine, Lund - Cemeteries

Parkin, Nona. *Cemetery Census of Lund, Nevada, White Pine County.*
979.3 A1 no.41, also on microfiche- 6018013

Nevada, White Pine, Lund - Church records
Church of Jesus Christ of Latter-day Saints. Lund Ward (Nevada). *Record of Members, 1901-1937; Annual Genealogical Report, Form E, 1907- 1948.*
Salt Lake City : Filmed by the Genealogical Society of Utah, 1951.
Microfilm of original records in the LDS Church Archives, Salt Lake City.
The Form E includes reports from the St. George and North Weber Stakes.
Microfilm- 0014904 item 1   Record of members 1901-1937
Microfilm- 0014904 item 2   Form E   1907-1948

Nevada, White Pine, Lund - History
White River Valley Then and Now, 1898-1980. Provo, Utah : Melayne Printing.
Q AREA 979.315 H2w, also on microfilm- 1035916 item 14

Nevada, White Pine, McGill - Church records
Church of Jesus Christ of Latter-day Saints. McGill Ward (Nevada). *Record of Members, 1912-1941; Annual Genealogical Report, Form E, 1912- 1948.*
Salt Lake City : Filmed by the Genealogical Society of Utah, 1951.
Microfilm of original records in the LDS Church Archives, Salt Lake City.
The Form E includes reports from the North Weber Stake.
Microfilm- 0014909 item 1-2   Record of members 1912-1941
Microfilm- 0014909 item 3   Form E, 1912-1948

Nevada, White Pine, Preston - Church records
Church of Jesus Christ of Latter-day Saints. Preston Ward (Nevada). *Record of Members, 1901-1947; Annual genealogical Report, Form E, 1907- 1947.*
Salt Lake City : Filmed by the Genealogical Society of Utah, 1951.
Microfilm of original records in the LDS Church Archives, Salt Lake City.
Preston Ward was a local unit of the St. George and Nevada Stakes. The Form E includes reports from the St. George and North Weber Stakes.
Microfilm- 0014917 item 1-2   Record of members 1901-1947
Microfilm- 0014917 item 3   Form E, 1907-1947

Nevada, White Pine, Ruth - Church records
Church of Jesus Christ of Latter-day Saints. Ruth Ward (Nevada). *Record of Members, 1924-1941; Annual Genealogical Report, Form E, 1926- 1948.*
Salt Lake City ; Salt Lake City : Filmed by the LDS Church Historian's Office : Filmed by the Genealogical Society of Utah, 1951, 1961.
Microfilm of original records in the LDS Church Archives, Salt Lake City.
Ruth Ward, created in 1936, was formerly known as Ruth Branch and was a local unit of the North Weber and Nevada Stakes. Includes index.
Microfilm- 0889343 item 7   Record of members 1924-1941
Microfilm- 0014918   Form E, 1926-1948

INDEX

This index only lists places because the book is set up alphabetically (chapters and topics) and it is easy to locate specific topics within the county of interest.

www.ingramcontent.com/pod-product-compliance
Lightning Source LLC
Chambersburg PA
CBHW070401270326
41926CB00014B/2646